The Unsettling of America

The Unsettling of America: Culture & Agriculture

by Wendell Berry

Sierra Club Books / San Francisco

FOR MAURICE TELLEEN

Portions of this book have appeared in slightly altered form in
The Nation and *The CoEvolution Quarterly*.

Library of Congress Cataloging-in-Publication Data

Berry, Wendell, 1934–
  The unsettling of America.

  Bibliography: p.
    1. Agriculture—Economic aspects—United States.
  2. Agriculture—Social aspects—United States.
  3. United States—Rural conditions.   I. Title.
  [HD1761.B47   1986]   338.1′0973   86-6426
  ISBN 0-87156-772-5 (pbk.)

book design by James Robertson, The Yolla Bolly Press
PRINTED IN THE UNITED STATES OF AMERICA

10 9 8 7 6 5 4 3 2 1

Preface

This book was meant to be a criticism of what I have called modern or orthodox agriculture. As I now realize, it is more a review than a criticism. Criticism requires a subject that is "finished." When agriculture is "finished," no would-be critic will be available. I am therefore constrained to accept my demotion as a privilege.

Nevertheless, there is a difficulty in writing a book on so inherently topical a subject as agricultural policy, and this difficulty is time: events that were the immediate cause of the book may be "finished" before the writing is. No reader of this book can fail to observe that it deals at length with the assumptions and policies of former Secretary of Agriculture Earl L. Butz, though Mr. Butz and the administration he served are now out of office.

I can only insist that my book is not for that reason out-of-date. Secretary Butz's tenure in the Department of Agriculture, and even his influence, are matters far more transient than the power and the values of those whose interests he represented. Moreover, the cultural issues that I attempt to deal with have been with us since our history began, and, barring miracle or catastophe, they will be with us for a long time to come.

As a matter of fact, this book's origins go back farther than the secretaryship of Mr. Butz. The first notes I made for it were incited by a news story in the summer of 1967 on the report of President Johnson's "special commission on federal food and fiber policies."

The commission said, according to an article in the *Louisville Courier-Journal*, that the country's biggest farm problem was a surplus of farmers: ". . . the technological advances in agriculture have so greatly reduced the need for manpower that too many people are trying to live on a national farm income wholly inadequate for them." The proposed solutions were to find "better opportunities for the farm people," "a more comprehensive national employment policy," "retraining programs," "improved general educational facilities," etc. Both the commission and the writer of the article had obviously *taken for granted* that the lives and communities of small farmers then still on the farm—and those of the 25 million who had left the farm since 1940—were of less value than "technological advances in agriculture." There seemed also to be no official doubt that adequate solutions were to be found in government-supplied "opportunities," facilities, and programs. Reading that article, I realized that my values were not only out of fashion, but under powerful attack. I saw that I was a member of a threatened minority. That is what set me off.

W.B.

Preface to
the Second Edition

When I was working on this book—from 1974 to 1977—the long agricultural decline that it deals with was momentarily disguised as a "boom." The big farmers were getting bigger with the help of inflated land prices and borrowed money, and the foreign demand for American farm products was strong, so from the official point of view the situation looked good. The big were *supposed* to get bigger. Foreigners were *supposed* to be in need of our products. The official point of view, foreshortened as usual by statistics, superstitious theory, and wishful prediction, was utterly complacent. Then Secretary of Agriculture Earl L. Butz issued the most optimistic, the most widely obeyed, and the worst advice ever given to farmers: that they should plow "fencerow to fencerow."

That the situation was *not* good—for farms or farmers or rural communities or nature or the general public—was even then evident to any experienced observer who would turn aside from the preconceptions of "agribusiness" and look at the marks of deterioration that were plainly visible. And now, almost a decade later, it is evident to everyone that, at least for farmers and rural communities, the situation is catastrophic: Farmers are losing their farms, some are killing themselves, some in the madness of despair are killing other people, and rural economy and rural life are gravely stricken. The agricultural economists chart the "liquidations of assets," the "shakeouts," and the "downturns," apparently amazed that now even the large "progressive" and "efficient" farmers are in trouble.

But this is not just a financial crisis for country people. Critical questions are being asked of our whole society: Are we, or are we not, going to take proper care of our land, our country? And do we, or do we not, believe in a democratic distribution of usable property? At present, these questions are being answered in the negative. Our soil erosion rates are worse now than during the years of the Dust Bowl. In the arid lands of the West, we are overusing and wasting the supplies of water. Toxic pollution from agricultural chemicals is a growing problem. We are closer every day to the final destruction of private ownership not only of small family farms, but of small usable properties of all kinds. Every problem I dealt with in this book, in fact, has grown worse since the book was written.

The one improvement has been in public concern about the problems. Among farmers there is growing distrust of the "agribusiness" line of talk and growing interest in agricultural health and sanity. Among city people there is a growing awareness that sane and healthy agriculture requires an informed urban constituency. There is hope in these developments and in the continued existence of a remnant of excellent small farms and farmers.

Some prominent agricultural economists are still finding it possible to pretend that the only issues involved are economic, but that possibility is diminishing. I recently attended a meeting at which an agricultural economist argued that there is no essential difference between owning and renting a farm. A farmer stood up in the audience and replied: "Professor, I don't think our ancestors came to America in order to *rent* a farm."

'Nough said.

w.b.
March 1986

Anything that I will ever have to say on the subject of agriculture can be little more than a continuation of talk begun in childhood with my father and with my late friend Owen Flood. Their conversation, first listened to and then joined, was my first and longest and finest instruction. From them, before I knew I was being taught, I learned to think of the meanings, the responsibilities, and the pleasures of farming.

But this book's greatest immediate debt is acknowledged in the dedication. Maury Telleen has been an indefatigable friend both to my book and to me. He has arranged indispensable meetings, written me letters, sent me clippings and books, talked to me on the phone, read my manuscript, borne up through hours of fervent conversation in his house, in my house, and over many hundreds of miles of happy agricultural travels. To his wife, Jeannine, I am indebted for understanding and for hospitality.

I am, of course, hopelessly in debt to my own wife, Tanya, for keeping farm and household together during my absences, and for enduring both my travels and my travails. But she has also participated in the thinking-out of this book, has been its critic, and, finally, its typist.

My neighbor, Tom Grissom, gave me invaluable help with the preliminary reading, and in many talks helped me to clarify my ideas.

For reading the manuscript and other kindnesses, I am grateful to Robert Rodale, Jerry Goldstein, Cia and Ed McClanahan, James Baker Hall, Joan Hall, Gary Snyder, Jim and Barbara Foote, and my father.

Stephen B. Brush, Clarence Van Sant, Gurney Norman, Ben Webb, and David Budbill generously gave me permission to quote from their letters, and Stephen Brush allowed me to make use of his excellent paper on Andean agriculture.

For hospitality and other kindnesses on my travels, I thank Tommy Shoup, Everett Hildebrandt, Roger Blobaum, Mr. and Mrs. Ilo Kusserow, Mr. and Mrs. Mike Jessen, Mr. and Mrs. Monroe J. Miller, Arnold Hockett, Clarence Van Sant, Mr. and Mrs. John Heinrich, Patty Kaminsky.

This list of my debts will make clear that much of the good of my book has been the gift of other people. Its flaws, on the other hand, have been furnished exclusively by me.

Contents

Who so hath his minde on taking,
hath it no more on what he hath taken.

MONTAIGNE, III. VI

So many goodly citties ransacked and razed; so many nations destroyed and made desolate; so infinite millions of harmelesse people of all sexes, states and ages, massacred, ravaged and put to the sword; and the richest, the fairest and the best part of the world topsiturvied, ruined and defaced for the traffick of Pearles and Pepper: Oh mechanicall victories, oh base conquest.

MONTAIGNE

CHAPTER ONE

The Unsettling
of America

One of the peculiarities of the white race's presence in America is how little intention has been applied to it. As a people, wherever we have been, we have never really intended to be. The continent is said to have been discovered by an Italian who was on his way to India. The earliest explorers were looking for gold, which was, after an early streak of luck in Mexico, always somewhere farther on. Conquests and foundings were incidental to this search—which did not, and could not, end until the continent was finally laid open in an orgy of goldseeking in the middle of the last century. Once the unknown of geography was mapped, the industrial marketplace became the new frontier, and we continued, with largely the same motives and with increasing haste and anxiety, to displace ourselves—no longer with unity of direction, like a migrant flock, but like the refugees from a broken ant hill. In our own time we have invaded foreign lands and the moon with the high-toned patriotism of the conquistadors, and with the same mixture of fantasy and avarice.

That is too simply put. It is substantially true, however, as a description of the dominant tendency in American history. The temptation, once that has been said, is to ascend altogether into rhetoric and inveigh equally against all our forebears and all present holders of office. To be just, however, it is necessary to remember that there has been another tendency: the tendency to stay put, to say, "No farther. This is the place." So far, this has been the weaker tendency, less glamorous, certainly less successful. It is also the older of these tendencies, having been the dominant one among the Indians.

The Indians did, of course, experience movements of population, but in general their relation to place was based upon old usage and association, upon inherited memory, tradition, veneration. The land was their homeland. The first and greatest American revolution, which has never been superseded, was the coming of people who did *not* look upon the land as a homeland. But there were always those among the newcomers who saw that they had come to a good place and who saw its domestic possibilities. Very early, for instance, there were men who wished to establish agricultural settlements rather than quest for gold or exploit the Indian trade. Later, we know that every advance of the frontier left behind families and communities who intended to remain and prosper where they were.

But we know also that these intentions have been almost systematically overthrown. Generation after generation, those who intended to remain and prosper where they were have been dispossessed and driven out, or subverted and exploited where they were, by those who were carrying out some version of the search for El Dorado. Time after time, in place after place, these conquerors have fragmented and demolished traditional communities, the beginnings of domestic cultures. They have always said that what they destroyed was outdated, provincial, and contemptible. And with alarming frequency they have been believed and trusted by their victims, especially when their victims were other white people.

If there is any law that has been consistently operative in American history, it is that the members of any *established* people or group or community sooner or later become "redskins"—that is, they become the designated victims of an utterly ruthless, officially sanctioned and subsidized exploitation. The colonists who drove off the Indians came to be intolerably exploited by their imperial governments. And that alien imperialism was thrown off only to be succeeded by a domestic version of the same thing; the class of independent small farmers who fought the war of independence has been exploited by, and recruited into, the industrial society until by now it is almost extinct. Today, the most numerous heirs of the farmers of Lexington and Concord are the little groups scattered all over the country whose names begin with "Save": Save Our Land, Save the Valley, Save Our Mountains, Save Our Streams, Save Our Farmland. As so often before, these are *designated* victims—people without official sanction, often without official friends, who are struggling to preserve their places, their values, and their lives as they know them and prefer to live them against the agencies of their own government which are using their own tax moneys against them.

The only escape from this destiny of victimization has been to "succeed"—that is, to "make it" into the class of exploiters, and then to remain so specialized and so "mobile" as to be unconscious of the effects of one's life or livelihood. This escape is, of course, illusory, for one man's producer is another's consumer, and even the richest and most mobile will soon find it hard to escape the noxious effluents and fumes of their various public services.

Let me emphasize that I am not talking about an evil that is merely contemporary or "modern," but one that is as old in America as the white man's presence here. It is an intention that was *organized* here almost from the start. "The New World," Bernard DeVoto wrote in *The Course of Empire*, "was a constantly expanding market. . . . Its value in gold was enormous but it had still greater value in that it expanded and integrated the industrial systems of Europe."

And he continues: "The first belt-knife given by a European to an Indian was a portent as great as the cloud that mushroomed over Hiroshima. . . . Instantly the man of 6000 B.C. was bound fast to a way of life that had developed seven and a half millennia beyond his own. He began to live better and he began to die."

The principal European trade goods were tools, cloth, weapons, ornaments, novelties, and alcohol. The sudden availability of these things produced a revolution that "affected every aspect of Indian life. The struggle for existence . . . became easier. Immemorial handicrafts grew obsolescent, then obsolete. Methods of hunting were transformed. So were methods—and the purposes—of war. As war became deadlier in purpose and armament a surplus of women developed, so that marriage customs changed and polygamy became common. The increased usefulness of women in the preparation of pelts worked to the same end. . . . Standards of wealth, prestige, and honor

5

changed. The Indians acquired commercial values and developed business cults. They became more mobile. . . .

"In the sum it was cataclysmic. A culture was forced to change much faster than change could be adjusted to. All corruptions of culture produce breakdowns of morale, of communal integrity, and of personality, and this force was as strong as any other in the white man's subjugation of the red man."

I have quoted these sentences from DeVoto because, the obvious differences aside, he is so clearly describing a revolution that did not stop with the subjugation of the Indians, but went on to impose substantially the same catastrophe upon the small farms and the farm communities, upon the shops of small local tradesmen of all sorts, upon the workshops of independent craftsmen, and upon the households of citizens. It is a revolution that is still going on. The economy is still substantially that of the fur trade, still based on the same general kinds of commercial items: technology, weapons, ornaments, novelties, and drugs. The one great difference is that by now the revolution has deprived the mass of consumers of any independent access to the staples of life: clothing, shelter, food, even water. Air remains the only necessity that the average user can still get for himself, and the revolution has imposed a heavy tax on that by way of pollution. Commercial conquest is far more thorough and final than military defeat. The Indian became a redskin, not by loss in battle, but by accepting a dependence on traders that made *necessities* of industrial goods. This is not merely history. It is a parable.

DeVoto makes it clear that the imperial powers, having made themselves willing to impose this exploitive industrial economy upon the Indians, could not then keep it from contaminating their own best intentions: "More than four-fifths of the wealth of New France was furs, the rest was fish, and it had no agricultural wealth. One trouble was that whereas the crown's imperial policy required it to develop the country's agriculture, the crown's economy required the colony's furs, an adverse interest." And La Salle's dream of developing Louisiana (agriculturally and otherwise) was frustrated because "The interest of the court in Louisiana colonization was to secure a bridgehead for an attack on the silver mines of northern Mexico. . . ."

One cannot help but see the similarity between this foreign colonialism and the domestic colonialism that, by policy, converts productive farm, forest, and grazing lands into strip mines. Now, as then, we see the abstract values of an industrial economy preying upon the native productivity of land and people. The fur trade was only the first establishment on this continent of a mentality whose triumph is its catastrophe.

My purposes in beginning with this survey of history are (1) to show how deeply rooted in our past is the mentality of exploitation; (2) to show how fundamentally revolutionary it is; and (3) to show how crucial to our history—hence, to our own minds—is the question of how we will relate to our land. This question, now that the corporate revolution has so determinedly invaded the farmland, returns us to our oldest crisis.

We can understand a great deal of our history—from Cortés' destruction of Tenochtitlán in 1521 to the bulldozer attack on the coalfields four-and-a-half centuries later—by thinking of ourselves as divided into conquerors and victims. In order to understand our own time and predicament and the work that is to be done, we would do well to shift the terms and say that we are divided between exploitation and nurture. The first set of terms is too simple for the purpose because, in any given situation, it proposes to divide people into two mutually exclusive groups; it becomes complicated only when we are dealing with situations in succession—as when a colonist who persecuted the Indians then resisted persecution by the crown. The terms exploitation and nurture, on the other hand, describe a division not only between persons but also within persons. We are all to some extent the products of an exploitive society, and it would be foolish and self-defeating to pretend that we do not bear its stamp.

Let me outline as briefly as I can what seem to me the characteristics of these opposite kinds of mind. I conceive a strip-miner to be a model exploiter, and as a model nurturer I take the old-fashioned idea or ideal of a farmer. The exploiter is a specialist, an expert; the nurturer is not. The standard of the exploiter is efficiency; the standard of the nurturer is care. The exploiter's goal is money, profit; the nurturer's goal is health—his land's health, his own, his family's, his community's, his country's. Whereas the exploiter asks of a piece of land only how much and how quickly it can be made to produce, the nurturer asks a question that is much more complex and difficult: What is its carrying capacity? (That is: How much can be taken from it without diminishing it? What can it produce *dependably* for an indefinite time?) The exploiter wishes to earn as much as possible by as little work as possible; the nurturer expects, certainly, to have a decent living from his work, but his characteristic wish is to work *as*

7

well as possible. The competence of the exploiter is in organization; that of the nurturer is in order—a human order, that is, that accommodates itself both to other order and to mystery. The exploiter typically serves an institution or organization; the nurturer serves land, household, community, place. The exploiter thinks in terms of numbers, quantities, "hard facts"; the nurturer in terms of character, condition, quality, kind.

It seems likely that all the "movements" of recent years have been representing various claims that nurture has to make against exploitation. The women's movement, for example, when its energies are most accurately placed, is arguing the cause of nurture; other times it is arguing the right of women to be exploiters—which men have no *right* to be. The exploiter is clearly the prototype of the "masculine" man—the wheeler-dealer whose "practical" goals require the sacrifice of flesh, feeling, and principle. The nurturer, on the other hand, has always passed with ease across the boundaries of the so-called sexual roles. Of necessity and without apology, the preserver of seed, the planter, becomes midwife and nurse. Breeder is always metamorphosing into brooder and back again. Over and over again, spring after spring, the questing mind, idealist and visionary, must pass through the planting to become nurturer of the real. The farmer, sometimes known as husbandman, is by definition half mother; the only question is how good a mother he or she is. And the land itself is not mother or father only, but both. Depending on crop and season, it is at one time receiver of seed, bearer and nurturer of young; at another, raiser of seed-stalk, bearer and shedder of seed. And in response to these changes, the farmer crosses back and forth from one zone of spousehood to another, first as planter and then as gatherer. Farmer and land are thus involved in a sort of dance in which the partners are always at opposite sexual poles, and the lead keeps changing: the farmer, as seed-bearer, causes growth; the land, as seed-bearer, causes the harvest.

The exploitive always involves the abuse or the perversion of nurture and ultimately its destruction. Thus, we saw how far the exploitive revolution had penetrated the official character when our recent secretary of agriculture remarked that "Food is a weapon." This was given a fearful symmetry indeed when, in discussing the possible use of nuclear weapons, a secretary of defense spoke of "palatable" levels of devastation. Consider the associations that have since ancient times clustered around the idea of food—associations of mutual care, generosity, neighborliness, festivity, communal joy, religious ceremony—and you will see that these two secretaries represent a cultural catastrophe. The concerns of farming and those of war, once thought to be diametrically opposed, have become identical. Here we have an example of men who have been made vicious, not presumably by nature or circumstance, but by their *values*.

Food is *not* a weapon. To use it as such—to foster a mentality willing to use it as such—is to prepare, in the human character and community, the destruction of the sources of food. The first casualties of the exploitive revolution are character and community. When those fundamental integrities are devalued and broken, then perhaps it is inevitable that food will be looked upon as a weapon, just as it is inevitable that the earth will be looked upon as fuel and people as numbers or machines. But character and community—that is, culture in the broadest, richest sense—constitute, just as much as nature, the source of food. Neither nature nor people alone can produce human sustenance, but only the two together, culturally wedded. The poet Edwin Muir said it unforgettably:

> *Men are made of what is made,*
> *The meat, the drink, the life, the corn,*
> *Laid up by them, in them reborn.*
> *And self-begotten cycles close*
> *About our way; indigenous art*
> *And simple spells make unafraid*
> *The haunted labyrinths of the heart*
> *And with our wild succession braid*
> *The resurrection of the rose.*

To think of food as a weapon, or of a weapon as food, may give an illusory security and wealth to a few, but it strikes directly at the life of all.

The concept of food-as-weapon is not surprisingly the doctrine of a Department of Agriculture that is being used as an instrument of foreign political and economic speculation. This militarizing of food is the greatest threat so far raised against the farmland and the farm communities of this country. If present attitudes continue, we may expect government policies that will encourage the destruction, by overuse, of farmland. This, of course, has already begun. To answer the official call for more production—evidently to be used to bait or bribe foreign countries—farmers are plowing their waterways and permanent pastures; lands that ought to remain in grass are being planted in row crops. Contour plowing, crop rotation, and other conservation measures seem to have gone out of favor or fashion in official circles and are practiced less and less on the farm. This exclusive emphasis on production will accelerate the mechanization and chemicalization of farming, increase the price of land, increase overhead and operating costs, and thereby further diminish the farm population. Thus the tendency, if not the intention, of Mr. Butz's confusion of farming and war, is to complete the deliverance of American agriculture into the hands of corporations.

The cost of this corporate totalitarianism in energy, land, and social disruption will be enormous. It will lead to the exhaustion of farmland and farm culture. Husbandry will become an extractive industry; because maintenance will entirely give way to production, the fertility of the soil will become a limited, unrenewable resource like coal or oil.

This may not happen. It *need* not happen. But it is necessary to recognize that it *can* happen. That it can happen is made evident not only by the words of such men as Mr. Butz, but more clearly by the large-scale industrial destruction of farmland already in progress. If it does happen, we are familiar enough with the nature of American salesmanship to know that it will be done in the name of the starving millions, in the name of liberty, justice, democracy, and brotherhood, and to free the world from communism. We must, I think, be prepared to see, and to stand by, the truth: that the land should not be destroyed for *any* reason, not even for any apparently good reason. We must be prepared to say that enough food, year after year, is possible only for a limited number of people, and that this possibility can be preserved only by the steadfast, knowledgeable *care* of those people. Such "crash programs" as apparently have been contemplated by the Department of Agriculture in recent years will, in the long run, cause more starvation than they can remedy.

Meanwhile, the dust clouds rise again over Texas and Oklahoma. "Snirt" is falling in Kansas. Snow drifts in Iowa and the Dakotas are black with blown soil. The fields lose their humus and porosity, become less retentive of water, depend more on pesticides, herbicides, chemical fertilizers. Bigger tractors become necessary because the compacted soils are harder to work—and their greater weight further compacts the soil. More and bigger machines, more chemical and methodological shortcuts are needed because of the shortage of manpower on the farm—and the problems of overcrowding and unemployment increase in the cities. It is estimated that it now costs (by erosion) two bushels of Iowa topsoil to grow one bushel of corn. It is variously estimated that from five to twelve calories of fossil fuel energy are required to produce one calorie of hybrid corn energy. An official of the National Farmers Union says that "a farmer who earns $10,000 to $12,000 a year typically leaves an estate valued at about $320,000"—which means that when that farm is financed again, either by a purchaser or by an heir (to pay the inheritance taxes), it simply cannot support its new owner and pay for itself. And the *Progressive Farmer* predicts the disappearance of 200,000 to 400,000 farms each year during the next twenty years if the present trend continues.

The first principle of the exploitive mind is to divide and conquer. And surely there has never been a people more ominously and painfully divided than we are—both against each other and within ourselves. Once the revolution of exploitation is under way, statesmanship and craftsmanship are gradually replaced by salesmanship.* Its stock in trade in politics is to sell despotism and avarice as freedom and democracy. In business it sells sham and frustration as luxury and satisfaction. The "constantly expanding market" first opened in the New World by the fur traders is still expanding—no longer so much by expansions of territory or population, but by the calculated outdating, outmoding, and degradation of goods and by the hysterical self-dissatisfaction of consumers that is indigenous to an exploitive economy.

This gluttonous enterprise of ugliness, waste, and fraud thrives in the disastrous breach it has helped to make between our bodies and our souls. As a people, we have lost sight of the profound communion—even the union—of the inner with the outer life. Confucius said: "If a man have not order within him / He can not spread order about him. . . ." Surrounded as we are by evidence of the disorders of our souls and our world, we feel the strong truth in those words as well as the possibility of healing that is in them. We see the likelihood that our surroundings, from our clothes to our countryside, are the products of our inward life—our spirit, our vision—as much as they are

*The craft of persuading people to buy what they do not need, and do not want, for more than it is worth.

products of nature and work. If this is true, then we cannot live as we do and be as we would like to be. There is nothing more absurd, to give an example that is only apparently trivial, than the millions who wish to live in luxury and idleness and yet be slender and good-looking. We have millions, too, whose livelihoods, amusements, and comforts are all destructive, who nevertheless wish to live in a healthy environment; they want to run their recreational engines in clean, fresh air. There is now, in fact, no "benefit" that is not associated with disaster. That is because power can be disposed morally or harmlessly only by thoroughly unified characters and communities.

What caused these divisions? There are no doubt many causes, complex both in themselves and in their interaction. But pertinent to all of them, I think, is our attitude toward work. The growth of the exploiters' revolution on this continent has been accompanied by the growth of the idea that work is beneath human dignity, particularly any form of hand work. We have made it our overriding ambition to escape work, and as a consequence have debased work until it is only fit to escape from. We have debased the products of work and have been, in turn, debased by them. Out of this contempt for work arose the idea of a nigger: at first some person, and later some thing, to be used to relieve us of the burden of work. If we began by making niggers of people, we have ended by making a nigger of the world. We have taken the irreplaceable energies and materials of the world and turned them into jimcrack "labor-saving devices." We have made of the rivers and oceans and winds niggers to carry away our refuse, which we think we are too good to dispose of decently ourselves. And in doing this to the world that is our common heritage and bond, we have returned to making niggers of people: we have become each other's niggers.

But is work something that we have a right to escape? And can we escape it with impunity? We are probably the first entire people ever to think so. All the ancient wisdom that has come down to us counsels otherwise. It tells us that work is necessary to us, as much a part of our condition as mortality; that good work is our salvation and our joy; that shoddy or dishonest or self-serving work is our curse and our doom. We have tried to escape the sweat and sorrow promised in Genesis—only to find that, in order to do so, we must forswear love and excellence, health and joy.

Thus we can see growing out of our history a condition that is physically dangerous, morally repugnant, ugly. Contrary to the blandishments of the salesmen, it is not particularly comfortable or happy. It is not even affluent in any meaningful sense, because its abundance is dependent on sources that are being rapidly exhausted by its methods. To see these things is to come up against the question: Then what *is* desirable?

One possibility is just to tag along with the fantasists in government and industry who would have us believe that we can pursue our ideals of affluence, comfort, mobility, and leisure indefinitely. This curious faith is predicated on the notion that we will soon develop unlimited new sources of energy: domestic oil fields, shale oil, gasified coal, nuclear power, solar energy, and so on. This is fantastical because the basic cause of the energy crisis is not scarcity; it is moral ignorance and weakness of character. We don't know *how* to use energy, or what to use it *for*. And we cannot restrain ourselves. Our time is characterized as much by the abuse and waste of human energy as it is by the abuse and waste of fossil fuel energy. Nuclear power, if we are to believe its advocates, is presumably going to be well used by the same mentality that has egregiously devalued and misapplied man- and womanpower. If we had an unlimited supply of solar or wind power, we would use that destructively, too, for the same reasons.

Perhaps all of those sources of energy are going to be developed. Perhaps all of them can sooner or later be developed without threatening our survival. But not all of them together can guarantee our survival, and they cannot define what is desirable. We will not find those answers in Washington, D.C., or in the laboratories of oil companies. In order to find them, we will have to look closer to ourselves.

I believe that the answers are to be found in our history: in its until now subordinate tendency of settlement, of domestic permanence. This was the ambition of thousands of immigrants; it is formulated eloquently in some of the letters of Thomas Jefferson; it was the dream of the freed slaves; it was written into law in the Homestead Act of 1862. There are few of us whose families have not at some time been moved to see its vision and to attempt to enact its possibility. I am talking about the idea that as many as possible should share in the ownership of the land and thus be bound to it by economic interest, by the investment of love and work, by family loyalty, by memory and tradition. How much land this should be is a question, and the answer will vary with geography. The Homestead Act said 160 acres. The freedmen of the 1860s hoped for forty. We know that, particularly in other countries, families have lived decently on far fewer acres than that.

The old idea is still full of promise. It is potent with healing and with health. It has the power to turn each person away from the big-time promising and planning of the government, to confront in himself, in the immediacy of his own circumstances and whereabouts, the question of what methods and ways are best. It proposes an economy of necessities rather than an economy based upon anxiety, fantasy, luxury, and idle wishing. It proposes the independent, free-standing citizenry that Jefferson thought to be the surest safeguard of democratic liberty. And perhaps most important of all, it proposes an agriculture based upon intensive work, local energies, care, and long-living communities—that is, to state the matter from a consumer's point of view: a dependable, long-term food supply.

This is a possibility that is obviously imperiled—by antipathy in high places, by adverse public fashions and attitudes, by the deterioration of our present farm communities and traditions, by the flawed education and the inexperience of our young people. Yet it alone can promise us the continuity of attention and devotion without which the human life of the earth is impossible.

Sixty years ago, in another time of crisis, Thomas Hardy wrote these stanzas:

> *Only a man harrowing clods*
> *In a slow silent walk*
> *With an old horse that stumbles and nods*
> *Half asleep as they stalk.*

> *Only thin smoke without flame*
> *From the heaps of couch-grass;*
> *Yet this will go onward the same*
> *Though Dynasties pass.*

Today most of our people are so conditioned that they do not wish to harrow clods either with an old horse or with a new tractor. Yet Hardy's vision has come to be more urgently true than ever. The great difference these sixty years have made is that, though we feel that this work *must* go onward, we are not so certain that it will. But the care of the earth is our most ancient and most worthy and, after all, our most pleasing responsibility. To cherish what remains of it, and to foster its renewal, is our only legitimate hope.

. . . wanting good government in their states, they first established order in their own families; wanting order in the home, they first disciplined themselves . . .

CONFUCIUS, *The Great Digest*

CHAPTER TWO

The Ecological
Crisis as a
Crisis of Character

In July of 1975 it was revealed by William Rood in the *Los Angeles Times* that some of our largest and most respected conservation organizations owned stock in the very corporations and industries that have been notorious for their destructiveness and for their indifference to the concerns of conservationists. The Sierra Club, for example, had owned stocks and bonds in Exxon, General Motors, Tenneco, steel companies "having the worst pollution records in the industry," Public Service Company of Colorado, "strip-mining firms with 53 leases covering nearly 180,000 acres and pulp-mill operators cited by environmentalists for their poor water pollution controls."

These investments proved deeply embarrassing once they were made public, but the Club's officers responded as quickly as possible by making appropriate changes in its investment policy. And so if it were only a question of policy, these investments could easily be forgotten, dismissed as aberrations of the sort that inevitably turn up now and again in the workings of organizations. The difficulty is that, although the investments were absurd, they were *not* aberrant; they were perfectly representative of the modern character. These conservation groups were behaving with a very ordinary consistency; they were only doing as organizations what many of their members were, and are, doing as individuals. They were making convenience of enterprises that they knew to be morally, and even practically, indefensible.

We are dealing, then, with an absurdity that is not a quirk or an accident, but is fundamental to our character as a people. The split between what we think and what we do is profound. It is not just possible, it is altogether to be expected, that our society would produce conservationists who invest in strip-mining companies, just as it must inevitably produce asthmatic executives whose industries pollute the air and vice-presidents of pesticide corporations whose children are dying of cancer. And these people will tell you that this is the way the "real world" works. They will pride themselves on their sacrifices for "our standard of living." They will call themselves "practical men" and "hardheaded realists." And they will have their justifications in abundance from intellectuals, college professors, clergymen, politicians. The viciousness of a mentality that can look complacently upon disease as "part of the cost" would be obvious to any child. But this is the "realism" of millions of modern adults.

There is no use pretending that the contradiction between what we think or say and what we do is a limited phenomenon. There is no group of the extra-intelligent or extra-concerned or extra-virtuous that is exempt. I cannot think of any American whom I know or have heard of, who is not contributing in some way to destruction. The reason is simple: to live undestructively in an economy that is overwhelmingly destructive would require of any one of us, or of any small group of us, a great deal more work than we have yet been able to do. How could we divorce ourselves completely and yet responsibly from the technologies and powers that are destroying our planet? The answer is not yet thinkable, and it will not be thinkable for some time —even though there are now groups and families and persons everywhere in the country who have begun the labor of thinking it.

And so we are by no means divided, or readily divisible, into environmental saints and sinners. But there *are* legitimate distinctions that need to be made. These are distinctions of degree and of consciousness. Some people are less destructive than others, and some are more conscious of their destructiveness than others. For some, their involvement in pollution, soil depletion, strip-mining, deforestation, industrial and commercial waste is simply a "practical" compromise, a necessary "reality," the price of modern comfort and convenience. For others, this list of involvements is an agenda for thought and work that will produce remedies.

People who thus set their lives against destruction have necessarily confronted in themselves the absurdity that they have recognized in their society. They have first observed the tendency of modern organizations to perform in opposition to their stated purposes. They have seen governments that exploit and oppress the people they are sworn to serve and protect, medical procedures that produce ill health, schools that preserve ignorance, methods of transportation that, as Ivan Illich says, have "created more distances than they . . . bridge." And they have seen that these public absurdities are, and can be, no more than the aggregate result of private absurdities; the corruption of community has its source in the corruption of character. This realization has become the typical moral crisis of our time. Once our personal connection to what is wrong becomes clear, then we have to choose: we can go on as before, recognizing our dishonesty and living with it the best we can, or we can begin the effort to change the way we think and live.

The disease of the modern character is specialization. Looked at from the standpoint of the social *system*, the aim of specialization may seem desirable enough. The aim is to see that the responsibilities of government, law, medicine, engineering, agriculture, education, etc., are given into the hands of the most skilled, best prepared people. The difficulties do not appear until we look at specialization from the opposite standpoint—that of individual persons. We then begin to see the grotesquery—indeed, the impossibility—of an idea of community wholeness that divorces itself from any idea of personal wholeness.

The first, and best known, hazard of the specialist system is that it produces specialists—people who are elaborately and expensively trained *to do one thing*. We get into absurdity very quickly here. There are, for instance, educators who have nothing to teach, communicators who have nothing to say, medical doctors skilled at expensive cures for diseases that they have no skill, and no interest, in preventing. More common, and more damaging, are the inventors, manufacturers, and salesmen of devices who have no concern for the possible effects of those devices. Specialization is thus seen to be a way of institutionalizing, justifying, and paying highly for a calamitous disintegration and scattering-out of the various functions of character: workmanship, care, conscience, responsibility.

Even worse, a system of specialization requires the abdication to specialists of various competences and responsibilities that were once personal and universal. Thus, the average—one is tempted to say, the ideal—American citizen now consigns the problem of food production to agriculturists and "agribusinessmen," the problems of health to doctors and sanitation experts, the problems of education to school teachers and educators, the problems of conservation to conservationists, and so on. This supposedly fortunate citizen is therefore left with only two concerns: making money and entertaining himself. He earns money, typically, as a specialist, working an eight-hour day at a job for the quality or consequences of which somebody else—or, perhaps more typically, nobody else—will be responsible. And not surprisingly, since he can do so little else for himself, he is even unable to entertain himself, for there exists an enormous industry of exorbitantly expensive specialists whose purpose is to entertain him.

The beneficiary of this regime of specialists ought to be the happiest of mortals—or so we are expected to believe. *All* of his vital concerns are in the hands of certified experts. He is a certified expert himself and as such he earns more money in a year than all his great-grandparents put together. Between stints at his job he has nothing to do but mow his lawn with a sit-down lawn mower, or watch other certified experts on television. At suppertime he may eat a tray of ready-prepared food, which he and his wife (also a certified expert) procure at the cost only of money, transportation, and the pushing of a button. For a few minutes between supper and sleep he may catch a glimpse of his children, who since breakfast have been in the care of education experts, basketball or marching-band experts, or perhaps legal experts.

The fact is, however, that this is probably the most unhappy average citizen in the history of the world. He has not the power to provide himself with anything but money, and his money is inflating like a balloon and drifting away, subject to historical circumstances and the power of other people. From morning to night he does not touch anything that he has produced himself, in which he can take pride. For all his leisure and recreation, he feels bad, he looks bad, he is overweight, his health is poor. His air, water, and food are all known to contain poisons. There is a fair chance that he will die of suffocation. He suspects that his love life is not as fulfilling as other people's. He wishes that he had been born sooner, or later. He does not know why his children are the way they are. He does not understand what they say. He does not care much and does not know why he does not care. He does not know what his wife wants or what he wants. Certain advertisements and pictures in magazines make him suspect that he is basically unattractive. He feels that all his possessions are under threat of pillage. He does not know what he would do if he lost his job, if the economy failed, if the utility companies failed, if the police went on strike, if the truckers went on strike, if his wife left him, if his children ran away, if he should be found to be incurably ill. And for these anxieties, of course, he consults certified experts, who in turn consult certified experts about *their* anxieties.

It is rarely considered that this average citizen is anxious because he *ought* to be—because he still has some gumption that he has not yet given up in deference to the experts. He ought to be anxious, because he is helpless. That he is dependent upon so many specialists, the beneficiary of so much expert help, can only mean that he is a captive, a potential victim. If he lives by the competence of so many other people, then he lives also by their indulgence; his own will and his own reasons to live are made subordinate to the mere tolerance of everybody else. He has *one* chance to live what he conceives to be his life: his own small specialty within a delicate, tense, everywhere-strained system of specialties.

From a public point of view, the specialist system is a failure because, though everything is done by an expert, very little is done well. Our typical industrial or professional product is both ingenious and shoddy. The specialist system fails from a personal point of view because a person who can do only one thing can do virtually nothing for himself. In living in the world by his own will and skill, the stupidest peasant or tribesman is more competent than the most intelligent worker or technician or intellectual in a society of specialists.

What happens under the rule of specialization is that, though society becomes more and more intricate, it has less and less structure. It becomes more and more organized, but less and less orderly. The community disintegrates because it loses the necessary understandings, forms, and enactments of the relations among materials and processes, principles and actions, ideals and realities, past and present, present and future, men and women, body and spirit, city and country, civilization and wilderness, growth and decay, life and death—just as the individual character loses the sense of a responsible involvement in these relations. No longer does human life rise from the earth like a pyramid, broadly and considerately founded upon its sources. Now it scatters itself out in a reckless horizontal sprawl, like a disorderly city whose suburbs and pavements destroy the fields.

The concept of country, homeland, dwelling place becomes simplified as "the environment"—that is, what surrounds us. Once we see our place, our part of the world, as *surrounding* us, we have already made a profound division between it and ourselves. We have given up the understanding—dropped it out of our language and so out of our thought—that we and our country create one another, depend on one another, are literally part of one another; that our land passes in and out of our bodies just as our bodies pass in and out of our land; that as we and our land are part of one another, so all who are living as neighbors here, human and plant and animal, are part of one another, and so cannot possibly flourish alone; that, therefore, our culture must be our response to our place, our culture and our place are images of each other and inseparable from each other, and so neither can be better than the other.

Because by definition they lack any such sense of mutuality or wholeness, our specializations subsist on conflict with one another. The rule is never to cooperate, but rather to follow one's own interest as far as possible. Checks and balances are all applied externally, by opposition, never by self-restraint. Labor, management, the military, the government, etc., never forbear until their excesses arouse enough opposition to *force* them to do so. The good of the whole of Creation, the world and all its creatures together, is never a consideration because it is never thought of; our culture now simply lacks the means for thinking of it.

It is for this reason that none of our basic problems is ever solved. Indeed, it is for this reason that our basic problems are getting worse. The specialists are profiting too well from the symptoms, evidently, to be concerned about cures—just as the myth of imminent cure (by some "breakthrough" of science or technology) is so lucrative and all-justifying as to foreclose any possibility of an interest in prevention. The problems thus become the stock in trade of specialists. The so-called professions survive by endlessly "processing" and talking about problems that they have neither the will nor the competence to solve. The doctor who is interested in disease but not in health is clearly in the same category with the conservationist who invests in the destruction of what he otherwise intends to preserve. They both have the comfort of "job security," but at the cost of ultimate futility.

One of the most troubling characteristics of the specialist mentality is its use of money as a kind of proxy, its willingness to transmute the powers and functions of life into money. "Time is money" is one of its axioms and the source of many evils—among them the waste of both time and money. Akin to the idea that time is money is the concept, less spoken but as commonly assumed, that we may be adequately represented by money. The giving of money has thus become our characteristic virtue.

But to give is not to do. The money is given *in lieu* of action, thought, care, time. And it is no remedy for the fragmentation of character and consciousness that is the consequence of specialization. At the simplest, most practical level, it would be difficult for most of us to give enough in donations to good causes to compensate for, much less remedy, the damage done by the money that is taken from us and used destructively by various agencies of the government and by the corporations that hold us in captive dependence on their products. More important, even if we *could* give enough to overbalance the official and corporate misuse of our money, we would still not solve the problem: the willingness to be represented by money involves a submission to the modern divisions of character and community. The remedy safeguards the disease.

This has become, to some extent at least, an argument against institutional solutions. Such solutions necessarily fail to solve the problems to which they are addressed because, by definition, they cannot consider the real causes. The only real, practical, hope-giving way to remedy the fragmentation that is the disease of the modern spirit is a small and humble way—a way that a government or agency or organization or institution will never think of, though a *person* may think of it: one must begin in one's own life the private solutions that can only *in turn* become public solutions.

If, for instance, one is aware of the abuses and extortions to which one is subjected as a modern consumer, then one may join an organization of consumers to lobby for consumer-protection legislation. But in joining a consumer organization, one defines oneself as a consumer *merely*, and a mere consumer is by definition a dependent, at the mercy of the manufacturer and the salesman. If the organization secures the desired legislation, then the consumer becomes the dependent not only of the manufacturer and salesman, but of the agency that enforces the law, and is at its mercy as well. The law enacted may be a good one, and the enforcers all honest and effective; even so, the consumer will understand that one result of his effort has been to increase the number of people of whom he must beware.

The consumer may proceed to organization and even to legislation by considering only his "rights." And most of the recent talk about consumer protection has had to do with the consumer's rights. Very little indeed has been said about the consumer's responsibilities. It may be that whereas one's rights may be advocated and even "served" by an organization, one's responsibilities cannot. It may be that when one hands one's responsibilities to an organization, one becomes by that divestiture irresponsible. It may be that responsibility is intransigently a personal matter—that a responsibility can be fulfilled or failed, but cannot be got rid of.

If a consumer begins to think and act in consideration of his responsibilities, then he vastly increases his capacities as a person. And he begins to be effective in a different way—a way that is smaller perhaps, and certainly less dramatic, but sounder, and able sooner or later to assume the force of example.

A responsible consumer would be a critical consumer, would refuse to purchase the less good. And he would be a moderate consumer; he would know his needs and would not purchase what he did not need; he would sort among his needs and study to reduce them. These things, of course, have been often said, though in our time they have not been said very loudly and have not been much heeded. In our time the rule among consumers has been to spend money recklessly. People whose governing habit is the relinquishment of power, competence, and responsibility, and whose characteristic suffering is the anxiety of futility, make excellent spenders. They are the ideal consumers. By inducing in them little panics of boredom, powerlessness, sexual failure, mortality, paranoia, they can be made to buy (or vote for) virtually anything that is "attractively packaged." The advertising industry is founded upon this principle.

What has not been often said, because it did not need to be said until fairly recent times, is that the responsible consumer must also be in some way a producer. Out of his own resources and skills, he must be equal to some of his own needs. The household that prepares its own meals in its own kitchen with some intelligent regard for nutritional value, and thus depends on the grocer only for selected raw materials, exercises an influence on the food industry that reaches from the store all the way back to the seedsman. The household that produces some or all of its own food will have a proportionately greater influence. The household that can provide some of its own pleasures will not be helplessly dependent on the entertainment industry, will influence it by not being helplessly dependent on it, and will not support it thoughtlessly out of boredom.

The responsible consumer thus escapes the limits of his own dissatisfaction. He can choose, and exert the influence of his choosing, because he has given himself choices. He is not confined to the negativity of his complaint. He influences the market by his freedom. This is no specialized act, but an act that is substantial and complex, both practically and morally. By making himself responsibly free, a person changes both his life and his surroundings.

It is possible, then, to perceive a critical difference between responsible consumers and consumers who are merely organized. The responsible consumer slips out of the consumer category altogether. He is a responsible consumer incidentally, almost inadvertently; he is a responsible consumer because he lives a responsible life.

The same distinction is to be perceived between organized conservationists and responsible conservationists. (A responsible consumer *is*, of course, a responsible conservationist.) The conservationists who are merely organized function as specialists who have lost sight of basic connections. Conservation organizations hold stock in exploitive industries because they have no clear perception of, and therefore fail to be responsible for, the connections between what they say and what they do, what they desire and how they live.

The Sierra Club, for instance, defines itself by a slogan which it prints on the flaps of its envelopes. Its aim, according to the slogan, is "... to explore, enjoy, and protect the nation's scenic resources ..." To some extent, the Club's current concerns and attitudes belie this slogan. But there is also a sense in which the slogan defines the limits of organized conservation—some that have been self-imposed, others that are implicit in the nature of organization.

The key word in the slogan is "scenic." As used here, the word is a fossil. It is left over from a time when our comforts and luxuries were accepted simply as the rewards of progress to an ingenious, forward-looking people, when no threat was perceived in urbanization and industrialization, and when conservation was therefore an activity oriented toward vacations. It was "good to get out of the city" for a few weeks or weekends a year, and there was understandable concern that there should remain pleasant places to go. Some of the more adventurous vacationers were even aware of places of unique beauty that would be defaced if they were not set aside and protected. These people were effective in their way and within their limits, and they started the era of wilderness conservation. The results will give us abundant reasons for gratitude as long as we have sense enough to preserve them. But wilderness conservation did little to prepare us either to understand or to oppose the general mayhem of the all-outdoors that the industrial revolution has finally imposed upon us.

Wilderness conservation, we can now see, is specialized conservation. Its specialization is memorialized, in the Sierra Club's slogan, in the word "scenic." A scene is a place "as seen by a viewer." It is a "view." The appreciator of a place perceived as scenic is merely its observer, by implication both different and distant or detached from it. The connoisseur of the scenic has thus placed strict limitations both upon the sort of place he is interested in and upon his relation to it.

But even if the slogan were made to read "... to explore, enjoy, and protect the nation's resources ... ," the most critical concern would still be left out. For while conservationists are exploring, enjoying, and protecting the nation's resources, they are also *using* them. They are drawing their lives from the nation's resources, scenic and unscenic. If the resolve to explore, enjoy, and protect does not create a moral energy that will define and enforce responsible use, then organized conservation will prove ultimately futile. And this, again, will be a failure of character.

Although responsible use may be defined, advocated, and to some extent required by organizations, it cannot be implemented or enacted by them. It cannot be effectively enforced by them. The use of the world is finally a personal matter, and the world can be preserved in health only by the forbearance and care of a multitude of persons. That is, the possibility of the world's health will have to be defined in the characters of persons as clearly and as urgently as the possibility of personal "success" is now so defined. Organizations may promote this sort of forbearance and care, but they cannot provide it.

CHAPTER THREE

The Ecological Crisis as a Crisis of Agriculture

One reason that an organization cannot properly enact our relationship to the world is that an organization cannot define that relationship except in general terms, and no matter how general may be a person's attitude toward the world, his impact upon it must become specific and tangible at some point. Sooner or later in his behalf —whether he approves or understands or not—a strip-miner's bulldozer tears into a mountainside, a stand of trees is clear-cut, a gully washes through a cornfield.

The conservation movement has never resolved this dilemma. It has never faced it. Until very recently—until pollution and strip-mining became critical issues—conservationists divided the country into that land which they wished to preserve and enjoy (the wilderness areas) and that which they consigned to use by *other* people. With the increase of pollution and mining, their interest has become two-branched, to include, along with the pristine, the critically abused. At present the issue of *use* is still in its beginning.

Because of this, the mentality of conservation is divided, and disaster is implicit in its division. It is divided between its intentional protection of some places and some aspects of "the environment" and its inadvertent destruction of others. It is variously either vacation-oriented or crisis-oriented. For the most part, it is not yet sensitive to the impact of daily living upon the sources of daily life. The typical present-day conservationist will fight to preserve what he enjoys; he will fight whatever directly threatens his health; he will oppose any ecological violence large or dramatic enough to attract his attention. But he has not yet worried much about the impact of his own livelihood, habits, pleasures, or appetites. He has not, in short, addressed himself to the problem of use. He does not have a definition of his relationship to the world that is sufficiently elaborate and exact.

The problem is well defined in a letter I received from David Budbill of Wolcott, Vermont:

"What I've noticed around here with the militant ecology people (don't get me wrong, I, like you, consider myself one of them) is a syndrome I call the Terrarium View of the World: nature always at a distance, under glass.

"Down-country people come up here, buy a 30-acre meadow, then when you ask them what they plan to *do* with it, they look at you like you're some kind of war criminal and say, 'Why, nothing! We want to leave it *just* the way it is!' They think they're protecting the environment, even though they've forgotten, or never knew, that nature abhors a vacuum . . . and in a couple of years their meadow is full of hardhack and berries and young gray birch and red maple. Pretty soon they can't even walk through the brush it's so thick. They treat the land like any other possession, object, they own, set it aside, watch it, passively, not wanting to, nay! thinking it abhorrent to engage in a living relationship with it. . . .

"Another thing folks like this do is buy land and immediately post it (to protect the animals, or their investment, I guess) then go back home. . . . The old guy or the young guy who has always hunted deer on that piece is mad. The excuse for posting (protection) is a thinly disguised cover for the real notion which has to do with the possessive, capitalist ideas about property. I'm not opposed to private property, like it even, but the folks I'm talking about, in their posting, violate . . . a strong local tradition of free trespass. There are disadvantages to free trespass, abuses, we've suffered them, but what's good about it is it understands something about use and sharing. The upper-class eco-folks lack this understanding . . .

". . . we always, with our neighbor, pick apples in the fall off trees on a down-country owner's land. There is a feeling we have the *right* to do that, a feeling that the sin is not trespass, the sin is letting the apples go to waste.

"What I'm trying to get at is that in the environmental movement there are some ugly, elitist, class-struggle type things operating. The best example of this around here is the controversy over trailers. The Audubon types (I'm a member of Audubon) are fighting . . . terribly hard to zone trailers out of areas like this, put them in trailer parks or eliminate them altogether. Well, a trailer is the only living space a working man around here can afford. And if he, say, inherits 3 acres from a parent and wants to put a trailer on it, the eco-folks would like to say no, which is a dandy way to ghettoize the poor. There are so many elements of class struggle lying under the attitudes of a lot of environmentalists; it's scary. . . . Their view of the natural world is so delicate and precious, terrarium-like, picture-windowish. I know nature is precious and delicate. I also know it is incredibly tough and resilient, has unbelievable power to respond to and flourish with kindly use.

". . . I don't care about the landscape if I am to be excluded from it. Why should I? In Audubon magazine almost always the beautiful pictures are without man; the ugly ones with him. Such self hatred! I keep wanting to write to them and say, 'Look! my name is David Budbill and I belong to the chain of being too, as a participant not an observer (nature is not television!) and the question isn't to use or not to use but rather *how* to use.'"

The conservationist congratulates himself, on the one hand, for his awareness of the severity of human influence on the natural world. On the other hand, in his own contact with that world, he can think of nothing but to efface himself—to leave it *just* the way it is.

This is an important issue, and I want to be careful not to oversimplify it. What has to be acknowledged at the outset is that wilderness conservation is important and that it has its place in any conservation program, just as the wilderness has its place in human memory and culture. It seems likely to me that the concern for wilderness must stand at the apex of the conservation effort, just as it probably must stand at the apex of consciousness in any decent culture. There are several reasons for this:

1. Our biological roots as well as our cultural roots are in nature. We began in a world that was pristine, undiminished by anything we had done, and at various times in our history the unspoiled wilderness has again imposed itself, its charming and forbidding *invitation*, upon our consciousness. It is important that we should preserve this memory. We need places in reach of every community where children

can imagine the prehistoric and the beginning of history: the un-known, the trackless, the first comers.

2. If we are to be properly humble in our use of the world, we need places that we do not use at all. We need the experience of leaving something alone. We need places that we forbear to change, or in-fluence by our presence, or impose on even by our understanding; places that we accept as influences upon us, not the other way around, that we enter with the sense, the pleasure, of having nothing to do there; places that we must enter in a kind of cultural nakedness, without comforts or tools, to submit rather than to conquer. We need what other ages would have called sacred groves. We need groves, anyhow, that we would treat as if they were sacred—in order, per-haps, to perceive their sanctity.

3. We need wilderness as a standard of civilization and as a cultural model. Only by preserving areas where nature's processes are undis-turbed can we preserve an accurate sense of the impact of civilization upon its natural sources. Only if we know how the land *was* can we tell how it *is*. Records, figures, statistics will not suffice; to know, in the true sense, is to see. We must see the difference—in rates of ero-sion, for instance, or in soil structure or fertility—in order to keep it as small as possible. As a cultural model, the wilderness is probably indispensable. Sir Albert Howard suggests that it is when he says that farmers should pattern the maintenance of their fields after the forest floor, for the forces of growth and the forces of decay are in balance there.

But we cannot hope—for reasons practical and humane, we cannot even wish—to preserve more than a small portion of the land in wilderness. Most of it we will have to use. The conservation mentality swings from self-righteous outrage to self-deprecation because it has neglected this issue. Its self-contradictions can only be reconciled—and the conservation impulse made to function as ubiquitously and variously as it needs to—by understanding, imagining, and living out the possibility of "kindly use." Only that can dissolve the boundaries that divide people from the land and its care, which together are the source of human life. There are many kinds of land use, but the one that is most widespread and in need of consideration is that of agri-culture.

For us, the possibility of kindly use is weighted with problems. In the first place, this is not ultimately an organizational or institutional solution. Institutional solutions tend to narrow and simplify as they approach action. A large number of people can act together only by defining the point or the line on which their various interests converge. Organizations tend to move toward single objectives—a ruling, a vote, a law—and they find it relatively simple to cohere under acronyms and slogans.

But kindly use is a concept that of necessity broadens, becoming more complex and diverse, as it approaches action. The land is too various in its kinds, climates, conditions, declivities, aspects, and histories to conform to any generalized understanding or to prosper under generalized treatment. The use of land cannot be both general and kindly—just as the forms of good manners, generally applied (applied, that is, without consideration of differences), are experienced as indifference, bad manners. To treat every field, or every part of every field, with the same consideration is not farming but industry. Kindly use depends upon intimate knowledge, the most sensitive responsiveness and responsibility. As knowledge (hence, use) is generalized, essential values are destroyed. As the householder evolves into a consumer, the farm evolves into a factory—with results that are potentially calamitous for both.

The understanding of kindly use in agriculture must encompass both farm and household, for the mutuality of influence between them is profound. Once, of course, the idea of a farm included the idea of a household: an integral and major part of a farm's economy was the economy of its own household; the family that owned and worked the farm lived from it. But the farm also helped to feed other households in towns and cities. These households were dependent on the farms, but not passively so, for their dependence was limited in two ways. For one thing, the town or city household was itself often a producer of food: at one time town and city lots routinely included garden space and often included pens and buildings to accommodate milk cows, fattening hogs, and flocks of poultry. For another thing, the urban household carefully selected and prepared the food that it bought; the neighborhood shops were suppliers of kitchen raw materials to local households, of whose needs and tastes the shopkeepers had personal knowledge. The shopkeepers were under the direct influence and discipline of their customers' wants, which they had to supply honestly if they hoped to prosper. The household was therefore not merely a unit in the economy of food production; its members practiced essential productive skills. The consumers of food were also producers or processors of food, or both.

31

This collaboration of household and farm was never, in America, sufficiently thrifty or sufficiently careful of soil fertility. It is tempting to suppose that, given certain critical historical and cultural differences, they might have developed sufficient thrift and care. As it happened, however, the development went in the opposite direction. The collaborators purified their roles—the household became simply a house or residence, purely consumptive in its function; the farm ceased to be a place to live and a way of life and became a unit of production—and their once collaborative relationship became competitive. Between them the merchant, who had been only a supplier of raw materials, began to usurp the previous functions of both household and farm, becoming increasingly both a processor and producer. And so an enterprise that once had some susceptibility to qualitative standards—standards of personal taste and preference at one end and of good husbandry at the other—has come more and more under the influence of standards that are merely economic or quantitative. The consumer wants food to be as cheap as possible. The producer wants it to be as expensive as possible. Both want it to involve as little labor as possible. And so the standards of cheapness and convenience, which are irresistibly simplifying and therefore inevitably exploitive, have been substituted for the standard of health (of both people and land), which would enforce consideration of essential complexities.

Social fashion, delusion, and propaganda have combined to persuade the public that our agriculture is for the best of reasons the envy of the Modern World. American citizens are now ready to believe without question that it is entirely good, a grand accomplishment, that each American farmer now "feeds himself and 56 others." They are willing to hear that "96 percent of America's manpower is freed from food production"—without asking what it may have been "freed" *for*, or how many as a consequence have been "freed" from employment of any kind. The "climate of opinion" is now such that a recent assistant secretary of agriculture could condemn the principle of crop rotation without even an acknowledgment of the probable costs in soil depletion and erosion, and former Secretary of Agriculture Butz could say with approval that in 1974 "only 4 percent of all U.S. farms . . . produced almost 50 percent of all farm goods," without acknowledging the human—and, indeed, the agricultural—penalties.

What these men were praising—what such men have been praising for so long that the praise can be uttered without thought—is a disaster that is both agricultural and cultural: the generalization of the relationship between people and land. That one American farmer can now feed himself and fifty-six other people may be, within the narrow view of the specialist, a triumph of technology; by no stretch of reason can it be considered a triumph of agriculture or of culture. It has been made possible by the substitution of energy for knowledge, of methodology for care, of technology for morality. This "accomplishment" is not primarily the work of farmers—who have been, by and large, its victims—but of a collaboration of corporations, university specialists, and government agencies. It is therefore an agricultural development not motivated by agricultural aims or disciplines, but by the ambitions of merchants, industrialists, bureaucrats, and academic careerists. We should not be surprised to find that its effect on both the farmland and the farm people has been ruinous. It has divided all land into two kinds—that which permits the use of large equipment and that which does not. And it has divided all farmers into two kinds—those who have sufficient "business sense" and managerial ability to handle the large acreages necessary to finance large machines and those who do not.

Those lands that are too steep or stony or small-featured to be farmed with big equipment are increasingly not farmed at all, but are abandoned to weeds and bushes, often with the gullies of previous bad use unrepaired. That these lands can often be made highly productive with kindly use is simply of no interest; we now have neither the small technology nor the small economics nor the available work force necessary to make use of them. What might be the importance of these "marginal" lands, and of an agricultural technology and economy appropriate to them, in light of population growth is a question that the agriculture experts apparently would be embarrassed to consider, so entranced are they by the glamor of bigness.

As for the farm families who cannot "get bigger" and therefore have to "get out," they are apparently written off as a reasonable, quite ordinary, and altogether bearable expense. Former Secretary Butz could praise the business acumen of the new big-time American farmer ("In all likelihood he knows as much about financing and business accountability as his banker"), evidently without wondering what may be the *agricultural* import or effect of such knowledge, or if somewhere there might not be an excellent farmer who is *not* more acute, in a business way, than his banker. But this is the catch in our almost religious dependence on experts: Mr. Butz is a farm expert, and a farm expert is by definition not a farmer; he has changed sides. I have at hand fifteen speeches by Mr. Butz and his assistant secretaries, all of which praise the productivity—that is, the business success—of the American farmer, and none of which mentions any problem of land maintenance or any problem of the small farmer.

A sampling of quotations from one of these speeches—one made by former Assistant Secretary Richard E. Bell—will give the gist and the manner of official agricultural thinking:

". . . true agripower . . . generates agridollars through agricultural exports."

"True agripower is the capacity of less than 5 percent of America's population to feed itself and the remaining 95 percent with enough food left over to meet market demands of other nations and still provide food assistance for poor people throughout the world."

"Agripower should not be a political tool. Feeding people . . . is too serious a matter to be left to political manipulation."

"Once again growth in U.S. farm productivity . . . is on the rise. . . . We no longer have the acreage limitations which for so many years served to restrict grain and cotton production. . . ."

". . . the real measure [of agricultural strength] is productivity, combined with processing and marketing efficiency."

"Years ago, farm operations were highly diversified, but today, farmers are concentrating on fewer and much larger crop or livestock enterprises. Now, many one- or two-enterprise farms exist where there were formerly three to five enterprises.

"And with the spread of sophisticated machinery, farm sizes have expanded as their numbers have declined—stretching from an average 195 acres in the 1940's to about 390 in the 1970's.

"Specialization and growth are aided by the ready availability of purchased inputs and custom services."

"With additional income earned from exports, U.S. farmers are able to purchase more household appliances, farm equipment, building supplies, and other capital and consumer goods."

34

"Agridollars have gone a long way toward offsetting our petro-dollar drain."

"Less than 5 percent . . . of all grain moving between countries goes for food assistance."

"It is evident that U.S. agripower is a major force in the world's exchange of goods and services. Agripower is, unquestionably, an even greater force than petropower in man's survival in the future. Man can and has survived without petroleum, but he cannot live without food."

And that was the official line on agriculture during the Butz years. There is nothing in it that was not representative: the self-congratu-lation, the confusions of purpose, the complacency, the jargon, the sprains and ruptures of sense, the ignorance or ignoring of conse-quence, the social and economic prejudices ritualized in progressivist clichés. And nowhere that I have seen was the official line more com-plicated than this, more aware of costs or inequities or conflicts or problems.

We would do well to examine these statements in more detail, for they are not just the political policies of ex-officials. They represent very well the prevalent assumptions of agricultural bureaucrats, aca-demicians, and businessmen.

"Agripower," it will be noted, is not measured by the fertility or health of the soil, or the health, wisdom, thrift, or stewardship of the farming community. It is measured by its ability to produce a mar-ketable surplus, which "generates agridollars." It is to be measured by "productivity, combined with processing and marketing effi-ciency." The income from this increased production, we are told, is spent by farmers not for soil maintenance or improvement, water conservation, or erosion control, but for "purchased inputs": "house-hold appliances, farm equipment, building supplies, and other capital and consumer goods." I do not mean that we should necessarily be-grudge the farmer these purchases; I am only noticing that, to Mr. Bell, the farmer does not prosper to become a better farmer, but to become a bigger spender. The assistant secretary was applying to farming a standard of judgment that is economic, not agricultural. Farming is defined here purely to suit the purposes of a businessman.

Mr. Bell makes the benign assertion that this "agripower" feeds people, including the poor of the world, and is therefore too important to be put to political use. But when this subject is reverted to at the end of the speech, we find that "U.S. agripower" is a major force in world trade, a force intended to offset the "petropower" of other countries. And we have the assurance that, after all, "Less than 5 percent . . . of all grain moving between countries goes for food assistance" to the poor. (And, of course, all of this must be weighed against former Secretary Butz's avowal that "Food is a weapon.")*

Next we hear the routine self-congratulation of the department on the increase of productivity following the removal of production controls (the only agricultural problem acknowledged in any of these speeches). Our agriculture policy is now based on the principle of "full production"—an obscure notion that former Secretary Butz and his colleagues paraded before their audiences like the True Cross. As businessmen and politicians, perhaps they did not know how strenuously agricultural production must be qualified by the restraints and disciplines of soil maintenance and conservation. Perhaps they did not know what "full production" means in present practice—present technology, methods, and economic urgencies having replaced those restraints and disciplines. In practice, however, "full production" means that on farm after farm fence rows, windbreaks, and waterways have been plowed, steep slopes put under cultivation, and soil stewardship generally neglected. It means that production is being paid for, not just with labor, money, and fuel, *but with land*.

But the most remarkable and significant part of Mr. Bell's speech is the one in which he applauds the most degenerative, dangerous, costly, and socially disruptive "achievements" of American agriculture: (1) "economy of size," which means the gathering of farmland into the ownership of fewer and fewer people—not farmers necessarily but an "agribusiness elite"—and the consequent dispossession of millions of small farmers and farm families; and (2) specialization, which means the abandonment of the ancient, proven principle of agricultural diversity—agricultural stability through diversity—with its attendant principles of mixed husbandry of plants and animals and crop rotation. It is now, for the first time, deemed provident and wise to put all the eggs in one basket.

The giveaway is in the curiously pleased-sounding statement that "specialization and growth are aided by the ready availability of purchased inputs. . . ." This betrays, for one thing, how far we have

*A friend has pointed out the "incredible cheek" of calling food "agripower" and then warning against its use as "a political tool."

abandoned the old ideal that the farm should aim at economic independence; that is, it should be far more productive than consumptive, more a source than a consumer of material goods. This old ideal sought to preserve the farmer on the farm; that was of necessity its first objective. But it also sought to keep the source of food independent of any but agricultural means—an aim that ought to recommend itself, it would seem, to a fairly ordinary intelligence. Its desirability becomes altogether clear when one considers that a farm —given the *appropriate* technology, the recovery and return of organic wastes to the soil, an economy that is not exploitive, and a sufficient human work force—can achieve a high measure of economic independence.

None of this was clear to the intellectuals of the Department of Agriculture, and no doubt they were thereby saved a good deal of worry. For one of the "purchased inputs," on the "ready availability" of which our agriculture now absolutely depends, is petroleum—for which we are not only dependent on non-agricultural sources, but on other nations. That we should have an agriculture based as much on petroleum as on the soil—that we need petroleum exactly as much as we need food and must have it *before* we can eat—may seem absurd. It *is* absurd. It is nevertheless true. And it exposes the hollowness of Mr. Bell's contention that "Agripower is, unquestionably, an even greater force than petropower in man's survival in the future. Man can and has survived without petroleum, but he cannot live without food." The two powers are now clearly the same. That the two are not only interdependent, but competitive as well, suggests more forcibly than Mr. Butz's words that "Food is a weapon."

And so, far from the concerns of "kindly use" that alone can assure a permanent agriculture and a permanent food supply, the Department of Agriculture is lost in the paper clouds of "agribusiness," propagating statistical proofs of visibly ruinous agricultural practices. One can imagine the average American nodding over these "expert" reports and projections. Whether he is nodding because he agrees or because he is asleep does not matter; there is no difference.

Thus the estrangement of consumer and producer, their evolution from collaborators in food production to competitors in the food market, involves a process of oversimplification on both sides. The consumer withdraws from the problems of food production, hence becomes ignorant of them and often scornful of them; the producer no longer sees himself as intermediary between people and land—the people's respresentative on the land—and becomes interested only in production. The consumer eats worse, and the producer farms worse. And, in their estrangement, waste is institutionalized. Without regret, with less and less interest in the disciplines of thrift and conservation, with, in fact, the assumption that this is the way of the world, our present agriculture wastes topsoil, water, fossil fuel, and human energy—to name only the most noticeable things. Consumers participate "innocently" or ignorantly in all these farm wastes and add to them wastes that are urban or consumptive in nature: mainly all the materials and energy that go into unnecessary processing and packaging, as well as tons of organic matter (highly valuable—and certainly, in the long run, necessary—as fertilizer) that they flush down their drains or throw out as garbage.

What this means for conservationists is that, as consumers, they may be using—and abusing—more land by proxy than they are conserving by the intervention of their organizations. We now have more people using the land (that is, living from it) and fewer thinking about it than ever before. We are eating thoughtlessly, as no other entire society ever has been able to do. We are eating—drawing our lives out of our land—thoughtlessly. If we study carefully the implications of that, we will see that the agricultural crisis is not merely a matter of supply and demand to be remedied by some change of government policy or some technological "breakthrough." It is a crisis of culture.

CHAPTER FOUR

The Agricultural
Crisis as a
Crisis of Culture

In my boyhood, Henry County, Kentucky, was not just a rural county, as it still is—it was a *farming* county. The farms were generally small. They were farmed by families who lived not only upon them, but within and *from* them. These families grew gardens. They produced their own meat, milk, and eggs. The farms were highly diversified. The main money crop was tobacco. But the farmers also grew corn, wheat, barley, oats, hay, and sorghum. Cattle, hogs, and sheep were all characteristically raised on the same farms. There were small dairies, the milking more often than not done by hand. Those were the farm products that might have been considered major. But there were also minor products, and one of the most important characteristics of that old economy was the existence of markets for minor products. In those days a farm family could easily market its surplus cream, eggs, old hens, and frying chickens. The power for field work was still furnished mainly by horses and mules. There was still a prevalent pride in workmanship, and thrift was still a forceful social ideal. The pride of most people was still in their homes, and their homes looked like it.

This was by no means a perfect society. Its people had often been violent and wasteful in their use of the land and of each other. Its present ills had already taken root in it. But I have spoken of its agricultural economy of a generation ago to suggest that there were also good qualities indigenous to it that might have been cultivated and built upon.

That they were not cultivated and built upon—that they were repudiated as the stuff of a hopelessly outmoded, unscientific way of life—is a tragic error on the part of the people themselves; and it is a work of monstrous ignorance and irresponsibility on the part of the experts and politicians, who have prescribed, encouraged, and applauded the disintegration of such farming communities all over the country.

In the decades since World War II the farms of Henry County have become increasingly mechanized. Though they are still comparatively diversified, they are less diversified than they used to be. The holdings are larger, the owners are fewer. The land is falling more and more into the hands of speculators and professional people from the cities, who—in spite of all the scientific agricultural miracles—still have much more money than farmers. Because of big technology and big economics, there is more abandoned land in the county than ever before. Many of the better farms are visibly deteriorating, for want of manpower and time and money to maintain them properly. The number of part-time farmers and ex-farmers increases every year. Our harvests depend more and more on the labor of old people and young children. The farm people live less and less from their own produce, more and more from what they buy. The best of them are more worried about money and more overworked than ever before. Among the people as a whole, the focus of interest has largely shifted from the household to the automobile; the ideals of workmanship and thrift have been replaced by the goals of leisure, comfort, and entertainment. For Henry County plays its full part in what Maurice Telleen calls "the world's first broad-based hedonism." The young people expect to leave as soon as they finish high school, and so they are without permanent interest; they are generally not interested in anything that cannot be reached by automobile on a good road. Few of the farmers' children will be able to afford to stay on the farm—perhaps even fewer will wish to do so, for it will cost too much, require too much work and worry, and it is hardly a fashionable ambition.

And nowhere now is there a market for minor produce: a bucket of cream, a hen, a few dozen eggs. One cannot sell milk from a few cows anymore; the law-required equipment is too expensive. Those markets were done away with in the name of sanitation—but, of course, to the enrichment of the large producers. We have always had to have "a good reason" for doing away with small operators, and in modern times the good reason has often been sanitation, for which there is apparently no small or cheap technology. Future historians will no doubt remark upon the inevitable association, with us, between sanitation and filthy lucre. And it is one of the miracles of science and hygiene that the germs that used to be in our food have been replaced by poisons.

In all this, few people whose testimony would have mattered have seen the connection between the "modernization" of agricultural techniques and the disintegration of the culture and the communities of farming—and the consequent disintegration of the structures of urban life. What we have called agricultural progress has, in fact, involved the forcible displacement of millions of people.

I remember, during the fifties, the outrage with which our political leaders spoke of the forced removal of the populations of villages in communist countries. I also remember that at the same time, in Washington, the word on farming was "Get big or get out"—a policy which is still in effect and which has taken an enormous toll. The only difference is that of method: the force used by the communists was military; with us, it has been economic—a "free market" in which the freest were the richest. The attitudes are equally cruel, and I believe that the results will prove equally damaging, not just to the concerns and values of the human spirit, but to the practicalities of survival.

And so those who could not get big have got out—not just in my community, but in farm communities all over the country. But as a social or economic goal, bigness is totalitarian; it establishes an inevitable tendency toward the *one* that will be the biggest of all. Many who got big to stay in are now being driven out by those who got bigger. The aim of bigness implies not one aim that is not socially and culturally destructive.

And this community-killing agriculture, with its monomania of bigness, is not primarily the work of farmers, though it has burgeoned on their weaknesses. It is the work of the institutions of agriculture: the university experts, the bureaucrats, and the "agribusinessmen," who have promoted so-called efficiency at the expense of community (and of real efficiency), and quantity at the expense of quality.

In 1973, 1000 Kentucky dairies went out of business. They were the victims of policies by which we imported dairy products to compete with our own and exported so much grain as to cause a drastic rise in the price of feed. And, typically, an agriculture expert at the University of Kentucky, Dr. John Nicolai, was optimistic about this failure of 1000 dairymen, whose cause he is supposedly being paid—partly with *their* tax money—to serve. They were inefficient producers, he said, and they needed to be eliminated.

He did not say—indeed, there was no indication that he had ever considered—what might be the limits of his criterion or his logic. Did he propose to applaud this process year after year until "biggest" and "most efficient" become synonymous with "only"? Did these dairymen have any value not subsumed under the heading of "efficiency"? And who benefited by their failure? Assuming that the benefit reached beyond the more "efficient" (that is, the bigger) producers to lower the cost of milk to consumers, do we then have a formula by which to determine how many consumer dollars are equal to the livelihood of one dairyman? Or is *any* degree of "efficiency" worth *any* cost? I do not think that this expert knows the answers. I do not think that he is under any pressure—scholarly, professional, moral, or otherwise—to ask the questions. This sort of regardlessness is invariably justified by pointing to the enormous productivity of American agriculture. But any abundance, in any amount, is illusory if it does not safeguard its producers, and in American agriculture it is now virtually the accepted rule that abundance will destroy its producers.

And along with the rest of society, the established agriculture has shifted its emphasis, and its interest, from quality to quantity, having failed to see that in the long run the two ideas are inseparable. To pursue quantity alone is to destroy those disciplines in the producer that are the only assurance of quantity. What is the effect on quantity of persuading a producer to produce an inferior product? What, in other words, is the relation of pride or craftsmanship to abundance? That is another question the "agribusinessmen" and their academic

42

collaborators do not ask. They do not ask it because they are afraid of the answer: The preserver of abundance is excellence.

My point is that food is a cultural product; it cannot be produced by technology alone. Those agriculturists who think of the problems of food production solely in terms of technological innovation are oversimplifying both the practicalities of production and the network of meanings and values necessary to define, nurture, and preserve the practical motivations. That the discipline of agriculture should have been so divorced from other disciplines has its immediate cause in the compartmental structure of the universities, in which complementary, mutually sustaining and enriching disciplines are divided, according to "professions," into fragmented, one-eyed specialties. It is suggested, both by the organization of the universities and by the kind of thinking they foster, that farming shall be the responsibility only of the college of agriculture, that law shall be in the sole charge of the professors of law, that morality shall be taken care of by the philosophy department, reading by the English department, and so on. The same, of course, is true of government, which has become another way of institutionalizing the same fragmentation.

However, if we conceive of a culture as one body, which it is, we see that all of its disciplines are everybody's business, and that the proper university product is therefore not the whittled-down, isolated mentality of expertise, but a mind competent in all its concerns. To such a mind it would be clear that there are agricultural disciplines that have nothing to do with crop production, just as there are agricultural obligations that belong to people who are not farmers.

A culture is not a collection of relics or ornaments, but a practical necessity, and its corruption invokes calamity. A healthy culture is a communal order of memory, insight, value, work, conviviality, reverence, aspiration. It reveals the human necessities and the human limits. It clarifies our inescapable bonds to the earth and to each other. It assures that the necessary restraints are observed, that the necessary work is done, and that it is done well. A healthy *farm* culture can be based only upon familiarity and can grow only among a people soundly established upon the land; it nourishes and safeguards a human intelligence of the earth that no amount of technology can satisfactorily replace. The growth of such a culture was once a strong possibility in the farm communities of this country. We now have only the sad remnants of those communities. If we allow another generation to pass without doing what is necessary to enhance and

43

embolden the possibility now perishing with them, we will lose it altogether. And then we will not only invoke calamity—we will deserve it.

Several years ago I argued with a friend of mine that we might make money by marketing some inferior lambs. My friend thought for a minute and then he said, "I'm in the business of producing *good* lambs, and I'm not going to sell any other kind." He also said that he kept the weeds out of his crops for the same reason that he washed his face. The human race has survived by that attitude. It can survive *only* by that attitude—though the farmers who have it have not been much acknowledged or much rewarded.

Such an attitude does not come from technique or technology. It does not come from education; in more than two decades in universities I have rarely seen it. It does not come even from principle. It comes from a passion that is culturally prepared—a passion for excellence and order that is handed down to young people by older people whom they respect and love. When we destroy the possibility of that succession, we will have gone far toward destroying ourselves.

It is by the measure of culture, rather than economics or technology, that we can begin to reckon the nature and the cost of the country-to-city migration that has left our farmland in the hands of only five percent of the people. From a cultural point of view, the movement from the farm to the city involves a radical simplification of mind and of character.

A competent farmer is his own boss. He has learned the disciplines necessary to go ahead on his own, as required by economic obligation, loyalty to his place, pride in his work. His workdays require the use of long experience and practiced judgment, for the failures of which he knows that he will suffer. His days do not begin and end by rule, but in response to necessity, interest, and obligation. They are not measured by the clock, but by the task and his endurance; they last as long as necessary or as long as he can work. He has mastered intricate formal patterns in ordering his work within the overlapping cycles—human and natural, controllable and uncontrollable—of the life of a farm.

Such a man, upon moving to the city and taking a job in industry, becomes a specialized subordinate, dependent upon the authority and judgment of other people. His disciplines are no longer implicit in his own experience, assumptions, and values, but are imposed on him from the outside. For a complex responsibility he has substituted a simple dutifulness. The strict competences of independence, the formal mastery, the complexities of attitude and know-how necessary to life on the farm, which have been in the making in the race of farmers since before history, all are replaced by the knowledge of some fragmentary task that may be learned by rote in a little while.

Such a simplification of mind is easy. Given the pressure of economics and social fashion that has been behind it and the decline of values that has accompanied it, it may be said to have been gravity-powered. The reverse movement—a reverse movement *is* necessary, and some have undertaken it—is uphill, and it is difficult. It cannot be fully accomplished in a generation. It will probably require several generations—enough to establish complex local cultures with strong communal memories and traditions of care.

There seems to be a rule that we can simplify our minds and our culture only at the cost of an oppressive social and mechanical complexity. We can simplify our society—that is, make ourselves free—only by undertaking tasks of great mental and cultural complexity. Farming, the *best* farming, is a task that calls for this sort of complexity, both in the character of the farmer and in his culture. To simplify either one is to destroy it.

That is because the best farming requires a farmer—a husbandman, a nurturer—not a technician or businessman. A technician or a businessman, given the necessary abilities and ambitions, can be made in a little while, by training. A good farmer, on the other hand, is a cultural product; he is made by a sort of training, certainly, in what his time imposes or demands, but he is also made by generations of experience. This essential experience can only be accumulated, tested, preserved, handed down in settled households, friendships, and communities that are deliberately and carefully native to their own ground, in which the past has prepared the present and the present safeguards the future.

The concentration of the farmland into larger and larger holdings and fewer and fewer hands—with the consequent increase of overhead, debt, and dependence on machines—is thus a matter of complex significance, and its agricultural significance cannot be disentangled from its cultural significance. It *forces* a profound revolution in the farmer's mind: once his investment in land and machines is large enough, he must forsake the values of husbandry and assume those of finance and technology. Thenceforth his thinking is not determined by agricultural responsibility, but by financial accountability and the capacities of his machines. Where his money comes from becomes less important to him than where it is going. He is caught up in the drift of energy and interest away from the land. Production begins to override maintenance. The economy of money has infiltrated and subverted the economies of nature, energy, and the human spirit. The man himself has become a consumptive machine.

For some time now ecologists have been documenting the principle that "you can't do one thing"—which means that in a natural system whatever affects one thing ultimately affects everything. Everything in the Creation is related to everything else and dependent on everything else. The Creation is one; it is a uni-verse, a whole, the parts of which are all "turned into one."

A good agricultural system, which is to say a durable one, is similarly unified. In the 1940s, the great British agricultural scientist, Sir Albert Howard, published *An Agricultural Testament* and *The Soil and Health*, in which he argued against the influence in agriculture of "the laboratory hermit" who had substituted "that dreary principle [official organization] for the soul-shaking principle of that essential freedom needed by the seeker after truth." And Howard goes on to speak of the disruptiveness of official organization: "The natural universe, which is one, has been halved, quartered, fractioned. . . . Real organization always involves real responsibility: the official organization of research tries to retain power and avoid responsibility by sheltering behind groups of experts." Howard himself began as a laboratory hermit: "I could not take my own advice before offering it to other people." But he saw the significance of the "wide chasm between science in the laboratory and practice in the field." He devoted his life to bridging that chasm. His is the story of a fragmentary intelligence seeking both its own wholeness and that of the world. The aim that he finally realized in his books was to prepare the way "for treating the whole problem of health in soil, plant, animal, and man as one great subject." He unspecialized his vision, in other words, so as to see the necessary unity of the concerns of agriculture, as well as the convergence of these concerns with concerns of other kinds: biological, historical, medical, moral, and so on. He sought to establish agriculture upon the same unifying cycle that preserves health, fertility, and renewal in nature: the Wheel of Life (as he called it, borrowing the term from religion), by which "Death supersedes life and life rises again from what is dead and decayed."

It remains only to say what has often been said before—that the best human cultures also have this unity. Their concerns and enterprises are not fragmented, scattered out, at variance or in contention with one another. The people and their work and their country are members of each other and of the culture. If a culture is to hope for any considerable longevity, then the relationships within it must, in recognition of their interdependence, be predominantly cooperative rather than competitive. A people cannot live long at each other's expense or at the expense of their cultural birthright—just as an agriculture cannot live long at the expense of its soil or its work force, and just as in a natural system the competitions among species must be limited if all are to survive.

In any of these systems, cultural or agricultural or natural, when a species or group exceeds the principle of usufruct (literally, the "use of the fruit"), it puts itself in danger. Then, to use an economic metaphor, it is living off the principal rather than the interest. It has broken out of the system of nurture and has become exploitive; it is destroying what gave it life and what it depends upon to live. In all of these systems a fundamental principle must be the protection of the source: the seed, the food species, the soil, the breeding stock, the old and the wise, the keepers of memories, the records.

And just as competition must be strictly curbed within these systems, it must be strictly curbed *among* them. An agriculture cannot survive long at the expense of the natural systems that support it and that provide it with models. A culture cannot survive long at the expense either of its agricultural or of its natural sources. To live at the expense of the source of life is obviously suicidal. Though we have no choice but to live at the expense of other life, it is necessary to recognize the limits and dangers involved: past a certain point in a unified system, "other life" is our own.

The definitive relationships in the universe are thus not competitive but interdependent. And from a human point of view they are analogical. We can build one system only within another. We can have agriculture only within nature, and culture only within agriculture. At certain critical points these systems have to conform with one another or destroy one another.

Under the discipline of unity, knowledge and morality come together. No longer can we have that paltry "objective" knowledge so prized by the academic specialists. To know anything at all becomes a moral predicament. Aware that there is no such thing as a specialized—or even an entirely limitable or controllable—effect, one becomes responsible for judgments as well as facts. Aware that as an agricultural scientist he had "one great subject," Sir Albert Howard could no longer ask, What can I do with what I know? without at the same time asking, How can I be responsible for what I know?

And it is within unity that we see the hideousness and destructiveness of the fragmentary—the kind of mind, for example, that can introduce a production machine to increase "efficiency" without troubling about its effect on workers, on the product, and on consumers; that can accept and even applaud the "obsolescence" of the small farm and not hesitate over the possible political and cultural effects; that can recommend continuous tillage of huge monocultures, with massive use of chemicals and no animal manure or humus, and worry not at all about the deterioration or loss of soil. For cultural patterns of responsible cooperation we have substituted this moral ignorance, which is the etiquette of agricultural "progress."

Dreams of the far future destiny of man were dragging up from its shallow and unquiet grave the old dream of Man as God. The very experience of the dissecting room and the pathological laboratory were breeding a conviction that the stifling of all deep-set repugnances was the first essential for progress.

C. S. LEWIS, *That Hideous Strength*

CHAPTER FIVE

Living in the Future: The "Modern" Agricultural Ideal

THE DOMESTICATION OF ABSENCE

It is impossible to divorce the question of what we do from the question of where we are—or, rather, where we think we are. That no sane creature befouls its own nest is accepted as generally true. What we conceive to be our nest, and where we think it is, are therefore questions of the greatest importance. Do we, for instance, carry on our work in our nest or do we only reside and get our mail there? Is our nest a place of consumption only or is it also a place of production? Is it the source of necessary goods, energies, and "services," or only their destination?

I have already spoken of the highly simplified role of the modern household with respect to the production and preparation of food: it has set itself increasingly aside from production and preparation and become more and more a place for the consumption of food produced and prepared elsewhere. But this setting aside of the nest or residence from the sources of life is more general and even more serious than that would indicate. The modern home, even more than the government and universities, has institutionalized the divisions and fragmentations of modern life.

With its array of gadgets and machines, all powered by energies that are destructive of land or air or water, and connected to work, market, school, recreation, etc., by gasoline engines, the modern home is a veritable factory of waste and destruction. It is the mainstay of the economy of money. But within the economies of energy and nature, it is a catastrophe. It takes in the world's goods and converts them into garbage, sewage, and noxious fumes—for none of which we have found a use.

And the modern household's direct destructiveness of the world bears a profound relation—as cause or effect or both—to the fundamental moral disconnections for which it also stands. It divorces us from the sources of our bodily life; as a people, we no longer know the earth we come from, have no respect for it, keep no responsibilities to it. And few who are acquainted with the young can doubt that the modern home has also failed as a place of instruction and that the schools are failing under the burden of that deeper failure.

But nowhere is the destructive influence of the modern home so great as in its remoteness from work. When people do not live where they work, they do not feel the effects of what they do. The people who make wars do not fight them. The people responsible for stripmining, clear-cutting of forests, and other ruinations do not live where their senses will be offended or their homes or livelihoods or lives immediately threatened by the consequences. The people responsible for the various depredations of "agribusiness" do not live on farms. They—like many others of less wealth and power—live in ghettos of their own kind in homes full of "conveniences" which signify that all is well. In an automated kitchen, in a gleaming, odorless bathroom, in year-round air-conditioning, in color TV, in an easy chair, the world is redeemed. If what God made can be made by humans into *this*, then what can be wrong?

The modern home is so destructive, I think, because it is a generalization, a product of factory and fashion, an everyplace or a noplace. Modern houses, like airports, are extensions of each other; they do not vary much from one place to another. A person standing in a modern room anywhere might imagine himself anywhere else—much as he could if he shut his eyes. The modern house is not a response to its place, but rather to the affluence and social status of its owner. It is the first means by which the modern mentality imposes itself upon the world. The industrial conquistador, seated in his living room in the evening in front of his TV set, many miles from his work, can easily forget where he is and what he has done. He is everywhere or nowhere. Everything around him, everything on TV, tells him of his success: *his* comfort is the redemption of the world. His home is the emblem of his status, but it is not the center of his interest or of his consciousness. The history of our time has been to a considerable extent the movement of the center of consciousness away from home.

Once, some farmers, particularly in Europe, lived in their barns— and so were both at work and at home. Work and rest, work and pleasure, were continuous with each other, often not distinct from each other at all. Once, shopkeepers lived in, above, or behind their shops. Once, many people lived by "cottage industries"—home production. Once, households were producers and processors of food, centers of their own maintenance, adornment, and repair, places of instruction and amusement. People were born in these houses, and lived and worked and died in them. Such houses were not generalizations. Similar to each other in materials and design as they might have been, they nevertheless looked and felt and smelled different from each other because they were articulations of particular responses to their places and circumstances.

THE VAGRANT SOVEREIGN

The modern specialist and/or industrialist in his modern house can probably have no very clear sense of where he is. His sense of his whereabouts is abstract: he is in a certain "line" as signified by his profession, in a certain "bracket" as signified by his income, and in a certain "crowd" as signified by his house and his amusements. Where he is matters only in proportion to the number of other people's effects he has to put up with. Geography is defined for him by his house, his office, his commuting route, and the interiors of shopping centers, restaurants, and places of amusement—which is to say that his geography is artificial; he could be anywhere, and he usually is.

This generalized sense of worldly whereabouts is a reflection of another kind of bewilderment: this modern person does not know where he is morally either. He assumes, as he has clearly been taught to assume, that as a member of the human race he is sovereign in the universe. He assumes that there is nothing that he *can* do that he should not do, nothing that he *can* use that he should not use. His "success" —which at present is indisputable—is that he has escaped any order that might imply restraints or impose limits. He has, like the heroes of fantasy, left home—left behind all domestic ties and restraints—and gone out into the world to seek his fortune.

This mentality has been long in the making, and its rise evidently parallels the exploitation of the New World. Carl Sauer wrote:
"The Modern Age began with the extension of royal absolution overseas. The crowns gave patents to individuals to discover, take possession, and govern islands or mainland, inhabited or uninhabited. The crown took to itself the title to land and people, first claimed for it by formal act. Thus Columbus planted the flag as he landed, the natives being bemused spectators. Thus Cabot without having sight of a native. Thus Juan de la Cosa entered on his map the flags of three nations. *The course of colonial empire began with disregard of native rights and persons* [my emphasis]. The Portuguese loaded the first cargo of black slaves when they reached the Bay of Arguin, and they did the same with Indians in New Foundland. Columbus estimated the prospects of slave trade when he landed in the West Indies. The Colonial idea as it took shape in the fifteenth century was untroubled by any concern other than to establish priority over other European nations."

Economic exploitation and competition as we now know them were thus established at the beginning of American history. Or perhaps it would be truer to say that they were established *by* the beginning of American history—for they do not seem to have risen so much out of theory or vision or desire or decree as out of newly opened distance and space. The new reaches of oceanic navigation, the discovery of new lands across what shortly before had been inconceivable distances, seem to have forced the European mind out of its old moral order. Those first discoverers carried the patents of their sovereigns, but they carried them into places altogether new to them, beyond what had been imagined, much less what had been culturally ordered. And so no matter the flags and pronouncements and the other trappings of fealty—the sovereignty that crossed the surf onto the shore of the New World was a new sovereignty of the human mind. What appeared to the eyes of the discoverers was not one of the orders of Creation that required respect or deference for its own sake. What they saw was a great concentration of "natural resources"—to be used according to purposes exterior to them. That some of those resources were human beings mattered not at all.

And so at the same time that they "discovered" America, these men invented the modern condition of being away from home. On the new shores the old orders of domesticity, respect, deference, humility fell away from them; they arrived contemptuous of whatever existed before their own coming, disdainful beyond contempt of native creatures or values or orders, ravenous for their own success. They began the era of absolute human sovereignty—which is to say the era of absolute human presumption. They invented us: the flag of Ferdinand and Isabella in the hand of Columbus on the shores of the Indies becomes Old Glory in the hand of Neil Armstrong on the moon. An infinitely greedy sovereign is afoot in the universe, staking his claims.

THE MANUFACTURED PARADISE

But our experience of sovereignty suggests that it becomes dangerous when it defines itself exclusively in terms of what is inferior to it, neglecting or ignoring what is superior to it. That is to say that sovereignty is a safe concept only when its place is symmetrically defined. Thus, once, the place of humans was thought to be above the animals and below the angels—between the natural and the divine. Then, by understanding and accepting that human place in the order of things, people could see that their privileges were limited and safeguarded by certain responsibilities. They could see, moreover, that only evil could be the result of the transgression of these limits: one could not escape the human condition except sinfully, by pride or by degradation.

The growth of what is called the Modern World has been, by turns, both the cause and the effect of the destruction of that old sense of universal order. The most characteristically modern behavior, or misbehavior, was made possible by a redefinition of humanity which allowed it to claim, not the sovereignty of its place, neither godly nor beastly, in the order of things, but rather an absolute sovereignty, placing the human will in charge of itself and of the universe.

And having thus usurped the whole Chain of Being, conceiving itself, in effect, both creature and creator, humanity set itself a goal that in those circumstances was fairly predictable: it would make an Earthly Paradise. This projected Paradise was no longer that of legend: the lost garden that might be rediscovered by some explorer or navigator. This new Paradise was to be invented and built by human intelligence and industry. And by machines. For the agent of our escape from our place in the order of Creation, and of our godlike ambition to make a Paradise, was the machine—not only as instrument, but even more powerfully as metaphor. Once, the governing human metaphor was pastoral or agricultural, and it clarified, and so preserved in human care, the natural cycles of birth, growth, death, and decay. But modern humanity's governing metaphor is that of the machine. Having placed ourselves in charge of Creation, we began to mechanize both the Creation itself and our conception of it. We began to see the whole Creation merely as raw material, to be transformed by machines into a manufactured Paradise.

And so the machine did away with mystery on the one hand and multiplicity on the other. The Modern World would respect the Creation only insofar as it could be *used* by humans. Henceforth, by definition, by principle, we would be unable to leave anything as it was. The usable would be used; the useless would be sacrificed in the use of something else. By means of the machine metaphor we have eliminated any fear or awe or reverence or humility or delight or joy that might have restrained us in our use of the world. We have indeed learned to act as if our sovereignty were unlimited and as if our intelligence were equal to the universe. Our "success" is a catastrophic demonstration of our failure. The industrial Paradise is a fantasy in the minds of the privileged and the powerful; the reality is a shambles.

THE COLONIZATION OF THE FUTURE

The generalization of vital connections and the assumption of unlimited human sovereignty go a long way toward explaining the displacement of the modern mind. But they do not explain *how* it happened. It can be said that the motive has often been greed, but even that does not satisfy, for greed has always existed. It is necessary to account for a new intensity of greed—a greed newly empowered, under no constraint to see itself as evil, allied (so it believes) with a manifest destiny and the way of the world. There must have been, not just a shift of basic assumptions, not just a motive, but also some kind of vision or dream or psychic lure.

It has been, I think, the future. What has drawn the Modern World into being is a strange, almost occult yearning for the future. The modern mind longs for the future as the medieval mind longed for Heaven. The great aim of modern life has been to improve the future—or even just to *reach* the future, assuming that the future will inevitably be "better." One of the oddest terms of praise in our language is "futuristic." "Far out," as a term of universal approbation, is perhaps a lineal descendant. Such terms are used to identify the signs and landmarks that confirm that we are indeed on the right road to the future, that we are getting there, that at any moment we may at last arrive. And this is no elitist obsession; it is commonplace. Politicians understand very well the power of the promise to build a better or more prosperous or more secure future. Parents characteristically strive and sacrifice to make a better or more secure future for their children. Workers work toward a secure future in which they will retire and enjoy themselves. Our obsession with security is a measure of the power we have granted the future to hold over us.*

The future has been envisioned, dreamed, projected, painted for us by prophets of every kind: scientists, comic-book writers, novelists, philosophers, politicians, industrialists, professors. And, of course, by ourselves; the cult of the future has turned us all into prophets. The future is the time when science will have solved all our problems, gratified all our desires; when we will all live in perfect ease in an air-conditioned, fully automated womb; when all the work will be done by machines so sophisticated that they will not only clothe, house, and feed us, but think for us, play our games, paint our pictures, write our poems. It is the Earthly Paradise, the Other Shore, where all will be well. And if we are living for the future, then history is on our side—or so we are at liberty to think, for the needed proofs are never at hand. That there has for some time been growing a cult of dread of the future testifies not only to the innate silliness and frivolity of this vision, but to its power. The adoration of the future may be beginning to falter, but it is still dominant, still available and useful to the exploitive mind.

There is no aspect of our life as a people that is not now under the dominance of this industrial dream of the future-as-Paradise. All our implements—automobiles, tractors, kitchen utensils, etc.—have always been conceived by the modern mind as in a kind of progress or pilgrimage toward their future forms. The automobile-of-the-future, the kitchen-of-the-future, the classroom-of-the-future have long figured more actively in our imaginations, plans, and desires than whatever versions of these things we may currently have. We long ago

*The following sentences are from a recent oil company advertisement:
"We have always been a nation more interested in the promise of the future than in the events of the past.
"Here at Atlantic Richfield we see the future as an exciting time. The best of times."

gave up the wish to have things that were adequate or even excellent; we have preferred instead to have things that were up-to-date. But to be up-to-date is an ambition with built-in panic: our possessions cannot be up-to-date more than momentarily unless we can stop time —or somehow get ahead of it. The only possibility of satisfaction is to be driving *now* in one's *future* automobile.

It is no doubt impossible to live without thought of the future; hope and vision can live nowhere else. But the only possible guarantee of the future is responsible behavior in the present. When supposed future needs are used to justify misbehavior in the present, as is the tendency with us, then we are both perverting the present and diminishing the future. But the most prolific source of justifications for exploitive behavior has been the future. The exploitive mind characteristically puts itself in charge of the future. The future is a time that cannot conceivably be reached except by industrial progress and economic growth.The future, so full of material blessings, is nevertheless threatened with dire shortages of food, energy, and security unless we exploit the earth even more "freely," with greater speed and less caution. The obvious paradoxes involved in this—that we are using up future necessities in order to make a more abundant future; that final loss has been made a calculated strategy of annual gain— have so far been understood to no great effect. The great convenience of the future as a context of behavior is that nobody knows anything about it. No rational person can *see* how using up the topsoil or the fossil fuels as quickly as possible can provide greater security for the future; but if enough wealth and power can conjure up the audacity to *say* that it can, then sheer fantasy is given the force of truth; the future becomes reckonable as even the past has never been. It is as if the future is a newly discovered continent which the corporations are colonizing. They have made "redskins" of our descendants, holding them subject to alien values, while their land is plundered of anything that can be shipped home and sold.

Nowhere is the cult of the future stronger than in agriculture. One reason for this is that farming has been harder to industrialize than manufacturing, and when industrialization has come, it has not brought shorter hours or greater ease or less worry. A great deal of the strain of the industrial revolution has been borne by farmers, and so it has been fairly easy to secure their allegiance to the future, when more industrialization will supposedly bring a better farm economy. The industrialization of farming as we now have it is not something that farmers would have bought all in a piece; as a group they have been too traditional or conservative for that. Instead, it has been sold to them in stages, one implement at a time. The reduction of available manpower by each new machine created the need for a better machine or a different one. In the practical circumstances of the modern farm, the popular yearning for the future is directly felt as a yearning for relief from weariness and worry.

Another reason for the dominance of the future over agriculture is that projected rates of population growth have become the all-purpose threat and justifier of the apologists of the agricultural establishment. Millions are threatened with starvation—so the argument runs—therefore we must continue to farm in larger monocultures on larger holdings with fewer farmers, larger and more expensive machines, more chemicals. The hunger of these future millions is now the foundation of policy in the Department of Agriculture. Hunger supports the department's charitable rhetoric ("Feeding people . . . is too serious a matter to be left to political manipulation"), its realpolitik ("Food is a weapon"), and its self-justification ("true agripower . . . generates agridollars through agricultural exports"). How the future might be served by careless and destructive practices in the present is a question that is simply overridden by the brazen glibness of official optimism. If there is a food crisis, then, according to specialist logic, we must produce more food more carelessly than ever before. The energy crisis has been used, by the same logic, to justify the squandering of fuels.

LET THEM EAT THE FUTURE

As a sampler both of prevalent agricultural trends and official attitudes, as well as of the popular gullibility with which they have been received, one could not do better than an article entitled "The Revolution in American Agriculture" in the *National Geographic* of February 1970.

We should remember that in 1970 revolution was a controversial subject in America. We had spent the past half century in various stages of panic over the fact or the alleged possibility of communist revolution. And, during the decade just past, a good many of our people, mostly young, had begun to think of themselves as revolutionaries; some of them had even begun to *act* like revolutionaries. That the *National Geographic* could speak at such a time of an agri-

59

cultural revolution could only indicate that a revolution of this kind, as opposed to a political revolution, was entirely acceptable to most Americans; it was simply part of the industrial revolution, which, after all, had become their way of life. That the industrial revolution, and the agricultural revolution along with it, had been real revolutions, surely the most powerful ever experienced, with real consequences, some of them political, and by no means all good—none of that mattered. The agricultural revolution, so far as the *National Geographic* and its readers were concerned, was a "good" revolution.

The author of the article, Mr. Jules B. Billard, is identified as a member of the magazine's senior editorial staff. But nowhere does he display the independence of judgment that one would expect either of a geographer or an editor. During most of the article he is in the grip of the ignorant awe, the greenhorn's ecstasy, that has been as necessary to this revolution as the ball bearing. During his encounters with the various manifestations of agricultural progress, Mr. Billard "marveled" twice; he was "staggered," "fascinated," "astounded," and "jolted" once each; he experienced two "jolting awakenings," the second more jolting than the first; and once his "mind churned."

The following is an inventory of Mr. Billard's revolutionary wonders:

"You can have strawberries in January, fresh oranges and lettuce the year round."

"Of the 6,000 to 8,000 items in the typical supermarket, 40 percent were not there a dozen years ago."

". . . in a single lifetime United States agriculture has advanced more than in all the preceding millenniums of man's labor on the land."

". . . I watched a factory-on-wheels move down celery rows . . . doing the work of forty men."

"I handled tomatoes bred for machine harvesting."

"I learned about heating cables buried underground to warm the soil so asparagus can grow in December . . ."

"Because only one person in 43 is needed to produce food, others can become doctors, teachers, shoemakers, janitors . . ." [This is a quote from former Agriculture Secretary Clifford Hardin.]

"Today 90 percent of the [California] tomato crop is picked mechanically."

". . . an incredible parade of machines are at work today on U.S. farms: acre-eaters . . . self-propelled combines that permit a man to ride in an air-conditioned cab to harvest a crop of corn that used to take a crew of 80 hands. Monster road-building machinery to level terraces or shape rice fields. Helicopters to spray cucumber fields. In all such a host of devices that today U.S. farmers are investing eight times as much capital as they did thirty years ago."

"Automated feeders, waterers, ventilators, and other labor savers make it possible for one man to take care of 100,000 broilers . . ."

"Block-long buildings, each housing 90,000 White Leghorns, cooped five birds to a 16-by-18 inch cage . . ."

". . . meatless dishes tasting like chicken, beef, or ham."

These accomplishments sort themselves readily into two categories: the frivolous and the problematic. The frivolity of strawberries in January, asparagus in December, and wheat or soybean products that taste like chicken is simply never acknowledged. Nor are the implications of the enormous increase of "items" in the supermarkets. By the values of gee-whiz journalism *any* increase is marvelous.

Nor is there any acknowledgment of the influence of "monster" technology ("acre-eaters") on the soil, the produce, the farm communities, and the lives and characters of farmers.

It is harder to ignore the enormous increase of indebtedness and overhead that has accompanied the enlargement of farm technology. Mr. Billard quotes an Iowa banker: "In 1920 . . . $5,000 was a big loan, and people hesitated to borrow. Now a $40,000 loan is commonplace, and having mortgage after mortgage is an accepted thing. I occasionally wonder whether the average farmer will ever get out of debt." The article gives examples of the enormous acreages and costs involved in several up-to-date operations. But these figures are simply left lying; in Mr. Billard's mind they evidently stand for nothing except the bigness of modern agriculture—which he approves of, so far as one can tell, because it amazes him. The Iowa banker's statement, doubtful as it may seem out of context, is made *in praise* of credit. Nowhere is there a question of the advisability of basing so large an enterprise on credit, or of the influence of routine indebtedness on a people's character. Nowhere is there a suspicion that there might be any worth in the old rural virtues of solvency and thrift.

The economic and moral uncertainty of living on credit is evidently —and typically—thought to be compensated by an improved standard of living: "Today [the farm wife is] as likely to be mini-skirted as her city sister, and as likely to own a dishwasher or self-cleaning oven or color television set. And her husband, who drives a tractor with an automatic transmission and uses power tools to eliminate backstraining labor, is as likely to have gone to college as his town cousin." That this standard of living is entirely material and entirely urban is characteristic of the prejudices that underlie the article.

The industrialization of animal husbandry is likewise seriously oversimplified. In addition to the ethical questions involved, the use of animals as machines—penning them in feed lots and cages— creates an enormous pollution problem. Mr. Billard acknowledges that this problem exists. He even cites a dubious solution: spreading the manure of 20,000 cattle on the pastures of a 320-acre farm which also contains the feed lots, a drainage pond, and a feed mill. But he also notes that in 1968 American farmers spread "nearly forty million tons" of chemical fertilizers, or "260 pounds for each acre under cultivation." The manure problem is separated from these figures on fertilizer consumption by fourteen pages. The dependence of our farmers on chemical fertilizers is not seen as a problem, and so the connection is missed. Mr. Billard forgot, or he never knew, that once plants and animals were raised together on the same farms—which therefore neither produced unmanageable surpluses of manure, to be wasted and to pollute the water supply, nor depended on such quantities of commercial fertilizer. The genius of American farm experts is very well demonstrated here: they can take a solution and divide it neatly into two problems.

That the agricultural revolution has displaced large numbers of people and put large numbers out of work is also acknowledged by Mr. Billard. But like the society as a whole, he has no trouble accepting this as part of the inevitable cost of progress. Lest anyone should become concerned about it, he includes early in his article a formula that makes it all right: " 'Machines do replace labor,' G. E. Vanden-Berg told me . . . in his office at the USDA's Agricultural Research Center in Beltsville, Maryland. 'However, it is the scarcity of labor that really spurs adoption of machines.' "

Nevertheless, twenty-four pages later, Mr. Billard is saying:

"Squeezed between higher operating costs and what he gets for his produce, the man on the farm must become more efficient or give up." So apparently there is a problem after all. But another "agribusiness" formula is immediately invoked to assuage the moral discomfort: when all else fails to disguise the indifference of official agriculture to all human concerns, one can always fall back on efficiency. And so it appears that the failure of so many small farmers over so many years is really a kind of justice: it is their own fault; they ought to have been more efficient; if they had to get bigger in order to be more efficient, then they ought to have got bigger.

But suppose there is no room to get bigger unless somebody is driven out. In that case, one must have recourse to the law of compensation. This is the favorite law of the exploiter. It holds that for every loss there is a gain that is opposite and at least equal. This law is good fortune itself, for it means that you can do no wrong. Mr. Billard is an ardent observer of the law of compensation. "How many have given up," he writes, "can be seen in such figures as these: In 1910 our farm population accounted for a third of the U.S. total. By 1969 it was a mere twentieth. People leave rural areas at an average rate of 650,000 a year; many drift into cities where they join past migrants in the ghettos—to become added tinder for the riots that can be labeled one of the social consequences of the agricultural revolution." And he goes on: "When people leave the farm, rural communities . . . likewise wither away."

Here surely is cause for mourning: a forced migration of people greater than any in history, the foretelling of riots in the cities and the failure of human community in the country. But no. On the contrary: "Not all small towns are dying. The smog and the traffic and the social unrest of megalopolis prompts a second look at advantages of living in smaller communities. Industry, freed by jet planes and superhighways from dependence on nearby markets, shifts its plants away from cities. Employees are drawn by such appeals as being able, ten minutes after leaving work, to be out on the golf course, or roaming the woods with gun and dog, or watching kids and crops grow in a handful of acres a man can call his own."

Thus, if country people are forced to move into the city, that is made up for, according to Mr. Billard, by the movement of city people, and the city itself, into the country. But that only *looks* like a balanced equation. The people who move into the city and those who move out into the country are hardly the same people. The country community (of "inefficient" and therefore socially negligible people) is broken up, to be replaced by an influx of urban people who (however "efficient") have no economic or cultural ties to the land and are not a community. In this exchange we lose country people, we lose community, and we lose land. And we also lose the "inner city," which is abandoned to those who cannot perform "efficiently" either in the city or in the country.

But probably the most interesting feature of Mr. Billard's account of this exchange is the importance he attaches to "watching kids and crops grow on a handful of acres a man can call his own." Why, one wonders, does this feeling assert itself when the handful of acres is owned by an urban migrant, but not when they are owned by a farmer? How, rationally, can one hold the small farm in contempt as the living of a farm family and then sentimentalize over it as the "country place" or hobby of an executive? It cannot be done unless it is assumed that an executive is more deserving of a small farm because, as an urban or a professional person, he is superior to a farmer.

The callousness and smugness of this attitude is fully displayed in the caption to two pictures, one showing several members of a black family in their house and the other showing a modern cotton-picking machine at work. The caption is headlined dramatically: "When machines displace people"—and it reads: "Through the years Ruth Anderson's husband had worked the sweltering cotton fields around Isola, Mississippi. In late spring Ed Anderson chopped cotton. . . . Summers he picked the cotton at $2.50 a hundred pounds. Between having her nine children, four of whom she tends above in the family's one-room shanty, Mrs. Anderson worked beside her husband. During picking season they brought home as much as $10 a day, and they got by.

"Then onto the fields rolled machines . . . that harvested as much in a day as could 80 men. Picking jobs vanished. Herbicides came on the market to kill weeds; they killed the chopping, too.

"Lacking a skill for steady work, the Andersons joined the hapless millions of rural refugees who, uprooted by mechanized farming, often drift to big cities seeking jobs.

"To help stem this flow, civil-rights groups, foundations, and the National Council of Churches support a self-help community called Freedom City . . ."

So much for the Andersons. We are evidently expected to assume that their plight, and the plight of millions like them, is exactly offset by Freedom City, which is trying "to help stem this flow"—as if the flow can be stemmed until every last "inefficient" field worker has entered a ghetto and gone on welfare. And then we are asked to turn away and marvel at the big machine that can do the work of eighty men, whose working conditions were, after all, "sweltering," and whose getting-by economy was out of fashion, if not slightly contemptible.

We are shown another farm family—three generations of them—at the dinner table on their 130-acre Long Island farm, part of which they have owned since 1737. These people, too, "stand at a crossroads: Either they mechanize and expand, or rising costs, high taxes, and big farm competition will drive them from the land." There is not a word or implication of so much as a doubt about the economic conditions that constitute this "crossroads," not the smallest curiosity as to what may be the cost. Nearly two-and-a-half centuries of family history on the same farm amounts simply to nothing if it can't pay the taxes. The fate of this family is offered as merely interesting, a kind of journal-fodder.

What excuses this human waste, this destruction of preserving traditions and associations, this moral indifference? It is the future—the future as both threat and lure—the secular Hell and Heaven of the enraptured booster.

Early in his article Mr. Billard refers to a possibility that is certainly grave, certainly to be taken seriously, but which has nevertheless become the routine curtain-raiser of "agribusiness" propagandists, who use it not for the rigorous self-evaluation that it requires, but shamelessly and tirelessly to justify themselves. They are fanatical believers in themselves, and like all fanatics they need an apocalypse—some ultimate bugaboo to shove into the face of doubt. What we have here is everybody's worry, but the farm experts and agribusinessmen would like us to leave it to them: "Earth's numbers now stand at 3.6 billion, and could double in 35 years. This . . . raises the specter of a famine more catastrophic than the world has ever seen."

Of course it does. And that means that we should be at work overhauling all our assumptions about ourselves and what we have done and what we are capable of doing, all our attitudes toward life and its complex sources, all our resources of technique and technology. If we are heading toward apocalypse, then obviously we must undertake an ordeal of preparation. We must cleanse ourselves of slovenliness, laziness, and waste. We must learn to discipline ourselves, to restrain ourselves, to need less, to care more for the needs of others. We must understand what the health of the earth requires, and we must put that before all other needs. If a catastrophic famine is possible, then let us undertake the labors of wisdom and make the necessary sacrifices of luxury and comfort.

But, according to Mr. Billard, this is not for ordinary people to worry about. The agriculture experts, industrialists, and scientists are going to take care of it: "The spread of modern agriculture can help assure the underdeveloped two-thirds of the world the freedom from hunger it gives the economically advanced one-third."

And by the end of his article Mr. Billard has entered into the glory of the true future-rapture. He talked to "Dr. Irving, of the Department of Agriculture," who said of the future: "Agriculture will be highly specialized. . . . Farms in one area will concentrate on growing oranges, those in another area tomatoes, in another potatoes—capitalizing on the competitive advantage soil or climate gives for a particular crop.

"Fields will be larger, with fewer trees, hedges, and roadways. Machines will be bigger and more powerful. . . . They'll be automated, even radio-controlled, with closed circuit TV to let an operator sitting on a front porch monitor what is going on. . . .

"Weather control may tame hailstorm and tornado dangers. . . . Atomic energy may supply power to level hills or provide irrigation water from the sea."

It was at this point that Mr. Billard's "mind churned with the implications of such developments building on the progress of the past." Gone are the fears of famine. Gone are any thoughts of displaced small farmers and farm workers, or of the threat of riots in the cities. Mr. Billard has risen right over apocalypse into Heaven itself. He ends by quoting triumphantly a remark by a Brazilian official: " 'We are concerned about the future of agriculture in Brazil. . . . In your country, you *are* in the future.' "

And so, of course, are the Andersons, with their nine children, their "one-room shanty," and no job—which ought to be reassuring to the people in the "underdeveloped two-thirds of the world," who are still trapped back there in the present.

The final two pages of Mr. Billard's article carry an "artist's conception" of the agricultural future, which is a veritable paradigm of the agribusiness ambition. The caption reads as follows:

"Farm of the future: Grainfields stretch like fairways and cattle pens resemble high-rise apartments in a farm of the early 21st century, as portrayed by artist David Meltzer *with the guidance of U.S. Department of Agriculture specialists* [my emphasis].

"Attached to a modernistic farm house, a bubble-topped control tower hums with a computer, weather reports, and a farm-price ticker tape. A remote-controlled tiller-combine glides across a 10-mile-long wheat field on tracks that keep the heavy machine from compacting the soil. Threshed grain, funneled into a pneumatic tube beside the field, flows into storage elevators rising close to a distant city. The same machine that cuts the grain prepares the land for another crop. A similar device waters neighboring strips of soybeans as a jet-powered helicopter sprays insecticides.

"Across a service road, conical mills blend feed for beef cattle, fattening in multilevel pens that conserve ground space. Tubes carry the feed to be mechanically distributed. A central elevator transports the cattle up and down, while a tubular side drain flushes wastes to be broken down for fertilizer. Beside the farther pen, a processing plant packs beef into cylinders for shipment to market by helicopter and monorail. Illuminated plastic domes provide controlled environments for growing high-value crops such as strawberries, tomatoes, and celery. Near a distant lake and recreation area, a pumping plant supplies water for the vast operation."

THE ORGANIZATION OF DISORDER

The cooperation of Department of Agriculture specialists in this visualization of a completely industrialized agriculture-of-the-future makes it as official, it would seem, as any vision of the future could be. And that this sort of thing is not an isolated aberration of overexcited journalism, but a confirmed habit—even the theoretical context—of agricultural expertise, is suggested by an article in the October 1974 issue of the *American Farmer* (voice of the American Farm Bureau Federation). This article is about a "dream farm" of 2076 A.D.—a model constructed by a group of South Dakota State University agricultural engineering students. This farm of the future is described as follows:

"The farm of 9 square miles will use only about 1,800 acres, less than one-fourth of which is for production.* The remainder will be a

*This sentence is hard to understand. The acreage to be used for production is evidently one-fourth of the nine square miles, not of the 1800 acres. But 1800 acres is *more* than one-fourth of nine square miles, not less.

buffer or 'relaxed' zone for recreation, wildlife, and living under the 'blending with human values' aspect of the overall planning.

"Livestock will be housed (and products processed) in a 15-story, 150' x 200' building. It will also contain power facilities, administrative headquarters, veterinary facilities, repair shops, refrigeration and packaging units, storage, research labs, water and waste treatment facilities. At capacity, the high-rise building will house 2,500 feeder cattle, 600 cow-calf units, 500 dairy cattle, 2,500 sheep, 6,750 finishing hogs, space for 150 sows and litters, 1,000 turkeys, and 15,000 chickens.

"Crops will be grown year around under plastic covers that provide precise climate control in three circular fields each a mile in diameter. At any given time, regardless of weather, one field or crop will be in the planting stage, another in the growing stage, and the third in the harvesting stage. Exceptionally high yields mean that only a fourth of the total 5,760-acre farm area would be needed for agricultural production.

"Only a half-inch of water will be needed for each crop. That's because evapotranspiration from growing plants would be recycled under massive, permanent plastic enclosures . . .

"Underground magnetic patterns, arranged to fit crop or machine, will attract specially-treated seed blasted from overhead tubes in the enclosures.

"If tillage is needed, it will be done by electromagnetic waves. Air-supported, remotely controlled machines will harvest entire plants because by 2076 A.D. the students believe multiple uses will be needed and found for most crops.

" 'Trickle' irrigation is to be electronically monitored to provide subsurface moisture automatically whenever needed.

"Recycling human, animal and crop wastes will be a key to the operation of the farm. Carbon dioxide from the respiration of livestock is to be piped into the circular enclosures for use by crops in exchange for the oxygen transpired by crops for use by livestock.

"Weed control is not anticipated as a problem because weeds would be eradicated under the field covers."

Soon after reading this article I wrote to Dr. Milo A. Hellickson, Associate Professor in Agricultural Engineering at South Dakota State University. My letter asked the following questions:

"1. Was any attention given to the possible social and economic effects of the projected innovations? Was it envisioned that this sort of farm would entirely replace the relatively small owner-operated farm? What would be its effect upon population patterns? Would it make food more or less expensive? What would be the energy requirements of such an operation, and what would be the sources of the required energy?

"2. What political consequences were anticipated? What, for instance, would be the impact . . . upon the doctrines of personal liberty and private property?

"3. What would be the effect upon the consumer? Would there be more or less choice of variety and quality?

"4. What would be the effect on the environment? For instance, roofing so large an acreage would present an unprecedented drainage problem. What did your students propose to do with the runoff? Would such a farm be built only in a desert area, or would it be feasible in an area of abundant rain fall?"

I received a prompt and very cordial reply from Dr. Hellickson, who responded to my questions as follows:

"Attention was given to the social and economic effect of the innovations. Essentially we feel that these developments would most likely fit individually into various farming operations and would not necessarily be all concentrated into one farmstead. As a matter of convenience in construction and so as not to alienate any particular phase of the agricultural industry, the model is constructed incorporating all the areas. Therefore, it would be equally possible in the future to maintain the smaller owner-operated farm and this then would cause little change in the distribution of the population. Specifically, we are thinking of energy captured from the sun, solar energy, as the sole energy source. I wouldn't even attempt to make a guess concerning expense, since this is such an area of dynamic change.

"Hopefully the above paragraph also answers question two. We are in no way advocating the elimination of the free enterprise system or the reduction of privately owned land.

"As per question three, I would see little change in the variety or quality of products available. . . . If anything, quality might be improved through the reduction or elimination of disease and through better handling systems.

"Hopefully this system would improve the environment by eliminating air pollution from the livestock building and also eliminating erosion from the cropped area. Runoff from the roof areas is proposed

69

to be used as the water source for the irrigation system and for live-stock and humans. Naturally, adequate facilities must be included to handle unusually large rainfalls."

There is no quarreling with the professed aim of either of these farms-of-the-future, which is an abundance of food. And they have other aspects that are praiseworthy: the conversion of wastes into fertilizer and the reliance of the South Dakota model on solar energy. But we are still left with the question of what will be the costs, not just of construction and materials, which would be passed on to consumers in the price of food, but costs of other kinds: social, cultural, political, nutritional, etc. And we still must ask if there may not be less costly ways to achieve the same ends.

The issue that is raised most directly by these farms-of-the-future is that of control. The ambition underlying these model farms is that of total control—a totally controlled agricultural environment. No-where is the essential totalitarianism and the essential weakness of the specialist mind more clearly displayed than in this ambition. Confronted with the living substance of farming—the complexly, even mysteriously interrelated lives on which it depends, from the microorganisms in the soil to the human consumers—the agriculture specialist can think only of subjecting it to total control, of turning it into a machine.

But total human control is just as impossible now as it ever was—or so the available evidence constrains one to believe. Nothing, for instance, could be more organized than one of our large cities, with its geometric streets, its numbered houses, its numbered citizens, its charted routes and zones, its great numbers of police and other func-tionaries charged to keep order—and yet nothing could be more chaotic than one of these same cities during rush hour or after dark or during a riot or a garbage collectors' strike. In the modern city un-precedented organization and unprecedented disorder exist side by side; one could argue that they have a symbiotic relationship, that they feed and thrive upon each other. It is not difficult to think of any number of such examples in government, education, industry, medi-cine, agriculture—wherever the specialist has come with his controls.

The reason would seem to be that the specialist and the idea of total control also have a symbiotic relationship, that neither can exist without the other. The specialist puts himself in charge of *one* possi-bility. By leaving out all other possibilities, he enfranchises his little fiction of total control. Leaving out all the "non-functional" or otherwise undesirable possibilities, he makes a rigid, exclusive boundary within which absolute control becomes, if not possible, at least conceivable.

But what the specialist never considers is that such a boundary is, in itself, profoundly disruptive. Its first disruption is in his mind, for having enclosed the possibility of control that is within his competence to imagine and desire, he becomes the enemy of all other possibilities. And, secondly, having chosen the possibility of total control within a small and highly simplified enclosure, he simply abandons the rest, leaves it totally *out* of control; that is, he forsakes or even repudiates the complex, partly mysterious patterns of interdependence and cooperation, controllable only within limits, by which human culture joins itself to its sources in the natural world.

This attempt at total control is an invitation to disorder. And the rule seems to be that the more rigid and exclusive is the specialist's boundary, and the stricter the control within it, the more disorder rages around it. One can make a greenhouse and grow summer vegetables in the wintertime, but in doing so one creates a vulnerability to the weather and a possibility of failure where none existed before. The control by which a tomato plant lives through January is much more problematic than the natural order by which an oak tree or a titmouse lives through January. The patterns of cooperation are safer than the mechanisms of exclusion, even though they lack the illusory safety of "control."

Because of his dependence on boundaries and controls, the genre or mode of the specialist is the "model." The necessary context of a model is the future. The qualifications of the present, of *living*, do not affect it, nor do the non-functional or the undesirable. It is remote even from probable difficulties of the future. Thus the language of the article in the *American Farmer*, having to do with the inward workings of the South Dakota State model, is confident and for the most part it is exact. But Dr. Hellickson's responses to my questions about its *influence* are tentative, conjectural, and hopeful. The model perfectly empowers the machine metaphor: only the "working parts" need be admitted. Therefore, if one is going to make a "model farm," one must give it a boundary, if possible a roof, that will keep out whatever does not "work." Weeds, insects, diseases do not work; leave them out. The weather works only sometimes, or on the average; leave the weather out. The work can be done by machines; leave the people out. But chemicals and drugs, no matter how dangerous, *do* work; they are part of the boundary, so they can be let in.

It may be a bit startling at this point to realize that what has been left out of this enclosure is health. As soon as pests, parasites, diseases, climatic fluctuations and extremes are left out, resistance to these things is also left out; and this resistance, in the soil and in the lives that come from the soil, is what we call health. And so for total control we have given up health—which is also a kind of control, safer by far than a plastic roof, but never total.

The model is an ideal and is surely meant to function as an ideal. But it is a *mechanical* ideal, and an exclusive one. Furthermore, its connections with the past and the present are severed; always implicit in a model is the idea of *replacing* what has survived of the past, what exists in the present. These characteristics divide the model radically from ideals of the more usual sort. Such ideals as honesty or generosity or gentleness or symmetry do indeed have an influence on the future, but we recognize them from what we have known of them in the past and from what they require of us in the present. Like health, they are required to survive among us in the presence of what they must resist; they survive in culture, in community, and in the characters of people. They are known and valued not because they have been modeled, but because they have been *exemplified*. The specialist, on the other hand, is interested only in the model, never in the example. He is interested in the future of farming, not in its history.

That is why the influence of his work does not interest him; if he puts a machine into the field to "save labor," he does not ask the fate of the replaced people.* He is working "in the future," which puts him at liberty simply to leave out whatever is displaced or whatever does not work. That is why there are no more people in these scenes of future farms than in the landscape photographs in conservation magazines; neither the agriculture specialist nor the conservation specialist has any idea where people belong in the order of things. Neither can conceive of a domesticated or a humane landscape. People

---

*This is the flaw in the doctrine of labor-saving. Labor-saving machines are *supposed* to make jobs easier. In fact, they destroy jobs. Instead of ameliorating work, they replace workers. What makes work easier and more pleasant without reducing employment is collaboration, neighbors helping each other. "Many hands make light work."

are complex, contradictory, unpredictable; they are perceived by the specialist as a kind of litter, pollutants of pure nature on the one hand and of pure technology, total control, on the other.

WHERE ARE THE PEOPLE?

By the power of a model, the specialist turns the future into a greenhouse of fantasies. But the model also empowers the fantasies with influence over present life—and, of course, over future life. And so, considering these model farms, one asks, Where are the people? out of self-interest and with some trepidation. The *National Geographic* model shows, as far as I can tell, only one "farmer." He is standing in the "bubble-topped control tower," presumably operating the whole farm by remote control. The article on the South Dakota State model mentions that "The hired hand gets the imposing new title of 'manager.'" Allowing for shifts, vacations, etc., these model farms evidently require a staff of only half a dozen or so to do the actual "work." Most of the jobs for people would evidently be non-agricultural: jobs of construction, maintenance, transport, etc.

And where are the *other* people—the ones who are not doing the computer-work of future farming? Well, the *National Geographic* picture shows some highway traffic that may or may not be remote-controlled. It shows "a distant city" and "a distant lake and recreation area." The South Dakota State model includes a zone for "recreation, wildlife, and living."

The agriculture prophets evidently think that they have left people pretty much to their own devices: they will have places to live and places to work and places for recreation, and, thanks to the completely controlled farms-of-the-future, they will have plenty to eat.

The specialists who conceived these models are American citizens. They undoubtedly believe in the doctrines of personal liberty and dignity, equality of opportunity, etc. If asked, they would undoubtedly say that the people outside the boundaries of these farms would benefit from them in every way: they would not only have areas especially allotted to them for living, working, and recreation, they would also have more freedom, dignity, and equality of opportunity than ever before.

But one must ask if they would not say these things thoughtlessly—because they are the right things to say in a democracy, or the most persuasive things to say, or because they are in the habit of saying them. It is clear, at least, that official policies—and these model farms represent official policy—have come to be *routinely* justified in this country on the grounds that they will uphold freedom, dignity, and equality of opportunity. There is no official depredation that one can think of that has not been initially so justified. The skids are greased with unctions of democracy.

But these assurances are always incidental, outside the boundary of whatever allegedly benign (and profitable) innovation is at hand. People are not going to be free or dignified or even well fed just because some specialist *says* that they will be. Or says that they will be *allowed to be, in certain areas*—for that is what these "agribusiness" visionaries are in fact saying. People will be *allowed* to be free to do *certain* things in *certain* places prescribed by *other* people. They will be free to work in the places set aside for work, free to play or relax in places set aside for recreation, free to live (whatever that may mean) in places set aside for living.

Thus there are several things that people will *not* be free to do in the nation-of-the-future that will be fed by these farms-of-the-future. They will not live where they work or work where they live. They will not work where they play. And they will not, above all, play where they work. There will be no singing in those fields. There will be no crews of workers or neighbors laughing and joking, telling stories, or competing at tests of speed or strength or skill. There will be no holiday walks or picnics in those fields because, in the first place, the fields will be ugly, all graces of nature having been ruled out, and, in the second place, they will be dangerous.

Very few people, more likely none of them, will own those farms. Very few will work on them. Most of them, more even than the ninety-five percent that *now* live in urban situations, will live remote from the farmland, divided from it by distance, by "buffer zones," by economics, by official structure. They will have nothing to say about how the land is used or the kind or quality of its produce. For these farms are obviously designed for the ownership and management of huge "agribusiness" corporations that will control them "privately" and control the market as well. The people will eat what the corporations decide for them to eat. They will be detached and remote from the sources of their life, joined to them only by corporate tolerance. They will have become consumers purely—consumptive machines—which is to say, the slaves of producers. What these model farms very powerfully suggest, then, is that the concept of total control may be impossible to confine within the boundaries of the specialist enterprise—that it is impossible to mechanize production without mechanizing consumption, impossible to make machines of soil, plants, and animals without making machines also of people.

It is important to recognize that in the minds both of the agribusiness specialists and of their believers and supporters among the public these representations of technological totalitarianism rest side by side with conventional good intentions. Mr. Billard, in his *National Geographic* article, is careful to write a paragraph of reassurance about the future of the family farm and the welfare of consumers: ". . . farms grossing more than $10,000 a year expand in number, with those in the more-than-$40,000 category increasing rapidly. The family farm figures largest in this growth. It accounts for 95% of all farms and 64 percent of total marketings. Corporate behemoths play no greater role today than 20 years ago; the specter of their progressively gobbling up all the farmland and in the end holding consumers at their mercy seems farfetched."

That, of course, depends on how you define "family farm" and "corporate behemoth." And beside the Department of Agriculture figures quoted earlier, and the testimony of his own article, Mr. Billard's reassurance is a mere hopeful assertion, not very reassuring.

And Dr. Hellickson, replying to my question about the possible influence of his students' work on personal liberty and private property, said: "We are in no way advocating the elimination of the free enterprise system or the reduction of privately owned land."

Sometimes I ask myself if it may not be that these reassurances are given cynically by people who know very well that they are turned against what they wish to appear to uphold. Though I leave open the possibility that this occasionally may be so, I have concluded so far that most often it is not. I believe that both Mr. Billard and Dr. Hellickson are sincere in their belief that the innovations they praise or advocate will not adversely affect traditional values, the supply or the quality of food, or the life of farming. I believe this of Dr. Hellickson in spite of his substitution of "the free enterprise system" for my phrase "personal liberty."

It is nevertheless a part of the significance of the statements of both men that they embody a large, if unconscious, moral contradiction. In this, it seems to me, they represent very accurately the flawed consciousness of our society, which is everywhere eagerly conniving in the destruction of what it says, and thinks, it wants to preserve.

75

For no matter what these gentlemen say, the private ownership of farmland and public concern for the health of farming are both diminishing at an alarming rate, and they are diminishing because of the big economics and big technology represented by these visions of future agriculture.

They are diminishing because as a society we have abandoned any interest in the survival of anything small. We seem to have adopted a moral rule of thumb according to which anything big is better than anything small. As a result, the agricultural establishment has simply looked away from the possibility of an economics and a technology suited to the needs and aims of the small farmer.

Some time ago I took part in a conference on agriculture, at which one of the speakers was an executive of Deere and Company. This man was asked by someone in the audience if he and his company were interested in small-farm technology. He replied that indeed they were. But as I remember that was all he said; he spoke of none of the particulars of such technology, in which he evidently had at least no personal interest. What did interest him, as I learned later in conversation, was the impending development of a 600-horsepower tractor, which eventually would be operated by remote control. In the face of such an interest, empowered as it is by official sanction, tax-supported research, and vast sums of money, the small farmer is not so much condemned as written off as a necessary expenditure. A price is put on his way of life which he is less and less able to meet.

DESERTS OF VAST TECHNOLOGY

As specialists, the agricultural scientists and "agribusinessmen" find it easy to talk as if the influence of big agricultural technology can be confined neatly to the "field" of agriculture. That it cannot be is already proven by the powerful *urban* influence that such technology has already had. And to the big-thinking, non-agricultural mind, food is merely a resource, like energy and raw materials, and so agricultural technology is not different from any other. About grain, fuel, and ore the only questions are: How much? and How fast?

Because big technology is so simplifying, the future looks, not bright, but absolutely perfect to F. M. Esfandiary, who teaches "long-range planning" in New York City's New School for Social Research. In an article entitled "Homo sapiens, the manna maker," Mr. Esfandiary sees the future as an earthly Heaven in which, by the miracles of technology, humans will usurp the role of God—who, it may be recalled, was once thought to be the only maker of manna. The following quotations will give the gist of his argument:

"The world is moving toward an age of limitless abundance— abundant energy, food, raw materials."

"Solar power, nuclear fusion, geothermal energy, recycled energy, wind energy, hydrogen fuel—these sources will soon provide cheap, nonpolluting, limitless energy, enough to last for millions of years."

"Agriculture is undergoing an epochal revolution. We are evolving from feudal and industrial agriculture to cybernated food production. Computers, remote control cultivators, television monitors, sensors, data banks can now automatically run thousands of acres of cultivated land. A couple of telefarm operators can feed a million people."

"We now have the capability to extract limitless raw materials from recycled wastes, rocks, the earth's interiors, the ocean floors, space."

That is the "objective" part of the argument. There follows a series of paragraphs that must hold the world record for rhetorical passion. It appears that Mr. Esfandiary is mad at us because we do not duck our heads and hurry right on into the future.

"How absurd the American panic over scarcity when we are entering an age of abundance. How absurd to focus on 'finiteness' at the period in evolution when our world is transcending finiteness, opening up the infinite resources of an infinite universe.
"How outrageous that after centuries of privation and sacrifice leaders can come up with nothing more than yet more sacrifice. How short-sighted the exhortation to no-growth at precisely the time when we urgently need more and more growth—growth not *within* but *beyond* industrialism.
"How retrogressive the preachings to lower living standards of the relatively rich to raise conditions of the poor, at a time when we can raise *everybody's* living conditions by vigorously developing and spreading abundance, not sharing scarcity."

The common assumption is that mechanization involves the giving over of certain tasks or functions to machines. In these paragraphs by Mr. Esfandiary a very different assumption, that may always have been implicit in the advocacy of industrial revolution, comes to the surface: he is proposing that we give over *everything* to machines. He is berating us, with the fervor of an evangelist, because we do not abandon ourselves to machines as people of faith abandon themselves to God. He is berating us, in fact, for not *being* gods or at least acting as if we were gods.

The crucial concept here is that of "limitless" or "infinite" quantity. By "limitless" and "infinite" Mr. Esfandiary undoubtedly means only "inconceivable." At any rate, people who have desired material *quantities* on such a scale have always been recognized as evil, and their stories have always involved a sort of ecological justice: godly appetite very quickly led beyond human competence, invariably with disastrous consequences. Mr. Esfandiary's unlimited, if theoretical, gluttony is licensed and given an illusory respectability because of its claim to be "scientific"—godly appetite may be within the competence of a computer—and because, as a "long-range planner," he does his theorizing in the future, where it cannot very handily be called to account.

It is nevertheless clear that Mr. Esfandiary's "future" calls for unprecedented violence. It would require the sacrifice of every value that is not quantitative. The technology of infinity (however that might be defined) would be vast and exclusive. It would be completely totalitarian, whether "publicly" or "privately" owned. It would overthrow the whole issue of control, for it would *be* the control. Since everyone would be totally dependent upon it, it would necessarily be everyone's first consideration. It might at first seem that enormous power would lie in the hands of the "couple of tele-farm operators" who would be feeding a million people; but it seems more likely that they, too, would be the absolute slaves of their machinery, no less dependent on it than the million. The machine would become an anti-god—if not infinite, at least absolute. To have even the illusion of infinite quantity, we would have to debase both the finite and the infinite; we would have to sacrifice both flesh and spirit. It is an old story. Evil is offering us the world: "All these things will I give thee, if thou wilt fall down and worship me." And we have only the old paradox for an answer: If we accept all on that condition, we lose all.

What is new is the *guise* of the evil: a limitless technology, dependent upon a limitless morality, which is to say upon no morality at all. How did such a possibility become thinkable? It seems to me that it is implicit in the modern separation of life and work. It is implicit in the assumption that we can live entirely apart from our way of making a living. It is implicit in the idea of the agricultural engineering students at South Dakota State University that their farm-of-the-future would require "blending with human values." To propose to blend such a farm with human values is simply to acknowledge that it *has* no human values, that human values have been removed from it. (The analogy is not accidental, I think, between this "blending with human values" and the "enrichment" of bread after the nutrients have been removed from the wheat.) If human values are removed from production, how can they be preserved in consumption? How can we value our lives if we devalue them in making a living?

If we do not live where we work, and when we work, we are wasting our lives, and our work too.

CHAPTER SIX

The Use
of Energy

"Energy," said William Blake, "is Eternal Delight." And the scientific prognosticators of our time have begun to speak of the eventual opening, for human use, of "infinite" sources of energy. In speaking of the use of energy, then, we are speaking of an issue of religion, whether we like it or not.

Religion, in the root sense of the word, is what binds us back to the source of life. Blake also said that "Energy is the only life . . ." And it is superhuman in the sense that humans cannot create it. They can only refine or convert it. And they are bound to it by one of the paradoxes of religion: they cannot have it except by losing it; they cannot use it except by destroying it. The lives that feed us have to be killed before they enter our mouths; we can only use the fossil fuels by burning them up. We speak of electrical energy as "current": it exists only while it runs away; we use it only by delaying its escape. To receive energy is at once to live and to die.

Perhaps from an "objective" point of view it is incorrect to say that we can destroy energy; we can only change it. Or we can destroy it only in its current form. But from a human point of view, we can destroy it also by wasting it—that is, by changing it into a form in which we cannot use it again. As users, we can preserve energy in cycles of use, passing it again and again through the same series of forms; or we can waste it by using it once in a way that makes it irrecoverable. The human pattern of cyclic use is exemplified in the small Oriental peasant farms described in F. H. King's *Farmers of Forty Centuries*, in which all organic residues, plant and animal and human, were returned to the soil, thus keeping intact the natural cycle of "birth, growth, maturity, death, and decay" that Sir Albert Howard identified as the "Wheel of Life." The pattern of wasteful use is exemplified in the modern sewage system and the internal combustion engine. With us, the wastes that escape use typically become pollutants. This kind of use turns an asset into a liability.

We have two means of bringing energy to use: by living things (plants, animals, our own bodies) and by tools (machines, energy-harnesses). For the use of these we have skills or techniques. All three together comprise our technology. Technology joins us to energy, to life. It is not, as many technologists would have us believe, a simple connection. Our technology is the practical aspect of our culture. By it we enact our religion, or our lack of it.

I began thinking about this by trying to make a clear distinction between the living organisms and skills of technology and its mechanisms, and to say that the living aspect was better than the mechanical. I found it impossible to make such a distinction. I thought of going back through history to a point at which such a distinction would become possible, but found that the farther back I went the less possible it became. When people had no machines other than throwing stones and clubs, their technology was all of a piece. It stayed that way through their development of more sophisticated tools, their mastery of fire, their domestication of plants and animals. Lives, skills, and tools were culturally indivisible.

The question at issue, then, is not of distinction but of balance. The ideal seems to be that the living part of our technology should not be devalued or overpowered by the mechanical. Because the biological limits are probably narrower than the mechanical, this calls for restraint on the proliferation of machines.

At some point in history the balance between life and machinery was overthrown. I think this began to happen when people began to desire long-term stores or supplies of energy—that is, when they began to think of energy as volume as well as force—and when machines ceased to enhance or elaborate skill and began to replace it.

Though it seems impossible to distinguish between the living and the mechanical aspects of technology, it is possible to distinguish between two kinds of energy: that which is made available by living things and that which is made available by machines.

The energy that comes from living things is produced by combining the four elements of medieval science: earth, air, fire (sunlight), and water. This is current energy. Though it is possible to speak of a *reserve* of such energy, as Sir Albert Howard does, in the sense of a surplus of fertility, it is impossible to conceive of a *reservoir* of it. It is not available in long-term supplies; in any form in which it can be preserved, as in humus, in the flesh of living animals, in cans or freezers or grain elevators, it still perishes fairly quickly in comparison, say, to coal or plutonium. It lasts over a long term only in the living cycle of birth, growth, maturity, death, and decay. The technology appropriate to the use of this energy, therefore, preserves its cycles. It is a technology that never escapes into its own logic but remains bound in analogy to natural law.

The energy that is made available, and consumed, by machines is typically energy that can be accumulated in stockpiles or reservoirs. Energy from wind and water obviously does not fit this category, but it suggests the possibility of bigger and better storage batteries, which one must assume will sooner or later be produced. And, of course, we already store water power behind hydroelectric dams. This mechanically derived energy is supposed to have set people free from work and other difficulties once considered native to the human condition. Whether or not it has done so in any meaningful sense is questionable—in my opinion, it is highly questionable. But there is no doubt that this sort of energy has freed machinery from the natural restraints that apply to the use of organic energy. We now have a purely mechanical technology that is very nearly a law unto itself.

And yet, in the long term, this liberation of the machine is illusory. Mechanical technology is based on quantities of materials and fuels that are finite. If the prophets of science foresee "limitless abundance" and "infinite resources," one must assume that they are speaking figuratively, meaning simply that they cannot comprehend how much there may be. In that sense, they are right: there are sources of energy that, given the necessary machinery, are inexhaustible *as far as we can see*.

The great difficulty, which these cheerful prophets do not acknowledge at all, is that we are trustworthy only so far as we can see. The

83

length of our vision is our moral boundary. Even if these foreseen supplies *are* limitless, we can use them only within limits. We can bring the infinite to bear only within the finite bounds of our biological circumstance and our understanding. It is already certain that our planet alone—not to mention potential sources in space—can provide us with more energy and materials than we can use safely or well. By our abuse of our finite sources, our lives and all life are already in danger. What might we bring into danger by the abuse of "infinite" sources?

The difficulty with mechanically extractable energy is that so far we have been unable to make it available without serious geological and ecological damage, or to effectively restrain its use, or to use or even neutralize its wastes. From birth, right now, we are carrying the physical and the moral poisons produced by our crude and ignorant use of this sort of energy. And the more abundant the energy of this sort that we use, the more abounding must be the consequences.

It is typical of the mentality of our age that we cannot conceive of infinity except as an enormous quantity. We cannot conceive of it as orderly process, as pattern or cycle, as shapeliness. We conceive of it as inconceivable quantity—that is, as the immeasurable. Any quantity that we cannot measure we assume must be infinite. That is about as sophisticated as saying that the world is flat because it *looks* flat. The talk about "infinite" resources is thus a kind of scientific-sounding foolishness. And it involves some quaint paradoxes. If we think, for instance, of infinite energy as immeasurable fuel, we are committed in the same thought to its destruction, for fuel must be destroyed to be used. We thus arrive at the curious idea of a destructible infinity. Furthermore, we have become guilty not only of the demonstrably silly assumption that we know what to do with infinite energy, but also of the monstrous pride of thinking ourselves somehow entitled to undertake infinite destruction.

This mechanically rendered infinitude of energy is an ambition surrounded by terrific problems. Such energy cannot be used constructively without at the same time being used destructively. And which way the balance will finally fall is a question that baffles the best minds. Nobody knows what will be the ultimate consequences of our present use of fossil fuel, much less those of our future use of atomic fuel. The sun may prove an "infinite" source of energy—at least one that may last several billion years. But who will control the use of that energy? How and for what purposes will it be used?

How much can be used without overthrowing ecological or social or political balances? Nobody knows.

The energy that is made available to us by living things, on the other hand, is made available not as an inconceivable quantity, but as a conceivable pattern. And for the mastery of this pattern—that is, the ability to see its absolute importance and to preserve it in use—one does not need a Ph.D. or a laboratory or a computer. One can master it in this sense, in fact, without having any analytic or scientific understanding of it at all. It was mastered, better than our scientific experts have mastered it, by "primitive" peasants and tribesmen thousands of years before modern science. It is conceivable not so much to the analytic intelligence, to which it may always remain in part mysterious, as to the imagination, by which we perceive, value, and imitate order beyond our understanding.

We cannot create biological energy any more than we can create atomic or fossil fuel energy. But we *can* preserve it in use; we can probably even augment it in use, in the sense that, by proper care, we can "build" soil. We cannot do that with machine-derived energy. This is an extremely important difference, with respect both to the energy economy itself and to the moral order that is undoubtedly determined by, as much as it determines, the value we put on energy.

The moral order by which we use machine-derived energy is comparatively simple. Whatever uses this sort of energy works simply as a conduit that carries it beyond use: the energy goes in as "fuel" and comes out as "waste." This principle sustains a highly simplified economy having only two functions: production and consumption.

The moral order appropriate to the use of biological energy, on the other hand, requires the addition of a third term: production, consumption, *and return*. It is the principle of return that complicates matters, for it requires responsibility, care, of a different and higher order than that required by production and consumption alone, and it calls for methods and economies of a different kind. In an energy economy appropriate to the use of biological energy, all bodies, plant and animal and human, are joined in a kind of energy community. They are not divided from each other by greedy, "individualistic" efforts to produce and consume large quantities of energy, much less to store large quantities of it. They are indissolubly linked in complex patterns of energy exchange. They die into each other's life, live into each other's death. They do not consume in the sense of using up. They do not produce waste. What they take in they change,

85

but they change it always into a form necessary for its use by a living body of another kind. And this exchange goes on and on, round and round, the Wheel of Life rising out of the soil, descending into it, through the bodies of creatures.

The soil is the great connector of lives, the source and destination of all. It is the healer and restorer and resurrector, by which disease passes into health, age into youth, death into life. Without proper care for it we can have no community, because without proper care for it we can have no life.

It is alive itself. It is a grave, too, of course. Or a healthy soil is. It is full of dead animals and plants, bodies that have passed through other bodies. For except for some humans—with their sealed coffins and vaults, their pathological fear of the earth—the only way into the soil is through other bodies. But no matter how finely the dead are broken down, or how many times they are eaten, they yet give into other life. If a healthy soil is full of death it is also full of life: worms, fungi, microorganisms of all kinds, for which, as for us humans, the dead bodies of the once living are a feast. Eventually this dead matter becomes soluble, available as food for plants, and life begins to rise up again, out of the soil into the light. Given only the health of the soil, nothing that dies is dead for very long. Within this powerful economy, it seems that death occurs only for the good of life. And having followed the cycle around, we see that we have not only a description of the fundamental biological process, but also a metaphor of great beauty and power. It is impossible to contemplate the life of the soil for very long without seeing it as analogous to the life of the spirit. No less than the faithful of religion is the good farmer mindful of the persistence of life through death, the passage of energy through changing forms.

And this living topsoil—living in both the biological sense and in the cultural sense, as metaphor—is the basic element in the technology of farming.

It is the nature of the soil to be highly complex and variable, to conform very inexactly to human conclusions and rules. It is itself a pattern of inexhaustible intricacy, and so it is easily damaged by the imposition of alien patterns. Out of the random grammar and lexicon of possibilities—geological, topographical, climatological, biological—the soil of any one place makes its own peculiar and inevitable sense. It makes an order, a pattern of forms, kinds, and processes, that includes any number of offsets and variables. By its permeability and absorbency, for example, the healthy soil corrects the irregularities of rainfall; by the diversity of its vegetation it protects against both disease and erosion. Most farms, even most fields, are made up of different kinds of soil patterns or soil sense. Good farmers have always known this and have used the land accordingly; they have been careful students of the natural vegetation, soil depth and structure, slope and drainage. They are not appliers of generalizations, theoretical or methodological or mechanical. Nor are they the active agents of their own economic will, working their way upon an inert and passive mass. They are responsive partners in an intimate and mutual relationship.

Because the soil is alive, various, intricate, and because its processes yield more readily to imitation than to analysis, more readily to care than to coercion, agriculture can never be an exact science. There is an inescapable kinship between farming and art, for farming depends as much on character, devotion, imagination, and the sense of structure, as on knowledge. It is a practical art.

But it is also a practical religion, a practice of religion, a rite. By farming we enact our fundamental connection with energy and matter, light and darkness. In the cycles of farming, which carry the elemental energy again and again through the seasons and the bodies of living things, we recognize the only infinitude within reach of the imagination. How long this cycling of energy will continue we do not know; it will have to end, at least here on this planet, sometime within the remaining life of the sun. But by aligning ourselves with it here, in our little time within the unimaginable time of the sun's burning, we touch infinity; we align ourselves with the universal law that brought the cycles into being and that will survive them.

The word *agriculture*, after all, does not mean "agriscience," much less "agribusiness." It means "cultivation of land." And *cultivation* is at the root of the sense both of *culture* and of *cult*. The ideas of tillage and worship are thus joined in *culture*. And these words all come from an Indo-European root meaning both "to revolve" and "to dwell." To live, to survive on the earth, to care for the soil, and to worship, all are bound at the root to the idea of a cycle. It is only by understanding the cultural complexity and largeness of the concept of agriculture that we can see the threatening diminishments implied by the term "agribusiness."

That agriculture is in so complex a sense a cultural endeavor—and that food is therefore a cultural product—would be regarded as

87

heresy by most of the agencies, institutions, and publications of modern farming. The spokesmen of the official reckoning would doubtless respond that they are not cultural but scientific, that they are specialists of "agriscience." If agriculture is acknowledged to have anything to do with culture, then its study has to include people. But the agriculture experts ruled people out when they made their discipline a specialty—or, rather, when they sorted it into a collection of specialties—and moved it into its own "college" in the university. This specialty collection is interested in soils (in the limited sense of soil chemistry), in plants and animals, and in machines and chemicals. It is not interested in people.

But what respect is one to give to a science that parcels a unified discipline into discrete fragments, that has no interest in its effects if they are not immediately measurable in a laboratory, and that is founded upon the waste of topsoil, energy, and manpower, and upon the dissolution of communities? Not much. And it has been my experience that, with respect to this science, farmers are divided into two kinds: those who endanger their solvency, and often their sanity, by trusting it and those who hold it in contempt.

In the view of the experts, then, agriculture is not only not a concern of culture, but not even a concern of science, for they have abandoned interest in the health of the farming communities on the one hand and in the health of the land on the other. They appear to have concluded that agriculture is purely a commercial concern; its purpose is to provide as much food as quickly and cheaply and with as few man-hours as possible and to be a market for machines and chemicals. It is, after all, "agribusiness"—not the land or the farming people—that now benefits most from agricultural research and that can promote humble academicians to highly remunerative and powerful positions in corporations and in government. Former Secretary Earl Butz's career exemplifies the predominant direction of interest of the agriculture specialist. According to Lauren Soth, writing in the *Nation*, "Butz is the perfect example of the agribusiness, commercial-farming, agricultural-education establishment man. When dean of agriculture at Purdue University, he also sat on the boards of directors of the Ralston-Purina Co., the J. I. Case Co., International Minerals and Chemicals Corp., Stokely-Van Camp Co. and Standard Life Insurance Co. of Indiana." By such men and such careers the land-grant college system, originally meant to enhance the small-farm possibility, has been captured for the corporations.

The discipline of agriculture—the "great subject," as Sir Albert Howard called it, "of health in soil, plant, animal, and man"—has been reduced to fit first the views of a piecemeal "science" and then the purposes of corporate commerce. I can see no possibility of a doubt that this is true, though I cannot explain exactly how it happened. But it seems to me that the way was prepared when the specialized shapers or makers of agricultural thought simplified their understanding of energy and began to treat current, living, biological energy as if it were a *store* of energy extractable by machinery. At that point the living part of technology began to be overpowered by the mechanical. The machine was on its own, to follow its own logic of elaboration and growth apart from life, the standard that had previously defined its purposes and hence its limits. Let loose from any moral standard or limit, the machine was also let loose in another way: it replaced the Wheel of Life as the governing cultural metaphor. Life came to be seen as a road, to be traveled as fast as possible, never to return. Or, to put it another way, the Wheel of Life became an industrial metaphor; rather than turning in place, revolving in order to dwell, it began to roll on the "highway of progress" toward an ever-receding horizon. The idea, the responsibility, of return weakened and disappeared from agricultural discipline. Henceforth, *any* resource would be regarded as an ore.

If agriculture is founded upon life, upon the use of living energy to serve human life, and if its primary purpose must therefore be to preserve the integrity of the life cycle, then agricultural technology must be bound under the rule of life. It must conform to natural processes and limits rather than to mechanical or economic models. The culture that sustains agriculture and that it sustains must form its consciousness and its aspiration upon the correct metaphor of the Wheel of Life. The appropriate agricultural technology would therefore be diverse; it would aspire to diversity; it would enable the diversification of economies, methods, and species to conform to the diverse kinds of land. It would always use plants and animals together. It would be as attentive to decay as to growth, to maintenance as to production. It would return all wastes to the soil, control erosion, and conserve water. To enable care and devotion and to safeguard the local communities and cultures of agriculture, it would use the land in small holdings. It would aspire to make each farm so far as possible the source of its own operating energy, by the use of human energy, work animals, methane, wind or water or solar power.

The mechanical aspect of the technology would serve to harness or enhance the energy available on the farm. It would not be permitted to replace such energies with imported fuels, to replace people, or to replace or reduce human skills.

The damages of our present agriculture all come from the determination to use the life of the soil as if it were an extractable resource like coal, to use living things as if they were machines, to impose scientific (that is, laboratory) exactitude upon living complexities that are ultimately mysterious.

If animals are regarded as machines, they are confined in pens remote from the source of their food, where their excrement becomes, instead of a fertilizer, first a "waste" and then a pollutant. Furthermore, because confinement feeding depends so largely on grains, grass is removed from the rotation of crops and more land is exposed to erosion.

If plants are regarded as machines, we wind up with huge monocultures, productive of elaborate ecological mischiefs, which are in turn productive of agricultural mischief: monocultures are much more susceptible to pests and diseases than mixed cultures and are therefore more dependent on chemicals.

If the soil is regarded as a machine, then its life, its involvement in living systems and cycles, must perforce be ignored. It must be treated as a dead, inert chemical mass. If its life is ignored, then so must be the natural sources of its fertility—and not only ignored, but scorned. Alfalfa and the clovers, according to some of the most up-to-date practitioners, are "weeds"; the only legitimate source of nitrogen is the fertilizer manufacturer. And animal manures are "wastes"; "efficiency" cannot use them. Not long ago I found that the manure from a saddle-horse barn belonging to the University of Kentucky was simply being dumped. When I asked why it was not used somewhere on the farm, I was told that it would interfere with the College of Agriculture's experiments. The result is absurd: our agriculture, potentially capable of a large measure of independence, is absolutely dependent on petroleum, on the oil companies, and on the vagaries of politics.

If people are regarded as machines, they must be regarded as replaceable by other machines. They are regarded, in other words, as dispensable. Their place on the farm is safe only as long as they are mechanically necessary.

In modern agriculture, then, the machine metaphor is allowed to usurp and wipe from consideration not merely *some* values, but the very *issue* of value. Once the expert's interest is focused on the question of "what will work" within the exclusive confines of his theoretical model, values are no longer of any concern whatever. The confines of his specialty enable him to impose a biological totalitarianism on—he thinks, since he is an agricultural expert—the farm. When he leaves his office or laboratory he will, he assumes, go "home" to value.

But then it must be asked if we can remove cultural value from one part of our lives without destroying it also in the other parts. Can we justify secrecy, lying, and burglary in our so-called intelligence organizations and yet preserve openness, honesty, and devotion to principle in the rest of our government? Can we subsidize mayhem in the military establishment and yet have peace, order, and respect for human life in the city streets? Can we degrade all forms of essential work and yet expect arts and graces to flourish on weekends? And can we ignore all questions of value on the farm and yet have them answered affirmatively in the grocery store and the household?

The answer is that, though such distinctions can be made theoretically, they cannot be preserved in practice. Values may be corrupted or abolished in only one discipline at the start, but the damage must sooner or later spread to all; it can no more be confined than air pollution. If we corrupt agriculture we corrupt culture, for in nature and within certain invariable social necessities we are one body, and what afflicts the hand will afflict the brain.

The effective knowledge of this unity must reside not so much in doctrine as in skill. Skill, in the best sense, is the enactment or the acknowledgment or the signature of responsibility to other lives; it is the practical understanding of value. Its opposite is not merely unskillfulness, but ignorance of sources, dependences, relationships.

Skill is the connection between life and tools, or life and machines. Once, skill was defined ultimately in qualitative terms: How *well* did a person work; how good, durable, and pleasing were his products? But as machines have grown larger and more complex, and as our awe of them and our desire for labor-saving have grown, we have tended more and more to define skill quantitatively: How speedily and cheaply can a person work? We have increasingly wanted a *measurable* skill. And the more quantifiable skills became, the easier they were to replace with machines. As machines replace skill, they disconnect themselves from life; they come between us and life. They begin to enact our ignorance of value—of essential sources, dependences, and relationships.

The catch is that we cannot live in machines. We can only live in the world, in life. To live, our contact with the sources of life must remain direct: we must eat, drink, breathe, move, mate, etc. When we let machines and machine skills obscure the values that represent these fundamental dependences, then we inevitably damage the world; we diminish life. We begin to "prosper" at the cost of a fundamental degradation.

The digging stick, for example, brought in a profound technological revolution: it made agriculture possible. Its use required skill. But its *effect* also required skill, and this kind of skill was higher and more complex than the first, for it involved restraint and responsibility. The digging stick made it possible to grow food; that was one thing. It also made it possible, and necessary, to disturb the earth; and that was another thing. The first skill required others that were its moral elaboration: the skill used in disturbing the earth called directly for other skills that would preserve the earth and restore its fertility.

Until fairly recently, as agricultural tools became more efficient or powerful or both, they required an increase of both kinds of skill. One could do more with stone implements than with sticks, and more with metal implements than with stone implements; the skilled use of these tools enabled one to disturb more ground and so called for further elaboration of the skills of responsibility.

This remained true after the beginning of the use of draft animals. The skills of use had to become much greater, for the human mind had to relate to the animal mind in a new way: not by the magic and cunning of the hunt, but in the practical intricacies of collaboration. And the skills of responsibility had to increase proportionately. More ground could now be disturbed, and so the technology of preservation had to become much larger. Also, the investment of life in work greatly increased; people had to take responsibility not only for their own appetites and excrements but for those of their animals as well.

It was only with the introduction of self-powering machines, and of machine-extracted energy, into the fields that something really new happened to agricultural skills: they began a radical diminishment.

In the first place, it requires more skill to use a team of horses or mules or oxen than to use a tractor. It is more difficult to learn to manage an animal than a machine; it takes longer. Two minds and two wills are involved. A relationship between a person and a work animal is analogous to a relationship between two people. Success depends upon the animal's willingness and upon its health; certain moral imperatives and restraints are therefore pragmatically essential. No such relationship is either necessary or possible with a machine. Within the range of the possible, a machine is directly responsive to human will; it neither starts nor stops because it wants to. A machine has no life, and for this reason it cannot of itself impose any restraint or any moral limit on behavior.

In the second place, the substitution of machines for work animals is justified mainly by their ability to increase the volume of work per man—that is, by their greater speed. But as speed increases, care declines. And so, necessarily, do the skills of responsibility. If this were not so, we would not restrict the speed of traffic in residential areas. We know that there is a limit to the capacity of attention, and that the faster we go the less we see. This law applies with equal force to work; the faster we work the less attention we can pay to its details, and the less skill we can apply to it.

This is true of *any* productive work, and it has great cultural importance; at present we are all suffering, in various ways, from dependence on goods that are poorly made. But its importance in agricultural production is probably more critical than elsewhere. In any biological system the first principle is restraint—that is, the natural or moral checks that maintain a balance between use and continuity. The life of one year must not be allowed to diminish the life of the next; nothing must live at the expense of the source. Thus, in nature, the food species is dependent on its predator, and pests and diseases are agents of health; so populations are controlled and balanced. In agriculture these natural checks are removed and therefore must be replaced by the skills of responsibility, which have to do with the prevention of erosion, the diversification and rotation of plant and animal species, the return of wastes to the soil, and all the other provisionings of the source. When productive power—that is, speed—in machines replaces the productive skills of people, there is a consequent narrowing of attention. The machines are expensive and they run on purchased fuels; they feed upon money. The work of production is immediately profitable, whereas the work of responsibility is not. Once the machine is in the field it creates an economic pressure that enforces haste; the machine concentrates all the energy of the farm and hurries it toward the marketplace. The demands of immediate use eclipse the demands of continuity. As the skills of production decline, the skills of responsibility perish.

To argue for a balance between people and their tools, between life and machinery, between biological and machine-produced energy, is to argue for restraint upon the use of machines. The arguments that rise out of the machine metaphor—arguments for cheapness, efficiency, labor-saving, economic growth, etc.—all point to infinite industrial growth and infinite energy consumption. The moral argument points to restraint; it is a conclusion that may be in some sense tragic, but there is no escaping it. Much as we long for infinities of power and duration, we have no evidence that these lie within our reach, much less within our responsibility. It is more likely that we will have either to live within our limits, within the human definition, or not live at all. And certainly the knowledge of these limits and of how to live within them is the most comely and graceful knowledge that we have, the most healing and the most whole.

The knowledge that purports to be leading us to transcendence of our limits has been with us a long time. It thrives by offering material means of fulfilling a spiritual, and therefore materially unappeasable, craving: we would all very much like to be immortal, infallible, free of doubt, at rest. It is because this need is so large, and so different in kind from all material means, that the knowledge of transcendence— our entire history of scientific "miracles"—is so tentative, fragmentary, and grotesque. Though there are undoubtedly mechanical limits, because there are human limits, there is no mechanical restraint. The only logic of the machine is to get bigger and more elaborate. In the absence of *moral* restraint—and we have never imposed adequate moral restraint upon our use of machines—the machine is out of control by definition. From the beginning of the history of machine-developed energy, we have been able to harness more power than we could use responsibly. From the beginning, these machines have created effects that society could absorb only at the cost of suffering and disorder.

And so the issue is not of supply but of use. The energy crisis is not a crisis of technology but of morality. We already have available more power than we have so far dared to use. If, like the strip-miners and the "agribusinessmen," we look on all the world as fuel or as extractable energy, we can do nothing but destroy it. The issue is restraint. The energy crisis reduces to a single question: Can we forbear to do anything that we are able to do? Or to put the question in the words of Ivan Illich: Can we, believing in "the effectiveness of power," see "the disproportionately greater effectiveness of abstaining from its use"?

The only people among us that I know of who have answered this question convincingly in the affirmative are the Amish. They alone, as a community, have carefully restricted their use of machine-developed energy, and so have become the only true masters of technology. They are mostly farmers, and they do most of their farm work by hand and by the use of horses and mules. They are pacifists, they operate their own local schools, and in other ways hold themselves aloof from the ambitions of a machine-based society. And by doing so they have maintained the integrity of their families, their community, their religion, and their way of life. They have escaped the mainstream American life of distraction, haste, aimlessness, violence, and disintegration. Their life is not idly wasteful, or destructive. The Amish no doubt have their problems; I do not wish to imply that they are perfect. But it cannot be denied that they have mastered one of the fundamental paradoxes of our condition: we can make ourselves whole only by accepting our partiality, by living within our limits, by being human—not by trying to be gods. By restraint they make themselves whole.

But just stop for a minute and think about what it means to live in a land where 95 percent of the people can be freed from the drudgery of preparing their own food.

JAMES E. BOSTIC, JR., FORMER DEPUTY
ASSISTANT SECRETARY OF AGRICULTURE
FOR RURAL DEVELOPMENT

Find the shortest, simplest way between the earth, the hands and the mouth.

LANZA DEL VASTO

CHAPTER SEVEN

The Body and
the Earth

ON THE CLIFF

The question of human limits, of the proper definition and place of human beings within the order of Creation, finally rests upon our attitude toward our biological existence, the life of the body in this world. What value and respect do we give to our bodies? What uses do we have for them? What relation do we see, if any, between body and mind, or body and soul? What connections or responsibilities do we maintain between our bodies and the earth? These are religious questions, obviously, for our bodies are part of the Creation, and they involve us in all the issues of mystery. But the questions are also agricultural, for no matter how urban our life, our bodies live by farming; we come from the earth and return to it, and so we live in agriculture as we live in flesh. While we live our bodies are moving particles of the earth, joined inextricably both to the soil and to the bodies of other living creatures. It is hardly surprising, then, that there should be some profound resemblances between our treatment of our bodies and our treatment of the earth.

That humans are small within the Creation is an ancient perception, represented often enough in art that it must be supposed to

97

have an elemental importance. On one of the painted walls of the Lascaux cave (20,000-15,000 B.C.), surrounded by the exquisitely shaped, shaded, and colored bodies of animals, there is the childish stick figure of a man, a huntsman who, having cast his spear into the guts of a bison, is now weaponless and vulnerable, poignantly frail, exposed, and incomplete. The message seems essentially that of the voice out of the whirlwind in the Book of Job: the Creation is bounteous and mysterious, and humanity is only a part of it—not its equal, much less its master.

Old Chinese landscape paintings reveal, among towering mountains, the frail outline of a roof or a tiny human figure passing along a road on foot or horseback. These landscapes are almost always populated. There is no implication of a dehumanized interest in nature "for its own sake." What is represented is a world in which humans belong, but which does not belong to humans in any tidy economic sense; the Creation provides a place for humans, but it is greater than humanity and within it even great men are small. Such humility is the consequence of an accurate insight, ecological in its bearing, not a pious deference to "spiritual" value.

Closer to us is a passage from the fourth act of *King Lear*, describing the outlook from one of the Dover cliffs:

> *The crows and choughs that wing the midway air*
> *Show scarce so gross as beetles. Halfway down*
> *Hangs one that gathers samphire, dreadful trade!*
> *Methinks he seems no bigger than his head.*
> *The fishermen that walk upon the beach*
> *Appear like mice, and yond tall anchoring bark*
> *Diminished to her cock—her cock, a buoy*
> *Almost too small for sight.*

And this is no mere description of a scenic "view." It is part of a play-within-a-play, a sort of ritual of healing. In it Shakespeare is concerned with the curative power of the perception we are dealing with: by understanding accurately his proper place in Creation, a man may be made whole.

In the lines quoted, Edgar, disguised as a lunatic, a Bedlamite, is speaking to his father, the Earl of Gloucester. Gloucester, having been blinded by the treachery of his false son, Edmund, has despaired and has asked the supposed madman to lead him to the cliff's edge, where he intends to destroy himself. But Edgar's description is from memory; the two are not standing on any such dizzy verge. What we are witnessing is the working out of Edgar's strategy to save his father from false feeling—both the pride, the smug credulity, that led to his suffering and the despair that is its result. These emotions are perceived as madness; Gloucester's blindness is literally the result of the moral blindness of his pride, and it is symbolic of the spiritual blindness of his despair.

Thinking himself on the edge of a cliff, he renounces this world and throws himself down. Though he falls only to the level of his own feet, he is momentarily stunned. Edgar remains with him, but now represents himself as an innocent bystander at the foot of what Gloucester will continue to think is a tall cliff. As the old man recovers his senses, Edgar persuades him that the madman who led him to the cliff's edge was in reality a "fiend." And Gloucester repents his self-destructiveness, which he now recognizes as another kind of pride; a human has no right to destroy what he did not create:

> You ever-gentle gods, take my breath from me.
> Let not my worser spirit tempt me again
> To die before you please.

What Gloucester has passed through, then, is a rite of death and rebirth. In his new awakening he is finally able to recognize his true son. He escapes the unhuman conditions of godly pride and fiendish despair and dies "smilingly" in the truly human estate " 'Twixt two extremes of passion, joy and grief . . ."

Until modern times, we focused a great deal of the best of our thought upon such rituals of return to the human condition. Seeking enlightenment or the Promised Land or the way home, a man would go or be forced to go into the wilderness, measure himself against the Creation, recognize finally his true place within it, and thus be saved both from pride and from despair. Seeing himself as a tiny member of a world he cannot comprehend or master or in any final sense possess, he cannot possibly think of himself as a god. And by the same token, since he shares in, depends upon, and is graced by all of which he is a part, neither can he become a fiend; he cannot descend into the final despair of destructiveness. Returning from the wilderness, he becomes a restorer of order, a preserver. He sees the truth, recognizes his true heir, honors his forebears and his heritage, and gives his blessing to his successors. He embodies the passing of human time, living and dying within the human limits of grief and joy.

ON THE TOWER

Apparently with the rise of industry, we began to romanticize the wilderness—which is to say we began to institutionalize it within the concept of the "scenic." Because of railroads and improved highways, the wilderness was no longer an arduous passage for the traveler, but something to be looked at as grand or beautiful from the high vantages of the roadside. We became viewers of "views." And because we no longer traveled in the wilderness as a matter of course, we forgot that wilderness still circumscribed civilization and persisted in domesticity. We forgot, indeed, that the civilized and the domestic continued to *depend* upon wilderness—that is, upon natural forces within the climate and within the soil that have never in any meaningful sense been controlled or conquered. Modern civilization has been built largely in this forgetfulness.

And as we transformed the wilderness into scenery, we began to feel in the presence of "nature" an awe that was increasingly statistical. We would not become appreciators of the Creation until we had taken its measure. Once we had climbed or driven to the mountain top, we were awed by the view, but it was an awe that we felt compelled to validate or prove by the knowledge of how high we stood and how far we saw. We are invited to "see seven states from atop Lookout Mountain," as if our political boundaries had been drawn in red on the third morning of Creation.

We became less and less capable of sensing ourselves as small within Creation, partly because we thought we could comprehend it statistically, but also because we were becoming creators, ourselves, of a mechanical creation by which we felt ourselves greatly magnified. We built bridges that stood imposingly in titanic settings, towers that stood around us like geologic presences, single machines that could do the work of hundreds of people. Why, after all, should one get excited about a mountain when one can see almost as far from the top of a building, much farther from an airplane, farther still from a space capsule? We have learned to be fascinated by the statistics of magnitude and power. There is apparently no limit in sight, no end, and so it is no wonder that our minds, dizzy with numbers, take refuge in a yearning for infinitudes of energy and materials.

And yet these works that so magnify us also dwarf us, reduce us to insignificance. They magnify us because we are capable of them.

They diminish us because, say what we will, once we build beyond a human scale, once we conceive ourselves as Titans or as gods, we are lost in magnitude; we cannot control or limit what we do. The statistics of magnitude call out like Sirens to the statistics of destruction. If we have built towering cities, we have raised even higher the cloud of megadeath. If people are as grass before God, they are as nothing before their machines.

If we are fascinated by the statistics of magnitude, we are no less fascinated by the statistics of our insignificance. We never tire of repeating the commonizing figures of population and population growth. We are entranced to think of ourselves as specks on the pages of our own overwhelming history. I remember that my high-school biology text dealt with the human body by listing its constituent elements, measuring their quantities, and giving their monetary worth—at that time a little less than a dollar. That was a bit of the typical fodder of the modern mind, at once sensational and belittling—no accidental product of the age of Dachau and Hiroshima.

In our time Shakespeare's cliff has become the tower of a bridge—not the scene of a wakening rite of symbolic death and rebirth, but of the real and final death of suicide. Hart Crane wrote its paradigm, as if against his will, in *The Bridge*:

> *Out of some subway scuttle, cell or loft*
> *A bedlamite speeds to thy parapets,*
> *Tilting there momentarily, shrill shirt ballooning,*
> *A jest falls from the speechless caravan.*

In Shakespeare, the real Bedlamite or madman is the desperate and suicidal Gloucester. The supposed Bedlamite is in reality his true son, and together they enact an eloquent ritual in which Edgar gives his father a vision of Creation. Gloucester abandons himself to this vision, literally casting himself into it, and is renewed; he finds his life by losing it. Gloucester is saved by a renewal of his sense of the world and of his proper place in it. And this is brought about by an enactment that is communal, both in the sense that he is accompanied in it by his son, who for the time being has assumed the disguise of a madman but the role of a priest, and in the sense that it is deeply traditional in its symbols and meanings. In Crane, on the other hand, the Bedlamite is alone, surrounded by speechlessness, cut off within the crowd from any saving or renewing vision. The height, which in Shakespeare is the traditional place of vision, has become in Crane a place of blindness; the bridge, which Crane intended as a unifying symbol, has become the symbol of a final estrangement.

HEALTH

After I had begun to think about these things, I received a letter containing an account of a more recent suicide. The following sentences from that letter seem both to corroborate Crane's lines and to clarify them:

"My friend _____ jumped off the Golden Gate Bridge two months ago. . . . She had been terribly depressed for years. There was no help for her. None that she could find that was sufficient. She was trying to get from one phase of her life to another, and couldn't make it. She had been terribly wounded as a child. . . . Her wound could not be healed. She destroyed herself."

The letter had already asked, "How does a human pass through youth to maturity without 'breaking down'?" And it had answered: "help from tradition, through ceremonies and rituals, rites of passage at the most difficult stages."

My correspondent went on to say: "Healing, it seems to me, is a necessary and useful word when we talk about agriculture." And a few paragraphs later he wrote: "The theme of suicide belongs in a book about agriculture . . ."

I agree. But I am also aware that many people will find it exceedingly strange that these themes should enter so forcibly into this book. It will be thought that I am off the subject. And so I want to take pains to show that I am *on* the subject—and on it, moreover, in the only way most people have of getting on it: by way of the issue of their own health. Indeed, it is when one approaches agriculture from any *other* issue than that of health that one may be said to be off the subject.

The difficulty probably lies in our narrowed understanding of the word *health*. That there is some connection between how we feel and what we eat, between our bodies and the earth, is acknowledged when we say that we must "eat right to keep fit" or that we should eat "a balanced diet." But by health we mean little more than how we feel. We are healthy, we think, if we do not feel any pain or too much pain, and if we are strong enough to do our work. If we become unhealthy, then we go to a doctor who we hope will "cure" us and restore us to health. By health, in other words, we mean merely the absence of disease. Our health professionals are interested almost exclusively in preventing disease (mainly by destroying germs) and in curing disease (mainly by surgery and by destroying germs).

But the concept of health is rooted in the concept of wholeness. To be healthy is to be whole. The word *health* belongs to a family of words, a listing of which will suggest how far the consideration of health must carry us: *heal, whole, wholesome, hale, hallow, holy*. And so it is possible to give a definition to health that is positive and far more elaborate than that given to it by most medical doctors and the officers of public health.

If the body is healthy, then it is whole. But how can it be whole and yet be dependent, as it obviously is, upon other bodies and upon the earth, upon all the rest of Creation, in fact? It becomes clear that the health or wholeness of the body is a vast subject, and that to preserve it calls for a vast enterprise. Blake said that "Man has no Body distinct from his Soul . . ." and thus acknowledged the convergence of health and holiness. In that, all the convergences and dependences of Creation are surely implied. Our bodies are also not distinct from the bodies of other people, on which they depend in a complexity of ways from biological to spiritual. They are not distinct from the bodies of plants and animals, with which we are involved in the cycles of feeding and in the intricate companionships of ecological systems and of the spirit. They are not distinct from the earth, the sun and moon, and the other heavenly bodies.

It is therefore absurd to approach the subject of health piecemeal with a departmentalized band of specialists. A medical doctor uninterested in nutrition, in agriculture, in the wholesomeness of mind and spirit is as absurd as a farmer who is uninterested in health. Our fragmentation of this subject cannot be our cure, because it is our disease. The body cannot be whole alone. Persons cannot be whole alone. It is wrong to think that bodily health is compatible with spiritual confusion or cultural disorder, or with polluted air and water or impoverished soil. Intellectually, we know that these patterns of interdependence exist; we understand them better now perhaps than we ever have before; yet modern social and cultural patterns contradict them and make it difficult or impossible to honor them in practice.

To try to heal the body alone is to collaborate in the destruction of the body. Healing is impossible in loneliness; it is the opposite of loneliness. Conviviality is healing. To be healed we must come with all the other creatures to the feast of Creation. Together, the above two descriptions of suicides suggest this very powerfully. The setting of both is urban, amid the gigantic works of modern humanity. The fatal sickness is despair, a wound that cannot be healed because it is encapsulated in loneliness, surrounded by speechlessness. Past the scale of the human, our works do not liberate us—they confine us. They cut off access to the wilderness of Creation where we must go to be reborn—to receive the awareness, at once humbling and exhilarating, grievous and joyful, that we are a part of Creation, one with all that we live from and all that, in turn, lives from us. They destroy the communal rites of passage that turn us toward the wilderness and bring us home again.

THE ISOLATION OF THE BODY

Perhaps the fundamental damage of the specialist system—the damage from which all other damages issue—has been the isolation of the body. At some point we began to assume that the life of the body would be the business of grocers and medical doctors, who need take no interest in the spirit, whereas the life of the spirit would be the business of churches, which would have at best only a negative interest in the body. In the same way we began to see nothing wrong with putting the body—most often somebody else's body, but frequently our own—to a task that insulted the mind and demeaned the spirit. And we began to find it easier than ever to prefer our own bodies to the bodies of other creatures and to abuse, exploit, and otherwise hold in contempt those other bodies for the greater good or comfort of our own.

The isolation of the body sets it into direct conflict with everything else in Creation. It gives it a value that is destructive of every other value. That this has happened is paradoxical, for the body was set apart from the soul in order that the soul should triumph over the body. The aim is stated in Shakespeare's Sonnet 146 as plainly as anywhere:

> *Poor soul, the center of my sinful earth,*
> *Lord of these rebel powers that thee array,*
> *Why dost thou pine within and suffer dearth,*
> *Painting thy outward walls so costly gay?*
> *Why so large cost, having so short a lease,*

> *Dost thou upon thy fading mansion spend?*
> *Shall worms, inheritors of this excess,*
> *Eat up thy charge? Is this thy body's end?*
> *Then, soul, live thou upon thy servant's loss,*
> *And let that pine to aggravate thy store;*
> *Buy terms divine in selling hours of dross;*
> *Within be fed, without be rich no more.*
> *So shalt thou feed on death, that feeds on men,*
> *And death once dead, there's no more dying then.*

The soul is thus set against the body, to thrive at the body's expense. And so a spiritual economy is devised within which the only law is competition. If the soul is to live in this world only by denying the body, then its relation to worldly life becomes extremely simple and superficial. Too simple and superficial, in fact, to cope in any meaningful or useful way with the world. Spiritual value ceases to have any worldly purpose or force. To fail to employ the body in this world at once for its own good and the good of the soul is to issue an invitation to disorder of the most serious kind.

What was not foreseen in this simple-minded economics of religion was that it is not possible to devalue the body and value the soul. The body, cast loose from the soul, is on its own. Devalued and cast out of the temple, the body does not skulk off like a sick dog to die in the bushes. It sets up a counterpart economy of its own, based also on the law of competition, in which it devalues and exploits the spirit. These two economies maintain themselves at each other's expense, living upon each other's loss, collaborating without cease in mutual futility and absurdity.

You cannot devalue the body and value the soul—or value anything else. The prototypical act issuing from this division was to make a person a slave and then instruct him in religion—a "charity" more damaging to the master than to the slave. Contempt for the body is invariably manifested in contempt for other bodies—the bodies of slaves, laborers, women, animals, plants, the earth itself. Relationships with all other creatures become competitive and exploitive rather than collaborative and convivial. The world is seen and dealt with, not as an ecological community, but as a stock exchange, the ethics of which are based on the tragically misnamed "law of the jungle." This "jungle" law is a basic fallacy of modern culture. The body is degraded and saddened by being set in conflict against the Creation itself, of which all bodies are members, therefore members of each other. The body is thus sent to war against itself.

Divided, set against each other, body and soul drive each other to extremes of misapprehension and folly. Nothing could be more absurd than to despise the body and yet yearn for its resurrection. In reaction to this supposedly religious attitude, we get, not reverence or respect for the body, but another kind of contempt: the desire to comfort and indulge the body with equal disregard for its health. The "dialogue of body and soul" in our time is being carried on between those who despise the body for the sake of its resurrection and those, diseased by bodily extravagance and lack of exercise, who nevertheless desire longevity above all things. These think that they oppose each other, and yet they could not exist apart. They are locked in a conflict that is really their collaboration in the destruction of soul and body both.

What this conflict has done, among other things, is to make it extremely difficult to set a proper value on the life of the body in this world—to believe that it is good, howbeit short and imperfect. Until we are able to say this and know what we mean by it, we will not be able to live our lives in the human estate of grief and joy, but repeatedly will be cast outside in violent swings between pride and despair. Desires that cannot be fulfilled in health will keep us hopelessly restless and unsatisfied.

COMPETITION

By dividing body and soul, we divide both from all else. We thus condemn ourselves to a loneliness for which the only compensation is violence—against other creatures, against the earth, against ourselves. For no matter the distinctions we draw between body and soul, body and earth, ourselves and others—the connections, the dependences, the identities remain. And so we fail to contain or control our violence. It gets loose. Though there are categories of violence, or so we think, there are no categories of victims. Violence against one is ultimately violence against all. The willingness to abuse other bodies is the willingness to abuse one's own. To damage the earth is to damage your children. To despise the ground is to despise its fruit; to despise the fruit is to despise its eaters. The wholeness of health is broken by despite.

If competition is the correct relation of creatures to one another and to the earth, then we must ask why exploitation is not more successful than it is. Why, having lived so long at the expense of other creatures and the earth, are we not healthier and happier than we are? Why does modern society exist under constant threat of the same suffering, deprivation, spite, contempt, and obliteration that it has imposed on other people and other creatures? Why do the health of the body and the health of the earth decline together? And why, in consideration of this decline of our worldly flesh and household, our "sinful earth," are we not healthier in spirit?

It is not necessary to have recourse to statistics to see that the human estate is declining with the estate of nature, and that the corruption of the body is the corruption of the soul. I know that the country is full of "leaders" and experts of various sorts who are using statistics to prove the opposite: that we have more cars, more super-highways, more TV sets, motorboats, prepared foods, etc., than any people ever had before—and are therefore better off than any people ever were before. I can see the burgeoning of this "consumer economy" and can appreciate some of its attractions and comforts. But that economy has an inside and an outside; from the outside there are other things to be seen.

I am writing this in the north-central part of Kentucky on a morning near the end of June. We have had rain for two days, hard rain during the last several hours. From where I sit I can see the Kentucky River swiftening and rising, the water already yellow with mud. I know that inside this city-oriented consumer economy there are many people who will never see this muddy rise and many who will see it without knowing what it means. I know also that there are many who will see it, and know what it means, and not care. If it lasts until the weekend there will be people who will find it as good as clear water for motorboating and waterskiing.

In the past several days I have seen some of the worst-eroded corn fields that I have seen in this country in my life. This erosion is occurring on the cash-rented farms of farmers' widows and city farmers, absentee owners, the doctors and businessmen who buy a farm for the tax breaks or to have "a quiet place in the country" for the weekends. It is the direct result of economic and agricultural policy; it might be said to *be* an economic and agricultural policy. The signs of the "agridollar," big-business fantasy of the Butz mentality are all present: the absenteeism, the temporary and shallow interest of the land-renter, the row-cropping of slopes, the lack of rotation, the plowed-out waterways, the rows running up and down the hills. Looked at from the field's edge, this is ruin, criminal folly, moral idiocy. Looked at from Washington, D.C., from inside the "economy," it is called "free enterprise" and "full production."

And around me here, as everywhere else I have been in this country—in Nebraska, Iowa, Indiana, New York, New England, Tennessee—the farmland is in general decline: fields and whole farms abandoned, given up with their scars unmended, washing away under the weeds and bushes; fine land put to row crops year after year, without rest or rotation; buildings and fences going down; good houses standing empty, unpainted, their windows broken.

And it is clear to anyone who looks carefully at any crowd that we are wasting our bodies exactly as we are wasting our land. Our bodies are fat, weak, joyless, sickly, ugly, the virtual prey of the manufacturers of medicine and cosmetics. Our bodies have become marginal; they are growing useless like our "marginal" land because we have less and less use for them. After the games and idle flourishes of modern youth, we use them only as shipping cartons to transport our brains and our few employable muscles back and forth to work.

As for our spirits, they seem more and more to comfort themselves by buying things. No longer in need of the exalted drama of grief and joy, they feed now on little shocks of greed, scandal, and violence. For many of the churchly, the life of the spirit is reduced to a dull preoccupation with getting to Heaven. At best, the world is no more than an embarrassment and a trial to the spirit, which is otherwise radically separated from it. The true lover of God must not be burdened with any care or respect for His works. While the body goes about its business of destroying the earth, the soul is supposed to lie back and wait for Sunday, keeping itself free of earthly contaminants. While the body exploits other bodies, the soul stands aloof, free from sin, crying to the gawking bystanders: "I am not enjoying it!" As far as this sort of "religion" is concerned, the body is no more than the lusterless container of the soul, a mere "package," that will nevertheless light up in eternity, forever cool and shiny as a neon cross. This separation of the soul from the body and from the world is no disease of the fringe, no aberration, but a fracture that runs through the mentality of institutional religion like a geologic fault. And this rift in the mentality of religion continues to characterize the modern mind, no matter how secular or worldly it becomes.

But I have not stated my point exactly enough. This rift is not *like* a geologic fault; it *is* a geologic fault. It is a flaw in the mind that runs inevitably into the earth. Thought affects or afflicts substance neither by intention nor by accident, but because, occurring in the Creation that is unified and whole, it must; there is no help for it.

The soul, in its loneliness, hopes only for "salvation." And yet what is the burden of the Bible if not a sense of the mutuality of influence, rising out of an essential unity, among soul and body and community and world? These are all the works of God, and it is therefore the work of virtue to make or restore harmony among them. The world is certainly thought of as a place of spiritual trial, but it is also the confluence of soul and body, word and flesh, where thoughts must become deeds, where goodness is to be enacted. This is the great meeting place, the narrow passage where spirit and flesh, word and world, pass into each other. The Bible's aim, as I read it, is not the freeing of the spirit from the world. It is the handbook of their interaction. It says that they cannot be divided; that their mutuality, their unity, is inescapable; that they are not reconciled in division, but in harmony. What else can be meant by the resurrection of the body? The body should be "filled with light," perfected in understanding. And so everywhere there is the sense of consequence, fear and desire, grief and joy. What is desirable is repeatedly defined in the tensions of the sense of consequence. False prophets are to be known "by their fruits." We are to treat others as we would be treated; thought is thus barred from any easy escape into aspiration or ideal, is turned around and forced into action. The following verses from Proverbs are not very likely the original work of a philosopher-king; they are overheard from generations of agrarian grandparents whose experience taught them that spiritual qualities become earthly events:

> *I went by the field of the slothful, and by the vineyard of the man void of understanding;*
>
> *And, lo, it was all grown over with thorns, and nettles had covered the face thereof, and the stone wall thereof was broken down.*
>
> *Then I saw, and considered it well. I looked upon it, and received instruction.*
>
> *Yet a little sleep, a little slumber, a little folding of the hands to sleep:*
>
> *So shall thy poverty come as one that traveleth; and thy want as an armed man.*

CONNECTIONS

I do not want to speak of unity misleadingly or too simply. Obvious distinctions can be made between body and soul, one body and other bodies, body and world, etc. But these things that appear to be distinct are nevertheless caught in a network of mutual dependence and influence that is the substantiation of their unity. Body, soul (or mind or spirit), community, and world are all susceptible to each other's influence, and they are all conductors of each other's influence. The body is damaged by the bewilderment of the spirit, and it conducts the influence of that bewilderment into the earth, the earth conducts it into the community, and so on. If a farmer fails to understand what health is, his farm becomes unhealthy; it produces unhealthy food, which damages the health of the community. But this is a network, a spherical network, by which each part is connected to every other part. The farmer is a part of the community, and so it is as impossible to say exactly where the trouble began as to say where it will end. The influences go backward and forward, up and down, round and round, compounding and branching as they go. All that is certain is that an error introduced anywhere in the network ramifies beyond the scope of prediction; consequences occur all over the place, and each consequence breeds further consequences. But it seems unlikely that an error can ramify endlessly. It spreads by way of the connections in the network, but sooner or later it must also begin to break them. We are talking, obviously, about a circulatory system, and a disease of a circulatory system tends first to impair circulation and then to stop it altogether.

Healing, on the other hand, complicates the system by opening and restoring connections among the various parts—in this way restoring the ultimate simplicity of their union. When all the parts of the body are working together, are under each other's influence, we say that it is whole; it is healthy. The same is true of the world, of which our bodies are parts. The parts are healthy insofar as they are joined harmoniously to the whole.

What the specialization of our age suggests, in one example after another, is not only that fragmentation is a disease, but that the diseases of the disconnected parts are similar or analogous to one another. Thus they memorialize their lost unity, their relation persisting in their disconnection. Any severance produces two wounds that are, among other things, the record of how the severed parts once fitted together.

The so-called identity crisis, for instance, is a disease that seems to have become prevalent after the disconnection of body and soul and the other piecemealings of the modern period. One's "identity" is apparently the immaterial part of one's being—also known as psyche, soul, spirit, self, mind, etc. The dividing of this principle from the body and from any particular worldly locality would seem reason enough for a crisis. Treatment, it might be thought, would logically consist in the restoration of these connections: the lost identity would find itself by recognizing physical landmarks, by connecting itself responsibly to practical circumstances; it would learn to stay put in the body to which it belongs and in the place to which preference or history or accident has brought it; it would, in short, find itself in finding its work. But "finding yourself," the pseudo-ritual by which the identity crisis is supposed to be resolved, makes use of no such immediate references. Leaving aside the obvious, and ancient, realities of doubt and self-doubt, as well as the authentic madness that is often the result of cultural disintegration, it seems likely that the identity crisis is a conventional illusion, one of the genres of self-indulgence. It can be an excuse for irresponsibility or a fashionable mode of self-dramatization. It is the easiest form of self-flattery—a way to construe procrastination as a virtue—based on the romantic assumption that "who I really am" is better in some fundamental way than the available evidence would suggest.

The fashionable cure for this condition, if I understand the lore of it correctly, has nothing to do with the assumption of responsibilities or the renewal of connections. The cure is "autonomy," another illusory condition, suggesting that the self can be self-determining and independent without regard for any determining circumstance or any of the obvious dependences. This seems little more than a jargon term for indifference to the opinions and feelings of other people. There is, in practice, no such thing as autonomy. Practically, there is only a distinction between responsible and irresponsible dependence. Inevitably failing this impossible standard of autonomy, the modern self-seeker becomes a tourist of cures, submitting his quest to the guidance of one guru after another. The "cure" thus preserves the disease.

It is not surprising that this strange disease of the spirit—the self's loss of self—should have its counterpart in an anguish of the body. One of the commonplaces of modern experience is dissatisfaction with the body—not as one has allowed it to become, but as it naturally is. The hardship is perhaps greater here because the body, unlike the self, is substantial and cannot be supposed to be inherently better than it was born to be. It can only be thought inherently worse than it *ought* to be. For the appropriate standard for the body—that is, health—has been replaced, not even by another standard, but by very exclusive physical *models*. The concept of "model" here conforms very closely to the model of the scientists and planners: it is an exclusive, narrowly defined ideal which affects destructively whatever it does not include.

Thus our young people are offered the ideal of health only by what they know to be lip service. What they are made to feel forcibly, and to measure themselves by, is the exclusive desirability of a certain physical model. Girls are taught to want to be leggy, slender, large-breasted, curly-haired, unimposingly beautiful. Boys are instructed to be "athletic" in build, tall but not too tall, broad-shouldered, deep-chested, narrow-hipped, square-jawed, straight-nosed, not bald, unimposingly handsome. Both sexes should look what passes for "sexy" in a bathing suit. Neither, above all, should look old.

Though many people, in health, are beautiful, very few resemble these models. The result is widespread suffering that does immeasurable damage both to individual persons and to the society as a whole. The result is another absurd pseudo-ritual, "accepting one's body," which may take years or may be the distraction of a lifetime. Woe to the man who is short or skinny or bald. Woe to the man with a big nose. Woe, above all, to the woman with small breasts or a muscular body or strong features; Homer and Solomon might have thought her beautiful, but she will see her own beauty only by a difficult rebellion. And like the crisis of identity, this crisis of the body brings a helpless dependence on cures. One spends one's life dressing and "making up" to compensate for one's supposed deficiencies. Again, the cure preserves the disease. And the putative healer is the guru of style and beauty aid. The sufferer is by definition a customer.

SEXUAL DIVISION

To divide body and soul, or body and mind, is to inaugurate an expanding series of divisions—not, however, an *infinitely* expanding series, because it is apparently the nature of division sooner or later to destroy what is divided; the principle of durability is unity. The divisions issuing from the division of body and soul are first sexual and then ecological. Many other divisions branch out from those, but those are the most important because they have to do with the fundamental relationships—with each other and with the earth—that we all have in common.

To think of the body as separate from the soul or as soulless, either to subvert its appetites or to "free" them, is to make an object of it. As a thing, the body is denied any dimension or rightful presence or claim in the mind. The concerns of the body—all that is comprehended in the term *nurture*—are thus degraded, denied any respected place among the "higher things" and even among the more exigent practicalities.

The first sexual division comes about when nurture is made the exclusive concern of women. This cannot happen until a society becomes industrial; in hunting and gathering and in agricultural societies, men are of necessity also involved in nurture. In those societies there usually have been differences between the work of men and that of women. But the necessity here is to distinguish between sexual difference and sexual division.

In an industrial society, following the division of body and soul, we have at the "upper" or professional level a division between "culture" (in the specialized sense of religion, philosophy, art, the humanities, etc.) and "practicality," and both of these become increasingly abstract. Thinkers do not act. And the "practical" men do not work with their hands, but manipulate the abstract quantities and values that come from the work of "workers." Workers are simplified or specialized into machine parts to do the wage-work of the body, which they were initially permitted to think of as "manly" because for the most part women did not do it.

Women traditionally have performed the most confining—though not necessarily the least dignified—tasks of nurture: housekeeping, the care of young children, food preparation. In the urban-industrial situation the confinement of these traditional tasks divided women more and more from the "important" activities of the new economy. Furthermore, in this situation the traditional nurturing role of men—that of provisioning the household, which in an agricultural society had become as constant and as complex as the women's role—became completely abstract; the man's duty to the household came to be simply to provide money. The only remaining *task* of provisioning—purchasing food—was turned over to women. This determination that nurturing should become *exclusively* a concern of women served to signify to both sexes that neither nurture nor womanhood was very important.

But the assignment to women of a kind of work that was thought both onerous and trivial was only the beginning of their exploitation. As the persons exclusively in charge of the tasks of nurture, women often came into sole charge of the household budget; they became family purchasing agents. The time of the household barterer was past. Kitchens were now run on a cash economy. Women had become customers, a fact not long wasted on the salesmen, who saw that in these women they had customers of a new and most promising kind. The modern housewife was isolated from her husband, from her school-age children, and from other women. She was saddled with work from which much of the skill, hence much of the dignity, had been withdrawn, and which she herself was less and less able to consider important. She did not know what her husband did at work, or after work, and she knew that her life was passing in his regardlessness and in his absence. Such a woman was ripe for a sales talk: this was the great commercial insight of modern times. Such a woman must be told—or subtly made to understand—that she must not be a drudge, that she must not let her work affect her looks, that she must not become "unattractive," that she must always be fresh, cheerful, young, shapely, and pretty. All her sexual and mortal fears would thus be given voice, and she would be made to reach for money. What was implied was always the question that a certain bank finally asked outright in a billboard advertisement: "Is your husband losing interest?"

Motivated no longer by practical needs, but by loneliness and fear, women began to identify themselves by what they bought rather than by what they did. They bought labor-saving devices which worked, as most modern machines have tended to work, to devalue or replace the skills of those who used them. They bought manufactured foods, which did likewise. They bought any product that offered to lighten the burdens of housework, to be "kind to hands," or to endear one to one's husband. And they furnished their houses, as they made up their faces and selected their clothes, neither by custom nor invention, but by the suggestion of articles and advertisements in "women's magazines." Thus housewifery, once a complex discipline acknowledged to be one of the bases of culture and economy, was reduced to the exercise of purchasing power.* The house-wife's only remaining productive capacity was that of reproduction. But even as a mother she remained a consumer, subjecting herself to an all-presuming doctor and again to written instructions calculated to result in the purchase of merchandise. Breast-feeding of babies became unfashionable, one suspects, because it was the last form of home production; no way could be found to persuade a woman to purchase her own milk. All these "improvements" involved a radical simplification of mind that was bound to have complicated, and ironic, results. As housekeeping became simpler and easier, it also became more boring. A woman's work became less accomplished and less satisfying. It became easier for her to believe that what she did was not important. And this heightened her anxiety and made her even more avid and even less discriminating as a consumer. The cure not only preserved the disease, it compounded it.

There was, of course, a complementary development in the minds of men, but there is less to say about it. The man's mind was not simplified by a degenerative process, but by a kind of coup: as soon as he separated working and living and began to work away from home, the practical considerations of the household were excerpted from his mind all at once.

In modern marriage, then, what was once a difference of work became a division of work. And in this division the household was destroyed as a practical bond between husband and wife. It was no longer a condition, but only a place. It was no longer a circumstance that required, dignified, and rewarded the enactment of mutual dependence, but the site of mutual estrangement. Home became a place for the husband to go when he was not working or amusing himself. It was the place where the wife was held in servitude.

A sexual difference is not a wound, or it need not be; a sexual division is. And it is important to recognize that this division—this destroyed household that now stands between the sexes—is a wound that is suffered inescapably by both men and women. Sometimes it is

---

*She did continue to do "housework," of course. But we must ask what this had come to mean. The industrial economy had changed the criterion of housekeeping from thrift to convenience. Thrift was a complex standard, requiring skill, intelligence, and moral character, and private thrift was rightly considered a public value. Once thrift was destroyed as a value, housekeeping became simply a corrupt function of a corrupt economy: its public "value" lay in the wearing out or using up of commodities.

assumed that the estrangement of women in their circumscribed "women's world" can only be for the benefit of men. But that interpretation seems to be based on the law of competition that is modeled in the exploitive industrial economy. This law holds that for everything that is exploited or oppressed there must be something else that is proportionately improved; thus, men must be as happy as women are unhappy.

There is no doubt that women have been deformed by the degenerate housewifery that is now called their "role"—but not, I think, for any man's benefit. If women are deformed by their role, then, insofar as the roles are divided, men are deformed by theirs. Degenerate housewifery is indivisible from degenerate husbandry. There is no escape. This is the justice that we are learning from the ecologists: you cannot damage what you are dependent upon without damaging yourself. The suffering of women is noticed now, is noticeable now, because it is not given any considerable status or compensation. If we removed the status and compensation from the destructive exploits we classify as "manly," men would be found to be suffering as much as women. They would be found to be suffering for the same reason: they are in exile from the communion of men and women, which is their deepest connection with the communion of all creatures.

For example: a man who is in the traditional sense a *good* farmer is husbandman and husband, the begetter and conserver of the earth's bounty, but he is also midwife and motherer. He is a nurturer of life. His work is domestic; he is bound to the household. But let "progress" take such a man and transform him into a technologist of production (that is, sever his bonds to the household, make useless or pointless or "uneconomical" his impulse to conserve and to nurture), and it will have made of him a creature as deformed, and as pained, as it has notoriously made of his wife.

THE DISMEMBERMENT OF THE HOUSEHOLD

We are familiar with the concept of the disintegral life of our time as a dismembered cathedral, the various concerns of culture no longer existing in reference to each other or within the discipline of any understanding of their unity. It may also be conceived, and its strains more immediately felt, as a dismembered household. Without the household—not just as a unifying ideal, but as a practical circumstance of mutual dependence and obligation, requiring skill, moral discipline, and work—husband and wife find it less and less possible to imagine and enact their marriage. Without much in particular that they can *do* for each other, they have a scarcity of practical reasons to be together. They may "like each other's company," but that is a reason for friendship, not for marriage. Aside from affection for any children they may have and their abstract legal and economic obligations to each other, their union has to be empowered by sexual energy alone.

Perhaps the most dangerous, certainly the most immediately painful, consequence of the disintegration of the household is this isolation of sexuality. The division of sexual energy from the functions of household and community that it ought both to empower and to grace is analogous to that other modern division between hunger and the earth. When it is no longer allied by proximity and analogy to the nurturing disciplines that bound the household to the cycles of fertility and the seasons, life and death, then sexual love loses its symbolic or ritualistic force, its deepest solemnity and its highest joy. It loses its sense of consequence and responsibility. It becomes "autonomous," to be valued only for its own sake, therefore frivolous, therefore destructive—even of itself. Those who speak of sex as "recreation," thinking to claim for it "a new place," only acknowledge its displacement from Creation.

The isolation of sexuality makes it subject to two influences that dangerously oversimplify it: the lore of sexual romance and capitalist economics. By "sexual romance" I mean the sentimentalization of sexual love that for generations has been the work of popular songs and stories. By means of them, young people have been taught a series of extremely dangerous falsehoods:

1. That people in love ought to conform to the fashionable models of physical beauty, and that to be unbeautiful by these standards is to be unlovable.

2. That people in love are, or ought to be, young—even though love is said to last "forever."

3. That marriage is a solution—whereas the most misleading thing a love story can do is to end "happily" with a marriage, not because there is no such thing as a happy marriage, but because marriage cannot be happy except by being *made* happy.

4. That love, alone, regardless of circumstances, can make harmony and resolve serious differences.

5. That "love will find a way" and so finally triumph over any kind of practical difficulty.

6. That the "right" partners are "made for each other," or that "marriages are made in Heaven."

7. That lovers are "each other's all" or "all the world to each other."

8. That monogamous marriage is therefore logical and natural, and "forsaking all others" involves no difficulty.

Believing these things, a young couple could not be more cruelly exposed to the abrasions of experience—or better prepared to experience marriage as another of those grim and ironic modern competitions in which the victory of one is the defeat of both.

As experience frets away gullibility, the exclusiveness of the sentimental ideal gives way to the possessiveness of sexual capitalism. Failing, as they cannot help but fail, to be each other's all, the husband and wife become each other's only. The sacrament of sexual union, which in the time of the household was a communion of workmates, and afterward tried to be a lovers' paradise, has now become a kind of marketplace in which husband and wife represent each other as sexual property. Competitiveness and jealousy, imperfectly sweetened and disguised by the illusions of courtship, now become governing principles, and they work to isolate the couple inside their marriage. Marriage becomes a capsule of sexual fate. The man must look on other men, and the woman on other women, as threats. This seems to have become particularly damaging to women; because of the progressive degeneration and isolation of their "role," their worldly stock in trade has increasingly had to be "their" men. In the isolation of the resulting sexual "privacy," the disintegration of the community begins. The energy that is the most convivial and unifying loses its communal forms and becomes divisive. This dispersal was nowhere more poignantly exemplified than in the replacement of the old ring dances, in which all couples danced together, by the so-called ballroom dancing, in which each couple dances alone. A significant part of the etiquette of ballroom dancing is, or was, that the exchange of partners was accomplished by a "trade." It is no accident that this capitalization of love and marriage was followed by a divorce epidemic—and by fashions of dancing in which each one of the dancers moves alone.

The disintegration of marriage, which completes the disintegration of community, came about because the encapsulation of sexuality, meant to preserve marriage from competition, inevitably *en-closed* competition. The principle that fenced everyone else out fenced the couple in; it became a sexual cul-de-sac. The model of economic competition proved as false to marriage as to farming. As with other capsules, the narrowness of the selective principle proved destructive of what it excluded, and what it excluded was essential to the life of what it enclosed: the nature of sexuality itself. Sexual romance cannot bear to acknowledge the generality of instinct, whereas sexual capitalism cannot acknowledge its particularity. But sexuality appears to be *both* general and particular. One cannot love a particular woman, for instance, unless one loves womankind—if not all women, at least other women. The capsule of sexual romance leaves out this generality, this generosity of instinct; it excludes Aphrodite and Dionysus. And it fails for that reason. Though sexual love can endure between the same two people for a long time, it cannot do so on the basis of this pretense of the exclusiveness of affection. The sexual capitalist—that is, the disillusioned sexual romantic—in reaction to disillusion makes the opposite oversimplification; one acknowledges one's spouse as one of a general, necessarily troublesome kind or category.

Both these attitudes look on sexual love as ownership. The sexual romantic croons, "You be-long to me." The sexual capitalist believes the same thing but has stopped crooning. Each holds that a person's sexual property shall be sufficient unto him or unto her, and that the morality of that sufficiency is to be forever on guard against expropriation. Within the capsule of marriage, as in that of economics, one intends to exploit one's property and to protect it. Once the idea of property becomes abstract or economic, both these motives begin to rule over it. They are, of course, contradictory; all that one can really protect is one's "right" or intention to exploit. The proprieties and privacies used to encapsulate marriage may have come from the tacit recognition that exploitive sex, like exploitive economics, is a very dirty business. One makes a secret of the sexuality of one's marriage for the same reason that one posts "Keep Out/Private Property" on one's strip mine. The tragedy, more often felt than acknowledged, is that what is exploited becomes undesirable.

The protective capsule becomes a prison. It becomes a household of the living dead, each body a piece of incriminating evidence. Or a greenhouse excluding the neighbors and the weather for the sake of some alien and unnatural growth. The marriage shrinks to a dull vigil of duty and legality. Husband and wife become competitors necessarily, for their only freedom is to exploit each other or to escape.

It is possible to imagine a more generous enclosure—a household welcoming to neighbors and friends; a garden open to the weather, between the woods and the road. It is possible to imagine a marriage bond that would bind a woman and a man not only to each other, but to the community of marriage, the amorous communion at which all couples sit: the sexual feast and celebration that joins them to all living things and to the fertility of the earth, and the sexual responsibility that joins them to the human past and the human future. It is possible to imagine marriage as a grievous, joyous human bond, endlessly renewable and renewing, again and again rejoining memory and passion and hope.

FIDELITY

But it is extremely difficult, now, to imagine marriage in terms of such dignity and generosity, and this difficulty is explained by the failure of these possessive and competitive forms of sexual love that have been in use for so long. This failure raises unavoidably the issue of fidelity: What is it, and what does it mean—in marriage, and also, since marriage is a fundamental relationship and metaphor, in other relationships?

No one can be glad to have this issue so starkly raised, for any consideration of it now must necessarily involve one's own bewilderment. We are apparently near the end of a degenerative phase of an evolutionary process—a long way from any large-scale regeneration. For that reason it is necessary to be hesitant and cautious, respectful of the complexity and importance of the problem. Marriage is not going to change because somebody thinks about it and recommends an "answer"; it can change only as its necessities are felt and as its circumstances change.

The idea of fidelity is perverted beyond redemption by understanding it as a grim, literal duty enforced only by willpower. This is the "religious" insanity of making a victim of the body as a victory of the soul. Self-restraint that is so purely negative is self-hatred. And one cannot be good, anyhow, just by not being bad. To be faithful merely out of duty is to be blinded to the possibility of a better faithfulness for better reasons.

It is reasonable to suppose, if fidelity is a virtue, that it is a virtue with a purpose. A purposeless virtue is a contradiction in terms. Virtue, like harmony, cannot exist alone; a virtue must lead to harmony between one creature and another. To be good for nothing is just that. If a virtue has been thought a virtue long enough, it must be assumed to have practical justification—though the very longevity that proves its practicality may obscure it. That seems to be what happened with the idea of fidelity. We heard the words "forsaking all others" repeated over and over again for so long that we lost the sense of their practical justification. They assumed the force of superstition: people came to be faithful in marriage not out of any understanding of the meaning of faith or of marriage, but out of the same fear of obscure retribution that made one careful not to break a mirror or spill the salt. Like other superstitions, this one was weakened by the scientific, positivist intellectuality of modern times and by the popular "sophistication" that came with it. Our age could be characterized as a manifold experiment in faithlessness, and if it has as yet produced no effective understanding of the practicalities of faith, it has certainly produced massive evidence of the damage and disorder of its absence.

It is possible to open this issue of the practicality of fidelity by considering that the modern age was made possible by the freeing, and concurrently by the cheapening, of energy. It can be said, of course, that the modern age was made possible by technologies that *control* energy and thus make it usable at an unprecedented rate. But such control is at best extremely limited: the devices by which industrial and military energies are used control them only momentarily; their moment of usefulness sets them loose in the world as social, ecological, and geological *forces*. We can use these energies only as explosives; we can control the rate, intensity, and time of combustion, but our effective control ends with the use of the small amount of the released energy that we are able to harness. Past that, the effects are on their own, to compound themselves as they will. In modern times we have never been able to subject our use of energy to a sense of responsibility anywhere near complex enough to be equal to its effects.

It may be that the principle of sexual fidelity, once it is again fully understood, will provide us with as good an example as we can find of the responsible use of energy. Sexuality is, after all, a form of energy, one of the most powerful. If we see sexuality as energy, then it becomes impossible to see sexual fidelity as merely a "duty," a virtue for the sake of virtue, or a superstition. If we made a superstition of fidelity, and thereby weakened it, by thinking of it as purely a moral or spiritual virtue, then perhaps we can restore its strength by recovering an awareness of its practicality.

At the root of culture must be the realization that uncontrolled energy is disorderly—that in nature all energies move in forms; that, therefore, in a human order energies must be *given* forms. It must have been plain at the beginning, as cultural degeneracy has made it plain again and again, that one can be indiscriminately sexual but not indiscriminately responsible, and that irresponsible sexuality would undermine any possibility of culture since it implies a hierarchy based purely upon brute strength, cunning, regardlessness of value and of consequence. Fidelity can thus be seen as the necessary discipline of sexuality, the practical definition of sexual responsibility, or the definition of the moral limits within which such responsibility can be conceived and enacted. The forsaking of all others is a keeping of faith, not just with the chosen one, but with the ones forsaken. The marriage vow unites not just a woman and a man with each other; it unites each of them with the community in a vow of sexual responsibility toward all others. The whole community is married, realizes its essential unity, in each of its marriages.

Another use of fidelity is to preserve the possibility of devotion against the distractions of novelty. What marriage offers—and what fidelity is meant to protect—is the possibility of moments when what we have chosen and what we desire are the same. Such a convergence obviously cannot be continuous. No relationship can continue very long at its highest emotional pitch. But fidelity prepares us for the *return* of these moments, which give us the highest joy we can know: that of union, communion, atonement (in the root sense of at-one-ment). The principle is stated in these lines by William Butler Yeats (by "the world" he means the world after the Fall):

> *Maybe the bride-bed brings despair,*
> *For each an imagined image brings*
> *And finds a real image there;*
> *Yet the world ends when these two things,*
> *Though several, are a single light . . .*

To forsake all others does not mean—because it *cannot* mean—to ignore or neglect all others, to hide or be hidden from all others, or to desire or love no others. To live in marriage is a responsible way to live in sexuality, as to live in a household is a responsible way to live in the world. One cannot enact or fulfill one's love for womankind or mankind, or even for all the women or men to whom one is attracted. If one is to have the power and delight of one's sexuality, then the generality of instinct must be resolved in a responsible relationship to a particular person. Similarly, one cannot live in the world; that is, one cannot become, in the easy, generalizing sense with which the phrase is commonly used, a "world citizen." There can be no such thing as a "global village." No matter how much one may love the world as a whole, one can live fully in it only by living responsibly in some small part of it. Where we live and who we live there with define the terms of our relationship to the world and to humanity. We thus come again to the paradox that one can become whole only by the responsible acceptance of one's partiality.

But to encapsulate these partial relationships is to entrap and condemn them in their partiality; it is to endanger them and to make them dangerous. They are enlivened and given the possibility of renewal by the double sense of particularity and generality: one lives in marriage *and* in sexuality, at home *and* in the world. It is impossible, for instance, to conceive that a man could despise women and yet love his wife, or love his own place in the world and yet deal destructively with other places.

HOME LAND AND HOUSE HOLD

What I have been trying to do is to define a pattern of disintegration that is at once cultural and agricultural. I have been groping for connections—that I think are indissoluble, though obscured by modern ambitions—between the spirit and the body, the body and other bodies, the body and the earth. If these connections do necessarily exist, as I believe they do, then it is impossible for material order to exist side by side with spiritual disorder, or vice versa, and impossible for one to thrive long at the expense of the other; it is impossible, ultimately, to preserve ourselves apart from our willingness to preserve other creatures, or to respect and care for ourselves except as we respect and care for other creatures; and, most to the point of this book, it is impossible to care for each other more or differently than we care for the earth.

This last statement becomes obvious enough when it is considered that the earth is what we all have in common, that it is what we are made of and what we live from, and that we therefore cannot damage it without damaging those with whom we share it. But I believe it goes farther and deeper than that. There is an uncanny *resemblance* between our behavior toward each other and our behavior toward the earth. Between our relation to our own sexuality and our relation to the reproductivity of the earth, for instance, the resemblance is plain and strong and apparently inescapable. By some connection that we do not recognize, the willingness to exploit one becomes the willingness to exploit the other. The conditions and the means of exploitation are likewise similar.

The modern failure of marriage that has so estranged the sexes from each other seems analogous to the "social mobility" that has estranged us from our land, and the two are historically parallel. It may even be argued that these two estrangements are very close to being one, both of them having been caused by the disintegration of the household, which was the formal bond between marriage and the earth, between human sexuality and its sources in the sexuality of Creation. The importance of this practical bond has not been often or very openly recognized in our tradition; in modern times it has almost disappeared under the burden of adverse fashion and economics. It is necessary to go far back to find it clearly exemplified.

To my mind, one of the best examples that we have is in Homer's *Odyssey*. Nowhere else that I know are the connections between marriage and household and the earth so fully and so carefully understood.

At the opening of the story Odysseus, after a twenty-year absence, is about to begin the last leg of his homeward journey. The sole survivor of all his company of warriors, having lived through terrible trials and losses, Odysseus is now a castaway on the island of the goddess Kalypso. He is Kalypso's lover but also virtually her prisoner. At night he sleeps with Kalypso in her cave; by day he looks across the sea toward Ithaka, his home, and weeps. Homer does not stint either feeling—the delights of Kalypso's cave, where the lovers "revel and rest softly, side by side," or the grief and longing of exile.

But now Zeus commands Kalypso to allow Odysseus to depart; she comes to tell him that he is free to go. And yet it is a tragic choice that she offers him: he must choose between her and Penélopê, his wife. If he chooses Kalypso, he will be immortal, but remain in exile; if he chooses Penélopê, he will return home at last, but will die in his time like other men:

If you could see it all, before you go—
all the adversity you face at sea—
you would stay here, and guard this house, and be
immortal—though you wanted her forever,
that bride for whom you pine each day.
Can I be less desirable than she is?
Less interesting? Less beautiful? Can mortals
compare with goddesses in grace and form?

And Odysseus answers:

My quiet Penélopê—how well I know—
would seem a shade before your majesty,
death and old age being unknown to you,
while she must die. Yet, it is true, each day
I long for home . . .

This is, in effect, a wedding ritual much like our own, in which Odysseus forsakes all others, in renouncing the immortal womanhood of the goddess, and renews his pledge to the mortal terms of his marriage. But unlike our ritual, this one involves an explicit loyalty to a home. Odysseus' far-wandering through the wilderness of the sea is not merely the return of a husband; it is a journey home. And a great deal of the power as well as the moral complexity of *The Odyssey* rises out of the richness of its sense of home.

By the end of Book XXIII, it is clear that the action of the narrative, Odysseus' journey from the cave of Kalypso to the bed of Penélopê, has revealed a structure that is at once geographical and moral. This structure may be graphed as a series of diminishing circles centered on one of the posts of the marriage bed. Odysseus makes his way from the periphery toward that center.

All around, this structure verges on the sea, which is the wilderness, ruled by the forces of nature and by the gods. In spite of the excellence of his ship and crew and his skill in navigation, a man is alien there. Only when he steps ashore does he enter a human order. From the shoreline of his island of Ithaka, Odysseus makes his way across a succession of boundaries, enclosed and enclosing, with the concentricity of a blossom around its pistil, a human pattern resembling a pattern of nature. He comes to his island, to his own lands, to his town, to his household and house, to his bedroom, to his bed.

As he moves toward this center he moves also through a series of recognitions, tests of identity and devotion. By these, his homecoming becomes at the same time a restoration of order. At first, having been for a while uncertain of his whereabouts, he recognizes his homeland by the conformation of the countryside and by a certain olive tree. He then becomes the guest of his swineherd, Eumaios, and tests his loyalty, though Eumaios will not be permitted to recognize his master until the story approaches its crisis. In the house of Eumaios, Odysseus meets and makes himself known to his son, Telémakhos. As he comes, disguised as a beggar, into his own house, he is recognized by Argus, his old hunting dog. That night, as the guest of Penélopê, who does not yet know who he is, he is recognized by his aged nurse, Eurýkleia, who sees a well-remembered scar on his thigh as she is bathing his feet.

He is scorned and abused as a vagabond by the band of suitors who, believing him dead, have been courting his wife, consuming his meat and wine, desecrating his household, and plotting the murder of his son. Penélopê proposes a trial by which the suitors will compete for her: she will become the bride of whichever one can string the bow of her supposedly dead husband and shoot an arrow through the aligned helve-sockets of twelve axe heads. The suitors fail. Odysseus performs the feat easily and is thereby recognized as "the great husband" himself. And then, with the help of the swineherd, the cowherd, and Telémakhos, he proceeds to trap the suitors and slaughter them all without mercy. To so distinguished a commentator as Richmond Lattimore, their punishment "seems excessive." But granting the acceptability of violent means to a warrior such as Odysseus, this outcome seems to me appropriate to the moral terms of the poem. It is made clear that the punishment is not merely the caprice of a human passion: Odysseus enacts the will of the gods; he is the agent of a divine judgment. The suitors' sin is their utter contempt for the domestic order that the poem affirms. They do not respect or honor the meaning of the household, and in *The Odyssey* this meaning is paramount.

It is therefore the recognition of Odysseus by Penélopê that is the most interesting and the most crucial. By the time Odysseus' vengeance and his purification of the house are complete, Penélopê is the only one in the household who has not acknowledged him. It is only reasonable that she should delay this until she is absolutely certain. After all, she has waited twenty years; it is not to be expected that she would be less than cautious now. Her faith has been equal and more than equal to his, and now she proves his equal also in cunning. She tells Eurýkleia to move their bed outside their bedroom and to make it up for Odysseus there. Odysseus' rage at hearing that identifies him beyond doubt, for she knew that only Odysseus would know —it is their "pact and pledge" and "secret sign"—that the bed could not be moved without destroying it. He built their bedroom with his own hands, and an old olive tree, as he says,

> *grew like a pillar on the building plot,*
> *and I laid out our bedroom round that tree . . .*
> *. . . I lopped off the silvery leaves and branches,*
> *hewed and shaped that stump from the roots up*
> *into a bedpost . . .*

She acknowledges him then, and only then does she give herself to his embrace.

> *Now from his heart into his eyes the ache*
> *of longing mounted, and he wept at last,*
> *his dear wife, clear and faithful in his arms,*
> *longed for*
> *as the sunwarmed earth is longed for by a swimmer*
> *spent in rough water where his ship went down . . .*

And so in the renewal of his marriage, the return of Odysseus and the restoration of order are complete. The order of the kingdom is centered on the marriage bed of the king and queen, and that bed is rooted in the earth. The figure last quoted makes explicit at last the long-hinted analogy between Odysseus' fidelity to his wife and his fidelity to his homeland. In Penélopê's welcoming embrace his two fidelities become one.

For Odysseus, then, marriage was not merely a legal bond, nor even merely a sacred bond, between himself and Penélopê. It was part of a complex practical circumstance involving, in addition to husband and wife, their family of both descendants and forebears, their household, their community, and the sources of all these lives in memory and tradition, in the countryside, and in the earth. These things, wedded together in his marriage, he thought of as his home, and it held his love and faith so strongly that sleeping with a goddess could not divert or console him in his exile.

In Odysseus' return, then, we see a complete marriage and a complete fidelity. To reduce marriage, as we have done, to a mere contract of sexual exclusiveness is at once to degrade it and to make it impossible. That is to take away its dignity and its potency of joy, and to make it only a pitiful little duty—not a union, but a division and a solitude.

The Odyssey's understanding of marriage as the vital link which joins the human community and the earth is obviously full of political implication. In this it will remind us of the Confucian principle that "The government of the state is rooted in family order." But *The Odyssey* goes further than the Confucian texts, it seems to me, in its understanding of agricultural value as the foundation of domestic order and peace.

I have considered the poem so far as describing a journey from the non-human order of the sea wilderness to the human order of the cleansed and reunited household. But it is also a journey between two kinds of human value; it moves from the battlefield of Troy to the terraced fields of Ithaka, which, through all the years and great deeds of Odysseus' absence, the peasants have not ceased to farm.

The Odyssey begins in the world of *The Iliad*, a world which, like our own, is war-obsessed, preoccupied with "manly" deeds of exploitation, anger, aggression, pillage, and the disorder, uprootedness, and vagabondage that are their result. At the end of the poem, Odysseus moves away from the values of that world toward the values of domesticity and peace. He restores order to his household by an awesome violence, it is true. But that finished and the house purified, he re-enters his marriage, the bedchamber and the marriage bed rooted in the earth. From there he goes into the fields.

The final recognition scene occurs between Odysseus and his old father, Laërtês:

> *Odysseus found his father in solitude*
> *spading the earth around a young fruit tree.*

> *He wore a tunic, patched and soiled, and leggings—*
> *oxhide patches, bound below his knees*
> *against the brambles . . .*

The point is not stated—the story is moving so evenly now toward its conclusion that it will not trouble to remind us that the man thus dressed is a *king*—but it is clear that Laërtês has survived his son's absence and the consequent grief and disorder *as a peasant*. Although Odysseus jokes about his father's appearance, the appropriateness of what he is doing is never questioned. In a time of disorder he has returned to the care of the earth, the foundation of life and hope. And Odysseus finds him in an act emblematic of the best and most responsible kind of agriculture: an old man caring for a young tree.

But the homecoming of Odysseus is still not complete. During his wanderings, he was instructed by the ghost of the seer Teirêsias to perform what is apparently to be a ritual of atonement. As the poem ends he still has this before him. Carrying an oar on his shoulder, he must walk inland until he comes to a place where men have no knowledge of the sea or ships, where a passerby will mistake his oar for a winnowing fan. There he must "plant" his oar in the ground and make a sacrifice to the sea god, Poseidon. Home again, he must sacrifice to all the gods. Like those people of the Biblical prophecy who will "beat their swords into plowshares, and their spears into pruning hooks" and not "learn war any more," Odysseus will not know rest until he has carried the instrument of his sea wanderings inland and planted it like a tree, until he has seen the symbol of his warrior life as a farming tool. But after his atonement has been made, a gentle death will come to him when he is weary with age, his countrymen around him "in blessed peace."

The Odyssey, then, is in a sense an anti-*Iliad*, posing against the warrior values of the other epic—the glories of battle and foreign adventuring—an affirmation of the values of domesticity and farming. But at the same time *The Odyssey* is too bountiful and wise to set these two kinds of value against each other in any purity or exclusiveness of opposition. Even less does it set into such opposition the two kinds of experience. The point seems to be that these apparently opposed experiences are linked together. The higher value may be given to domesticity, but this cannot be valued or understood alone. Odysseus' fidelity and his homecoming are as moving and instructive as they are precisely because they are the result of *choice*. We know—as Odysseus undoubtedly does also—the extent of his love for Penélopê because he can return to her only by choosing her, at the price of death, over Kalypso. We feel and understand, with Odysseus, the value of Ithaka as a homeland, because bound inextricably to the experience of his return is the memory of his absence, of his long wandering at sea, and even of the excitement of his adventures. The prophecy of the peaceful death that is to come to him is so deeply touching because the poem has so fully realized the experiences of discord and violent death. The farm life of the island seems so sweet and orderly because we know the dark wilderness of natural force and mystery within which the fields are cleared and lighted.

THE NECESSITY OF WILDNESS

Domestic order is obviously threatened by the margin of wilderness that surrounds it. Marriage may be destroyed by instinctive sexuality; the husband may choose to remain with Kalypso or the wife may run away with godlike Paris. And the forest is always waiting to overrun the fields. These are real possibilities. They must be considered, respected, even feared.

And yet I think that no culture that hopes to endure can afford to destroy them or to set up absolute safeguards against them. Invariably the failure of organized religions, by which they cut themselves off from mystery and therefore from sanctity, lies in the attempt to impose an absolute division between faith and doubt, to make belief perform as knowledge; when they forbid their prophets to go into the wilderness, they lose the possibility of renewal. And the most dangerous tendency in modern society, now rapidly emerging as a scientific-industrial ambition, is the tendency toward encapsulation of human order—the severance, once and for all, of the umbilical cord fastening us to the wilderness or the Creation. The threat is not only in the totalitarian desire for absolute control. It lies in the willingness to ignore an essential paradox: the natural forces that so threaten us are the same forces that preserve and renew us.

An enduring agriculture must never cease to consider and respect and preserve wildness. The farm can exist only within the wilderness of mystery and natural force. And if the farm is to last and remain in health, the wilderness must survive within the farm. That is what agricultural fertility *is*: the survival of natural process in the human order. To learn to preserve the fertility of the farm, Sir Albert Howard wrote, we must study the forest.

Similarly, the instinctive sexuality within which marriage exists must somehow be made to thrive within marriage. To divide one from the other is to degrade both and ultimately to destroy marriage.

Fidelity to human order, then, if it is fully responsible, implies fidelity also to natural order. Fidelity to human order makes devotion possible. Fidelity to natural order preserves the possibility of choice, the possibility of the renewal of devotion. Where there is no possibility of choice, there is no possibility of faith. One who returns home—to one's marriage and household and place in the world—

desiring anew what was previously chosen, is neither the world's stranger nor its prisoner, but is at once in place and free.

The relation between these two fidelities, inasmuch as they sometimes appear to contradict one another, cannot help but be complex and tricky. In our present stage of cultural evolution, it cannot help but be baffling as well. And yet it is only the double faith that is adequate to our need. If we are to have a culture as resilient and competent in the face of necessity as it needs to be, then it must somehow involve within itself a ceremonious generosity toward the wilderness of natural force and instinct. The farm must yield a place to the forest, not as a wood lot, or even as a necessary agricultural principle, but as a sacred grove—a place where the Creation is let alone, to serve as instruction, example, refuge; a place for people to go, free of work and presumption, to let themselves alone. And marriage must recognize that it survives because of, as well as in spite of, Kalypso and Paris and the generosity of instinct that they represent. It must give some ceremonially acknowledged place to the sexual energies that now thrive outside all established forms, in the destructive freedom of moral ignorance or disregard. Without these accommodations we will remain divided: some of us will continue to destroy the world for purely human ends, while others, for the sake of nature, will abandon the task of human order.

What forms or revisions of forms may be adequate to this double faith, I do not know. Cultural solutions are organisms, not machines, and they cannot be invented deliberately or imposed by prescription. Perhaps all that one can do is to clarify as well as possible the needs and pressures that bear upon the process of cultural evolution. I am certain, however, that no satisfactory solution can come from considering marriage alone or agriculture alone. These are our basic connections to each other and to the earth, and they tend to relate analogically and to be reciprocally defining: our demands upon the earth are determined by our ways of living with one another; our regard for one another is brought to light in our ways of using the earth. And I am certain that neither can be changed for the better in the experimental, prescriptive ways we have been using. Ways of life change only in living. To live by expert advice is to abandon one's life.

"FREEDOM" FROM FERTILITY

The household is the bond of marriage that is most native to it, that grows with it and gives it substantial being in the world. It is the practical condition within which husband and wife can enact devotion and loyalty to each other. The motive power of sexual love is thus joined directly to constructive work and is given communal and ecological value. Without the particular demands and satisfactions of the making and keeping of a household, the sanctity and legality of marriage remain abstract, in effect theoretical, and its sexuality becomes a danger. Work is the health of love. To last, love must enflesh itself in the materiality of the world—produce food, shelter, warmth or shade, surround itself with careful acts, well-made things. This, I think, is what Millen Brand means in *Local Lives* when he speaks of the "threat" of love—"so that perhaps acres of earth and its stones are needed and drawn-out work and monotony/to balance that danger..."

Marriage and the care of the earth are each other's disciplines. Each makes possible the enactment of fidelity toward the other. As the household has become increasingly generalized as a function of the economy and, as a consequence, has become increasingly "mobile" and temporary, these vital connections have been weakened and finally broken. And whatever has been thus disconnected has become a ground of exploitation for some breed of salesman, specialist, or expert.

A direct result of the disintegration of the household is the division of sexuality from fertility and their virtual takeover by specialists. The specialists of human sexuality are the sexual clinicians and the pornographers, both of whom subsist on the increasing possibility of sex between people who neither know nor care about each other. The specialists of human fertility are the evangelists, technicians, and salesmen of birth control, who subsist upon our failure to see any purpose or virtue in sexual discipline. In this, as in our use of every other kind of energy, our inability to contemplate any measure of restraint or forbearance has been ruinous. Here the impulse is characteristically that of the laboratory scientist: to encapsulate sexuality by separating it absolutely from the problems of fertility.

This division occurs, it seems to me, in a profound cultural failure: the loss of any sense that sexuality and fertility might exist together compatibly in this world. We have lost this possibility because we do not understand, because we cannot bear to consider, the meaning consider, the meaning of restraint.* The sort of restraint I am talking

---

*At the root of this failure is probably another sexual division: the assignment to women of virtually all responsibility for sexual discipline.

of restraint.* The sort of restraint I am talking about is illustrated in a recent *National Geographic* article about the people of Hunza in northern Pakistan. The author is a woman, Sabrina Michaud, and she is talking with a Hunza woman in her kitchen:

" 'What have you done to have only one child?' she asks me. Her own children range from 12 to 30 years of age, and seem evenly spaced, four to five years apart. 'We leave our husband's bed until each child is weaned,' she explains simply. But this natural means of birth control has declined, and population has soared."

The woman's remark is thus passed over and not returned to; but if I understand the significance of this paragraph, it is of great importance. The decline of "this natural means of birth control" seems to have been contemporaneous with the coming of roads and "progress" and the opening up of a previously isolated country. What is of interest is that in their isolation in arid, narrow valleys surrounded by the stone and ice of the Karakoram Mountains, these people had practiced sexual restraint as a form of birth control. They had neither our statistical expertise nor our doom-prophets of population growth; it just happened that, placed geographically as they were, they lived always in sight of their agricultural or ecological limits, and they made a competent response.

We have been unable to see the difference between this kind of restraint—a cultural response to an understood practical limit—and the obscure, self-hating, self-congratulating Victorian self-restraint, of which our attitudes and technologies of sexual "freedom" are merely the equally obscure other side. This so-called freedom fragments us and turns us more vehemently and violently than before against our own bodies and against the bodies of other people.

For the care or control of fertility, both that of the earth and that of our bodies, we have allowed a technology of chemicals and devices to replace entirely the cultural means of ceremonial forms, disciplines, and restraints. We have gathered up the immense questions that surround the coming of life into the world and reduced them to simple problems for which we have manufactured and marketed simple solutions. An infertile woman and an infertile field both receive a dose of chemicals, at the calculated risk of undesirable consequences, and are thus equally reduced to the status of productive machines. And for unwanted life—sperm, ova, embryos, weeds, insects, etc.—we have the same sort of ready remedies, for sale, of course, and characteristically popularized by advertisements that speak much of advantages but little of problems.

The result is that we are bringing up a generation of young people who feel that they are "free from worry" about fertility. The pharmacist or the doctor will look after the fertility of the body, and the farming experts and agribusinessmen will look after the fertility of the earth. This is to short-circuit human culture at its source. It is, in effect, to remove from consciousness the two fundamental issues of human life. It permits two great powers to be regarded and used as if they were unimportant.

More serious is the resort to "authorized" modes of direct violence. In land use, this is the permanent diminishment or destruction of fertility as an allowable cost of production, as in strip-mining or in the sort of agriculture that good farmers have long referred to also as "mining." This use of technological means cuts across all issues of health and culture for the sake of an annual quota of production.

The human analogue is in the "harmless" and "simple" surgeries of permanent sterilization, which are now being promoted by a propaganda of extreme oversimplification. The publicity on this subject is typically evangelical in tone and simplistically moral; the operations are recommended like commercial products by advertisings complete with exuberant testimonials of satisfied customers and appeals to the prospective customer's maturity, sexual pride, and desire for "freedom"; and the possible physical and psychological complications are played down, misrepresented, not mentioned at all, or simply not known. It is altogether possible that the operations will be performed by doctors as perfunctory, simplistic, presumptuous, and uninforming as the public literature.

I am fully aware of the problem of overpopulation, and I do not mean to say that birth control is unnecessary. What I do mean to say is that any means of birth control is a serious matter, both culturally and biologically, and that sterilization is the most serious of all: to give up fertility is a major change, as important as birth, puberty, marriage, or death.

The great changes having to do with a woman's fertility—puberty, childbirth, and menopause—have, like sexual desire, the unarguable sanction of biological determinism. They belong to a kind of natural tradition. As a result, they are not only endurable, but they belong to a process—the life process or the Wheel of Life—that we have learned to affirm with some understanding. We know, among other things, that this process includes tragedy and survives it, even triumphs over it. The same applies to the occasions of a man's fertility, although not so formidably, a man being less involved, physically, in the *predicament* of fertility and consciously involved in it only if he wants to be. Nevertheless, he comes to fertility and, if he is a moral person, to the same issues of responsibility that it poses for women.

One of the fundamental interests of human culture is to impose this responsibility, to subject fertility to moral will. Culture articulates needs and forms for sexual restraint and involves issues of value in the process of mating. It is possible to imagine that the resulting tension creates a distinctly human form of energy, highly productive of works of the hands and the mind. But until recently there was no division between sexuality and fertility, because none was possible.

This division was made possible by modern technology, which subjected human fertility, like the fertility of the earth, to a new kind of will: the technological will, which may not *necessarily* oppose the moral will, but which has not only tended to do so, but has tended to replace it. Simply because it became possible—and simultaneously profitable—we have cut the cultural ties between sexuality and fertility, just as we have cut those between eating and farming. By "freeing" food and sex from worry, we have also set them apart from thought, responsibility, and the issue of quality. The introduction of "chemical additives" has tended to do away with the issue of taste or preference; the specialist of sex, like the specialist of food, is dealing with a commodity, which he can measure but cannot value.

What is horrifying is not only that we are relying so exclusively on a technology of birth control that is still experimental, but that we are using it *casually*, in utter cultural nakedness, unceremoniously, without sufficient understanding, and as a substitute for cultural solutions—exactly as we now employ the technology of land use. And to promote these means without cultural and ecological insight, as merely a way to divorce sexuality from fertility, pleasure from responsibility—or to *sell* them that way for ulterior "moral" motives— is to try to cure a disease by another disease. That is only a new battle in the old war between body and soul—as if we were living in front of a chorus of the most literal fanatics chanting: "If thy right eye offend thee, pluck it out! If thy right hand offend thee, cut it off!"

The technologists of fertility exercise the powers of gods and the social function of priests without community ties or cultural responsibilities. The clinicians of sex change the lives of people—as the clinicians of agriculture change the lives of places and communities—

to whom they are strangers and whom they do not know. These specialists thrive in a profound cultural rift, and they are always accompanied by the exploiters who mine that rift for gold. The pornographer exploits sexual division. And working the similar division between us and our land we have the "agribusinessmen," the pornographers of agriculture.

FERTILITY AS WASTE

But there is yet another and more direct way in which the isolation of the body has serious agricultural effects. That is in our society's extreme oversimplification of the relation between the body and its food. By regarding it as merely a consumer of food, we reduce the function of the body to that of a conduit which channels the nutrients of the earth from the supermarket to the sewer. Or we make it a little factory which transforms fertility into pollution—to the enormous profit of "agribusiness" and to the impoverishment of the earth. This is another technological and economic interruption of the cycle of fertility.

Much has already been said here about the division between the body and its food in the productive phase of the cycle. It is the alleged wonder of the Modern World that so many people take energy from food in which they have invested no energy, or very little. Ninety-five percent of our people, boasted the former deputy assistant secretary of agriculture, are now free of the "drudgery" of food production. The meanings of that division, as I have been trying to show, are intricate and degenerative. But that is only half of it. Ninety-five percent (at least) of our people are also free of any involvement or interest in the maintenance phase of the cycle. As their bodies take in and use the nutrients of the soil, those nutrients are transformed into what we are pleased to regard as "wastes"—and are duly wasted.

This waste also has its cause in the old "religious" division between body and soul, by which the body and its products are judged offensive. Once, living with this offensiveness was considered a condemnation, and that was bad enough. But modern technology "saved" us with the flush toilet and the water-borne sewage system. These devices deal with the "wastes" of our bodies by simply removing them from consideration. The irony is that this technological purification of the body requires the pollution of the rivers and the starvation of the fields. It makes the alleged offensiveness of the body truly and inescapably offensive and blinds an entire society to the knowledge that these "offensive wastes" are readily purified in the topsoil—that, indeed, from an ecological point of view, these are not wastes and are not offensive, but are valuable agricultural products essential both to the health of the land and to that of the "consumers."

Our system of agriculture, by modeling itself on economics rather than biology, thus removes food from the *cycle* of its production and puts it into a finite, linear process that in effect destroys it by transforming it into waste. That is, it transforms food into fuel, a form of energy that is usable only once, and in doing so it transforms the body into a consumptive machine.

It is strange, but only apparently so, that this system of agriculture is institutionalized, not in any form of rural life or culture, but in what we call our "urban civilization." The cities subsist in competition with the country; they live upon a one-way movement of energies out of the countryside—food and fuel, manufacturing materials, human labor, intelligence, and talent. Very little of this energy is ever returned. Instead of gathering these energies up into coherence, a cultural consummation that would not only return to the countryside what belongs to it, but also give back generosities of learning and art, conviviality and order, the modern city dissipates and wastes them. Along with its glittering "consumer goods," the modern city produces an equally characteristic outpouring of garbage and pollution—just as it produces and/or collects unemployed, unemployable, and otherwise wasted people.

Once again it must be asked, if competition is the appropriate relationship, then why, after generations of this inpouring of rural wealth, materials, and humanity into the cities, are the cities and the countryside in equal states of disintegration and disrepair? Why have the rural and urban communities *both* fallen to pieces?

HEALTH AND WORK

The modern urban-industrial society is based on a series of radical disconnections between body and soul, husband and wife, marriage and community, community and the earth. At each of these points of disconnection the collaboration of corporation, government, and expert sets up a profit-making enterprise that results in the further dismemberment and impoverishment of the Creation.

Together, these disconnections add up to a condition of critical ill

137

health, which we suffer in common—not just with each other, but with all other creatures. Our economy is based upon this disease. Its aim is to separate us as far as possible from the sources of life (material, social, and spiritual), to put these sources under the control of corporations and specialized professionals, and to sell them to us at the highest profit. It fragments the Creation and sets the fragments into conflict with one another. For the relief of the suffering that comes of this fragmentation and conflict, our economy proposes, not health, but vast "cures" that further centralize power and increase profits: wars, wars on crime, wars on poverty, national schemes of medical aid, insurance, immunization, further industrial and economic "growth," etc.; and these, of course, are followed by more regulatory laws and agencies to see that our health is protected, our freedom preserved, and our money well spent. Although there may be some "good intention" in this, there is little honesty and no hope.

Only by restoring the broken connections can we be healed. Connection *is* health. And what our society does its best to disguise from us is how ordinary, how commonly attainable, health is. We lose our health—and create profitable diseases and dependences—by failing to see the direct connections between living and eating, eating and working, working and loving. In gardening, for instance, one works with the body to feed the body. The work, if it is knowledgeable, makes for excellent food. And it makes one hungry. The work thus makes eating both nourishing and joyful, not consumptive, and keeps the eater from getting fat and weak. This is health, wholeness, a source of delight. And such a solution, unlike the typical industrial solution, does not cause new problems.

The "drudgery" of growing one's own food, then, is not drudgery at all. (If we make the growing of food a drudgery, which is what "agribusiness" does make of it, then we also make a drudgery of eating and of living.) It is—in addition to being the appropriate fulfillment of a practical need—a sacrament, as eating is also, by which we enact and understand our oneness with the Creation, the conviviality of one body with all bodies. This is what we learn from the hunting and farming rituals of tribal cultures.

As the connections have been broken by the fragmentation and isolation of work, they can be restored by restoring the wholeness of work. There is work that is isolating, harsh, destructive, specialized or trivialized into meaninglessness. And there is work that is restorative, convivial, dignified and dignifying, and pleasing. Good work is not just the maintenance of connections—as one is now said to work "for a living" or "to support a family"—but the *enactment* of connections. It *is* living, and a way of living; it is not support for a family in the sense of an exterior brace or prop, but is one of the forms and acts of love.

To boast that now "95 percent of the people can be freed from the drudgery of preparing their own food" is possible only to one who cannot distinguish between these kinds of work. The former deputy assistant secretary cannot see work as a vital connection; he can see it only as a trade of time for money, and so of course he believes in doing as little of it as possible, especially if it involves the use of the body. His ideal is apparently the same as that of a real-estate agency which promotes a rural subdivision by advertising "A homelife of endless vacation." But the society that is so glad to be free of the drudgery of growing and preparing food also boasts a thriving medical industry to which it is paying $500 per person per year. And that is only the down payment.

We embrace this curious freedom and pay its exorbitant cost because of our hatred of bodily labor. We do not want to work "like a dog" or "like an ox" or "like a horse"—that is, we do not want to use ourselves as beasts. This as much as anything is the cause of our disrespect for farming and our abandonment of it to businessmen and experts. We remember, as we should, that there have been agricultural economies that used people as beasts. But that cannot be remedied, as we have attempted to do, by using people as machines, or by not using them at all.

Perhaps the trouble began when we started using animals disrespectfully: as "beasts"—that is, as if they had no more feeling than a machine. Perhaps the destructiveness of our use of machines was prepared in our willingness to abuse animals. That it was never necessary to abuse animals in order to use them is suggested by a passage in *The Horse in the Furrow*, by George Ewart Evans. He is speaking of how the medieval ox teams were worked at the plow: ". . . the ploughman at the handles, the team of oxen—yoked in pairs or four abreast—and the driver who walked alongside with his goad." And then he says: "It is also worth noting that in the Welsh organization . . . the counterpart of the driver was termed *y geilwad* or the *caller*. He walked *backwards* in front of the oxen singing to them as they worked. Songs were specially composed to suit the rhythm of the oxen's work . . ."

That seems to me to differ radically from our present customary use of any living thing. The oxen were not used as beasts or machines, but as fellow creatures. It may be presumed that this work used people the same way. It is possible, then, to believe that there is a kind of work that does not require abuse or misuse, that does not use anything as a substitute for anything else. We are working well when we use ourselves as the fellow creatures of the plants, animals, materials, and other people we are working with. Such work is unifying, healing. It brings us home from pride and from despair, and places us responsibly within the human estate. It defines us as we are: not too good to work with our bodies, but too good to work poorly or joylessly or selfishly or alone.

Instead of sending the experimenter into the fields and meadows to question the farmer and the land worker so as to understand how important quality is, and above all to take up a piece of land himself, the new authoritarian doctrine demands that he shut himself up in a study...

SIR ALBERT HOWARD, *The Soil and Health*

... his education had had the curious effect of making things that he read and wrote more real to him than things he saw. Statistics about agricultural labourers were the substance; any real ditcher, ploughman, or farmer's boy, was the shadow. Though he had never noticed it himself, he had a great reluctance, in his work, ever to use such words as "man" or "woman." He preferred to write about "vocational groups," "elements," "classes" and "populations": for, in his own way, he believed as firmly as any mystic in the superior reality of the things that are not seen.

C. S. LEWIS, *That Hideous Strength*

CHAPTER EIGHT

Jefferson, Morrill, and the Upper Crust

THE CONVICTION OF THOMAS JEFFERSON

In the mind of Thomas Jefferson, farming, education, and democratic liberty were indissolubly linked. The great conviction of his life, which he staked his life upon and celebrated in a final letter two weeks before his death, was "that the mass of mankind has not been born with saddles on their backs, nor a favored few booted and spurred, ready to ride them legitimately, by the grace of God." But if liberty was in that sense a right, it was nevertheless also a privilege to be earned, deserved, and strenuously kept; to keep themselves free, he thought, a people must be stable, economically independent, and virtuous. He believed—on the basis, it should be remembered, of extensive experience both in this country and abroad—that these qualities were most dependably found in the farming people: "Cultivators of the earth are the most valuable citizens. They are the most vigorous, the most independent, the most virtuous, and they are tied to their country, and wedded to its liberty and interests by the most lasting bonds." These bonds were not merely those of economics and property, but those, at once more feeling and more practical, that come from the investment in a place and a community of work, devotion, knowledge, memory, and association.

By contrast, Jefferson wrote: "I consider the class of artificers as the panders of vice, and the instruments by which the liberties of a country are generally overturned." By "artificers" he meant manufacturers, and he made no distinction between "management" and "labor." The last-quoted sentence is followed by no explanation, but its juxtaposition with the one first quoted suggests that he held manufacturers in suspicion because their values were already becoming abstract, enabling them to be "socially mobile" and therefore subject pre-eminently to the motives of self-interest.

To foster the strengths and virtues necessary to citizenship in a democracy, public education was obviously necessary, and Jefferson never ceased to be thoughtful of that necessity: ". . . I do most anxiously wish to see the highest degrees of education given to the higher degrees of genius, and to all degrees of it, so much as may enable them to read and understand what is going on in the world, and to keep their part of it going on right: for nothing can keep it right but their own vigilant and distrustful superintendence."

And all these statements must be read in the light of Jefferson's apprehension of the disarray of agriculture and of agricultural communities in his time: ". . . the long succession of years of stunted crops, of reduced prices, the general prostration of the farming business, under levies for the support of manufacturers, etc., with the calamitous fluctuations of value in our paper medium, have kept agriculture in a state of abject depression, which has peopled the Western States by silently breaking up those on the Atlantic . . ."

JUSTIN MORRILL AND THE LAND-GRANT COLLEGE ACTS

On July 2, 1862, two days less than thirty-six years after the death of Jefferson, the first of the land-grant college acts became law. This was the Morrill Act, which granted "an amount of public land, to be apportioned to each State a quantity equal to thirty thousand acres for each Senator and Representative in Congress . . ." The interest on the money from the sale of these lands was to be applied by each state "to the endowment, support, and maintenance of at least one college where the leading object shall be . . . to teach such branches of learning as are related to agriculture and the mechanic arts . . . in order to promote the liberal and practical education of the industrial classes in the several pursuits and professions in life."

In 1887 Congress passed the Hatch Act, which created the state agricultural experiment stations, with the purpose, among others, of promoting "a sound and prosperous agriculture and rural life as indispensable to the maintenance of maximum employment and national prosperity and security." This act states that "It is also the intent of Congress to assure agriculture a position in research *equal to that of industry*, which will aid in maintaining an equitable balance between agriculture and other segments of the economy." (Emphasis mine—to call attention to the distinction made between agriculture and industry.) The act declares, further, that "It shall be the object and duty of the State agricultural experiment stations . . . to conduct . . . researches, investigations, and experiments bearing directly on and contributing to the establishment and maintenance of a permanent and effective agricultural industry . . . including . . . such investigations as have for their purpose the development and improvement of the rural home and rural life . . ."

And in 1914 the Smith-Lever Act created the cooperative extension service "In order to aid in diffusing among the people . . . useful and practical information on subjects relating to agriculture and home economics, and to encourage the application of the same . . ."

Together, these acts provide for what is known as the land-grant college complex. They fulfill the intention of Justin Smith Morrill, representative and later senator from Vermont. In clarification of the historical pertinence and the aims of the language of the several bills, it is useful to have Morrill's statement of his intentions in a memoir written "apparently in 1874."

Morrill was aware, as Jefferson had been, of an agricultural disorder manifested both by soil depletion and by the unsettlement of population: ". . . the very cheapness of our public lands, and the facility of purchase and transfer, tended to a system of bad-farming or strip and waste of the soil, by encouraging short occupancy and a speedy search for new homes, entailing upon the first and older settlements a rapid deterioration of the soil, which would not be likely to be arrested except by more thorough and scientific knowledge of agriculture and by a higher education of those who were devoted to its pursuit."

But Morrill, unlike Jefferson, had personal reason to be generously concerned for "the class of artificers": ". . . being myself the son of a hard-handed blacksmith . . . who felt his own deprivation of schools . . . I could not overlook mechanics in any measure intended to aid the industrial classes in the procurement of an education that might exalt their usefulness."

And he wished to break what seemed to him "a monopoly of education": ". . . most of the existing collegiate institutions and their feeders were based upon the classic plan of teaching those only destined to pursue the so-called learned professions, leaving farmers and mechanics and all those who must win their bread by labor, to the haphazard of being self-taught or not scientifically taught at all, and restricting the number of those who might be supposed to be qualified to fill places of higher consideration in private or public employments to the limited number of the graduates of the literary institutions."

THE LAND GRANT-COLLEGES

To understand what eventually became of the land-grant college complex, it will be worthwhile to consider certain significant differences between the thinking of Jefferson and that of Morrill. The most important of these is the apparent absence from Morrill's mind of Jefferson's complex sense of the dependence of democratic citizenship upon education. For Jefferson, the ideals and aims of education appear to have been defined directly by the requirements of political liberty. He envisioned a local system of education with a double purpose: to foster in the general population the critical alertness necessary to good citizenship and to seek out and prepare a "natural aristocracy" of "virtue and talents" for the duties and trusts of leadership. His plan of education for Virginia did not include any form of specialized or vocational training. He apparently assumed that if communities could be stabilized and preserved by the virtues of citizenship and leadership, then the "practical arts" would be improved as a matter of course by local example, reading, etc. Morrill, on the other hand, looked at education from a strictly practical or utilitarian viewpoint. He believed that the primary aims of education were to correct the work of farmers and mechanics and "exalt their usefulness." His wish to break the educational monopoly of the professional class was Jeffersonian only in a very limited sense: he wished to open the professional class to the children of laborers. In distinguishing among the levels of education, he did not distinguish, as Jefferson did, among "degrees of genius."

Again, whereas Jefferson regarded farmers as "the most valuable citizens," Morrill looked upon the professions as "places of higher consideration." We are thus faced with a difficulty in understanding Morrill's wish to "exalt the usefulness" of "those who must win their bread by labor." Would education exalt their usefulness by raising the quality of their work or by making them eligible for promotion to "places of higher consideration"?

Those differences and difficulties notwithstanding, the apparent intention in regard to agriculture remains the same from Jefferson to Morrill to the land-grant college acts. That intention was to promote the stabilization of farming populations and communities and to establish in that way a "permanent" agriculture, enabled by better education to preserve both the land and the people.

The failure of this intention, and the promotion by the land-grant colleges of an *impermanent* agriculture destructive of land and people, was caused in part by the lowering of the educational standard from Jefferson's ideal of public or community responsibility to the utilitarianism of Morrill, insofar as this difference in the aims of the two men represented a shift of public value. The land-grant colleges have, in fact, been very little—and have been less and less—concerned "to promote the liberal and practical education of the industrial classes" or of any other classes. Their history has been largely that of the whittling down of this aim—from education in the broad, "liberal" sense to "practical" preparation for earning a living to various "programs" for certification. They first reduced "liberal and practical" to "practical," and then for "practical" they substituted "specialized." And the standard of their purpose has shifted from usefulness to careerism. And if this has not been caused by, it has certainly accompanied a degeneration of faculty standards, by which professors and teachers of disciplines become first upholders of "professional standards" and then careerists in pursuit of power, money, and prestige.

The land-grant college legislation obviously calls for a system of local institutions responding to local needs and local problems. What we have instead is a system of institutions which more and more resemble one another, like airports and motels, made increasingly uniform by the transience or rootlessness of their career-oriented faculties and the consequent inability to respond to local conditions. The professor lives in his career, in a ghetto of career-oriented fellow professors. Where he may be geographically is of little interest to him. One's career is a vehicle, not a dwelling; one is concerned less for where it is than for where it will go.

The careerist professor is by definition a specialist professor. Utterly dependent upon his institution, he blunts his critical intelligence and blurs his language so as to exist "harmoniously" within it—and so serves his school with an emasculated and fragmentary intelligence, deferring "realistically" to the redundant procedures and meaningless demands of an inflated administrative bureaucracy whose educational purpose is written on its paychecks.

But just as he is dependent on his institution, the specialist professor is also dependent on his students. In order to earn a living, he must teach; in order to teach, he must have students. And so the tendency is to make a commodity of education: to package it attractively, reduce requirements, reduce homework, inflate grades, lower standards, and deal expensively in "public relations."

As self-interest, laziness, and lack of conviction augment the general confusion about what an education is or ought to be, and as standards of excellence are replaced by sliding scales of adequacy, these schools begin to depend upon, and so to institutionalize, the local problems that they were founded to solve. They begin to need, and so to promote, the mobility, careerism, and moral confusion that are victimizing the local population and destroying the local communities. The stock in trade of the "man of learning" comes to be ignorance.

The colleges of agriculture are focused somewhat more upon their whereabouts than, say, the colleges of arts and sciences because of the local exigencies of climate, soils, and crop varieties; but like the rest they tend to orient themselves within the university rather than within the communities they were intended to serve. The impression is unavoidable that the academic specialists of agriculture tend to validate their work experimentally rather than practically, that they would rather be professionally reputable than locally effective, and that they pay little attention, if any, to the social, cultural, and political consequences of their work. Indeed, it sometimes appears that they pay very little attention to its economic consequences. There is nothing more characteristic of modern agricultural research than its divorcement from the sense of consequence and from all issues of value.

This is facilitated on the one hand by the academic ideal of "objectivity" and on the other by a strange doctrine of the "inevitabil-

ity" of undisciplined technological growth and change. "Objectivity" has come to be simply the academic uniform of moral cow-
ardice: one who is "objective" never takes a stand. And in the
fashionable "realism" of technological determinism, one is shed of
the embarrassment of moral and intellectual standards and of any
need to define what is excellent or desirable. Education is relieved of
its concern for truth in order to prepare students to live in "a changing world." As soon as educational standards begin to be dictated by
"a changing world" (changing, of course, to a tune called by the
governmental-military-academic-industrial complex), then one is
justified in teaching virtually anything in any way—for, after all, one
never knows for sure what "a changing world" is going to become.
The way is thus opened to run a university as a business, the main
purpose of which is to sell diplomas—after a complicated but un-
demanding four-year ritual—and thereby give employment to professors.

COLLEGES OF "AGRIBUSINESS" AND UNSETTLEMENT

That the land-grant college complex has fulfilled its obligation "to
assure agriculture a position in research equal to that of industry"
simply by failing to distinguish between the two is acknowledged in
the term "agribusiness." The word does not denote any real identity
either of function or interest, but only an expedient confusion by
which the interests of industry have subjugated those of agriculture.
This confusion of agriculture with industry has utterly perverted the
intent of the land-grant college acts. The case has been persuasively
documented by a task force of the Agribusiness Accountability Proj-
ect. In the following paragraphs, Jim Hightower and Susan DeMarco
give the task force's central argument:

"Who is helped and who is hurt by this research?

"It is the largest-scale growers, the farm machinery and chemicals
input companies and the processors who are the primary beneficiaries. Machinery companies such as John Deere, International
Harvester, Massey-Ferguson, Allis-Chalmer and J. I. Case almost
continually engage in cooperative research efforts at land grant colleges. These corporations contribute money and some of their own
research personnel to help land grant scientists develop machinery.
In return, they are able to incorporate technological advances in
their own products. In some cases they actually receive exclusive
licences to manufacture and sell the products of tax-paid research.

149

"If mechanization has been a boon to agribusiness, it has been a bane to millions of rural Americans. Farmworkers have been the earliest victims. There were 4.3 million hired farm workers in 1950. Twenty years later that number had fallen to 3.5 million . . .

"Farmworkers have not been compensated for jobs lost to mechanized research. They were not consulted when that work was designed, and their needs were not a part of the research that resulted. They simply were left to fend on their own—no re-training, no unemployment compensation, no research to help them adjust to the changes that came out of the land grant colleges.

"Independent family farmers also have been largely ignored by the land grant colleges. Mechanization research by land grant colleges is either irrelevant or only incidentally adaptable to the needs of 87 to 99 percent of America's farmers. The public subsidy for mechanization actually has weakened the competitive position of the family farmer. Taxpayers, through the land grant college complex, have given corporate producers a technological arsenal specifically suited to their scale of operation and designed to increase their efficiency and profits. The independent family farmer is left to strain his private resources to the breaking point in a desperate effort to clamber aboard the technological treadmill."

The task force also raised the issue of academic featherbedding—irrelevant or frivolous research or instruction carried on by colleges of agriculture, experiment stations, and extension services. Evidently, people in many states may expect to be "served" by such studies as one at Cornell that discovered that "employed homemakers have less time for housekeeping tasks than non-employed homemakers." An article in the *Louisville Courier-Journal* lately revealed, for example, that "a 20-year-old waitress . . . recently attended a class where she learned 'how to set a real good table.'

"She got some tips on how to save steps and give faster service by 'carrying quite a few things' on the same tray. And she learned most of the highway numbers in the area, so she could give better directions to confused tourists.

"She learned all of that from the University of Kentucky College of Agriculture. Specialists in restaurant management left the Lexington campus to give the training to waitresses . . .

"The UK College of Agriculture promotes tourism.

"The college also helps to plan highways, housing projects, sewer systems and industrial developments throughout the state.

"It offers training in babysitting, 'family living'..."

This sort of "agricultural" service is justified under the Smith-Lever Act, Section 347a, inserted by amendment in 1955, and by Representative Lever's "charge" to the Extension Service in 1913. Both contain language that requires some looking at.

Section 347a is based mainly upon the following congressional insight: that "in certain agricultural areas," "there is concentration of farm families on farms either too small or too unproductive or both...." For these "disadvantaged farms" the following remedies were provided: "(1) Intensive on-the-farm educational assistance to the farm family in appraising and resolving its problems; (2) assistance and counseling to local groups in appraising resources for capability of improvement in agriculture or introduction of industry designed to supplement farm income; (3) cooperation with other agencies and groups in furnishing all possible information as to existing employment opportunities, particularly to farm families having underemployed workers; and (4) in cases where the farm family, after analysis of its opportunities and existing resources, finds it advisable to seek a new farming venture, the providing of information, advice, and counsel in connection with making such change."

The pertinent language of Representative Lever's "charge," which is apparently regarded as having the force of law, at least by the University of Kentucky Cooperative Extension Service, places upon extension agents the responsibility "to assume leadership in every movement, whatever it may be, the aim of which is better farming, better living, more happiness, more education and better citizenship."

If Section 347a is an example—as it certainly is—of special-interest legislation, its special interest is only ostensibly and vaguely in the welfare of small ("disadvantaged") farmers. To begin with, it introduces into law and into land-grant philosophy the startling concept that a farm can be "too small" or "too unproductive." The only standard for this judgment is implied in the clauses that follow it: the farmers of such farms "are unable to make adjustments and investments required to establish profitable operations"; such a farm "does not permit profitable employment of available labor"; and—most revealing—"many of these farm families are not able to make full use of current extension programs...."

The first two of these definitions of a "too small" or "too unproductive" farm are not agricultural but economic: the farm must provide, not a living, but a profit. And it must be profitable, more-over, in an economy that—in 1955, as now—favors "agribusiness." (Section 347a is a product of the era in which then Assistant Secre-tary of Agriculture John Davis and Earl Butz were advocating "corporate control to 'rationalize' agriculture production"; in which Mr. Davis himself invented the term "agribusiness"; in which then Secretary of Agriculture Ezra Taft Benson told farmers to "Get big or get out.") Profitability may be a standard of a sort, but a most relative sort and by no means sufficient. It leaves out of considera-tion, for instance, the possibility that a family might farm a small acreage, take excellent care of it, make a decent, honorable, and in-dependent living from it, and yet fail to make what the authors of Section 347a would consider a profit.

But the third definition is, if possible, even more insidious: a farm is "too small" or "too unproductive" if it cannot "make full use of current extension programs." The farm is not to be the measure of the service; the service is to be the measure of the farm.

It will be argued that Section 347a was passed in response to real conditions of economic hardship on the farm and that the aim of the law was to permit the development of *new* extension programs as remedies. But that is at best only half true. There certainly were economic hardships on the farm in 1955; we have proof of that in the drastic decline in the number of farms and farmers since then. But there was plenty of land-grant legislation at that time to permit the extension service to devise any program necessary to deal with agri-cultural problems *as such*. What is remarkable about Section 347a is that it permitted the land-grant colleges to abandon these problems as such, to accept the "agribusiness" revolution as inevitable, and to undertake non-agricultural solutions to agricultural problems. And the assistances provided for in Section 347a are so general and vague as to allow the colleges to be most inventive. After 1955, the agri-cultural academicians would have a vested interest, not in the welfare of farmers, but in virtually anything at all that might happen to ex-farmers, their families, and their descendants forevermore. They have, in other words, a vested interest in their own failure—foolproof job security.

But it is hard to see how the language of Section 347a, loose as it is, justifies the teaching of highway numbers to waitresses, the promo-tion of tourism, and the planning of industrial developments, sewer systems, and housing projects. For justification of these programs we apparently must look to the language of Representative Lever's "charge," which in effect tells the extension agents to do anything they can think of.

These new "services" seem little more than desperate maneuvers on the part of the land-grant colleges to deal with the drastic reduction in the last thirty years of their lawful clientele—a reduction for which the colleges themselves are in large part responsible because of their eager collaboration with "agribusiness." As the conversion of farming into agribusiness has depopulated the farmland, it has become necessary for the agriculture specialists to develop "programs" with which to follow their erstwhile beneficiaries into the cities—either that or lose their meal ticket in the colleges. If the colleges of agriculture have so assiduously promoted the industrialization of farming and the urbanization of farmers that now "96 percent of America's manpower is freed from food production," then the necessary trick of survival is to become colleges of industrialization and urbanization—that is, colleges of "agribusiness"—which, in fact, is what they have been for a long time. Their success has been stupendous: as the number of farmers has decreased, the colleges of agriculture have grown larger.

The bad faith of the program-mongering under Section 347a may be suggested by several questions:

Why did land-grant colleges not address themselves to the *agricultural* problems of small or "disadvantaged" farmers?

Why did they not undertake the development of small-scale technologies and methods appropriate to the small farm?

Why have they assumed that the turn to "agribusiness" and big technology was "inevitable"?

Why, if they can promote tourism and plan sewer systems, have they not promoted cooperatives to give small farmers some measure of protection against corporate suppliers and purchasers?

Why have they watched in silence the destruction of the markets of the small producers of poultry, eggs, butter, cream, and milk—once the mainstays of the small-farm economy?

Why have they never studied or questioned the necessity or the justice of the sanitation laws that have been used to destroy such markets?

Why have they not tried to calculate the real (urban and rural) costs of the migration from farm to city?

Why have they raised no questions of social, political, or cultural value?

153

That the colleges of agriculture should have become colleges of "agribusiness"—working, in effect, *against* the interests of the small farmers, the farm communities, and the farmland—can only be explained by the isolation of specialization.

First we have the division of the study of agriculture into specialties. And then, within the structure of the university, we have the separation of these specialties from specialties of other kinds. This problem is outlined with forceful insight by André Mayer and Jean Mayer in an article entitled "Agriculture, the Island Empire," published in the summer 1974 issue of *Daedalus*. Like other academic professions, agriculture has gone its separate way and aggrandized itself in its own fashion: "As it developed into an intellectual discipline in the nineteenth century, it did so in academic divisions which were isolated from the liberal arts center of the university . . ." It "produced ancillary disciplines parallel to those in the arts and sciences . . ." And it "developed its own scientific organizations; its own professional, trade, and social organizations; its own technical and popular magazines; and its own public. It even has a separate political system . . ."

The founding fathers, these authors point out, "placed agriculture at the center of an Enlightenment concept of science broad enough to include society, politics, and sometimes even theology." But the modern academic structure has alienated agriculture from such concerns. The result is an absurd "independence" which has produced genetic research "without attention to nutritional values," which has undertaken the so-called Green Revolution without concern for its genetic oversimplification or its social, political, and cultural dangers, and which keeps agriculture in a separate "field" from ecology.

A BETRAYAL OF TRUST

The educational *ideal* that concerns us here was held clearly in the mind of Thomas Jefferson, was somewhat diminished or obscured in the mind of Justin Morrill, but survived indisputably in the original language of the land-grant college acts. We see it in the intention that education should be "liberal" as well as "practical," in the wish to foster "a sound and prosperous agriculture and rural life," in the distinction between agriculture and industry, in the purpose of establishing and maintaining a "permanent" agriculture, in the implied perception that this permanence would depend on the stability of "the rural home and rural life." This ideal is simply that farmers should be educated, liberally and practically, *as farmers*; education should be given and acquired with the understanding that those so educated would return to their home communities, not merely to be farmers, corrected and improved by their learning, but also to assume the trusts and obligations of community leadership, the highest form of that "vigilant and distrustful superintendence" without which the communities could not preserve themselves. This leadership, moreover, would tend to safeguard agriculture's distinction from and competitiveness with industry. Conceivably, had it existed, this leadership might have resulted in community-imposed restraints upon technology, such as those practiced by the Amish.

Having stated the ideal, it becomes possible not merely to perceive the degeneracy and incoherence of the land-grant colleges within themselves, but to understand their degenerative influence on the farming communities. It becomes possible to see that their failure goes beyond the disintegration of intellectual and educational standards; it is the betrayal of a trust.

The land-grant acts gave to the colleges not just government funds and a commission to teach and to do research, but also a purpose which may be generally stated as the preservation of agriculture and rural life. That this purpose is a practical one is obvious from the language of the acts; no one, I dare say, would deny that this is so. It is equally clear, though far less acknowledged, that the purpose is also moral, insofar as it raises issues of value and of feeling. It may be that pure practicality can deal with agriculture so long as agriculture is defined as a set of problems that are purely technological (though such a definition is in itself a gross falsification), but it inevitably falters at the meanings of "liberal," "sound and prosperous," "permanent and effective," "development and improvement"; and it fails altogether to address the concepts of "the rural home and rural life." When the Hatch Act, for instance, imposed upon the colleges the goals of "a permanent and effective agricultural industry" and "the development and improvement of the rural home and rural life," it implicitly required of them an allegiance to the agrarian values that have constituted one of the dominant themes of American history and thought.

The tragedy of the land-grant acts is that their moral imperative came finally to have nowhere to rest except on the careers of specialists whose standards and operating procedures were amoral: the "objective" practitioners of the "science" of agriculture, whose minds have no direction other than that laid out by career necessity and the logic of experimentation. They have no apparent moral allegiances or bearings or limits. Their work thus inevitably serves whatever power is greatest. That power at present is the industrial economy, of which "agribusiness" is a part. Lacking any moral force or vision of its own, the "objective" expertise of the agriculture specialist points like a compass needle toward the greater good of the "agribusiness" corporations. The objectivity of the laboratory functions in the world as indifference; knowledge without responsibility is merchandise, and greed provides its applications. Far from developing and improving the rural home and rural life, the land-grant colleges have blindly followed the drift of virtually the whole population away from home, blindly documenting or "serving" the consequent disorder and blindly rationalizing this disorder as "progress" or "miraculous development."

At this point one can begin to understand the violence that has been done to the Morrill Act's provision for a "liberal and practical education." One imagines that Jefferson might have objected to the inclusion of the phrase "and practical," and indeed in retrospect the danger in it is clearly visible. Nevertheless, the law evidently sees "liberal and practical" as a description of *one* education, not two. And as long as the two terms are thus associated, the combination remains thinkable: the "liberal" side, for instance, might offer necessary restraints of value to the "practical"; the "practical" interest might direct the "liberal" to crucial issues of use and effect.

In practice, however, the Morrill Act's formula has been neatly bisected and carried out as if it read "a liberal *or* a practical education." But though these two kinds of education may theoretically be divided and given equal importance, in fact they are no sooner divided than they are opposed. They enter into competition with one another, and by a kind of educational Gresham's Law the practical curriculum drives out the liberal.

This happens because the *standards* of the two kinds of education are fundamentally different and fundamentally opposed. The standard of liberal education is based upon definitions of excellence in the various disciplines. These definitions are in turn based upon example. One learns to order one's thoughts and to speak and write coherently by studying exemplary thinkers, speakers, and writers of the past.

One studies *The Divine Comedy* and the Pythagorean theorem not to acquire something to be exchanged for something else, but to understand the orders and the kinds of thought and to furnish the mind with subjects and examples. Because the standards are rooted in examples, they do not change.

The standard of practical education, on the other hand, is based upon the question of what will work, and because the practical is by definition of the curriculum set aside from issues of value, the question tends to be resolved in the most shallow and immediate fashion: what is practical is what makes money; what is most practical is what makes the most money. Practical education is an "investment," something acquired to be exchanged for something else—a "good" job, money, prestige. It is oriented entirely toward the future, toward what *will* work in the "changing world" in which the student is supposedly being prepared to "compete." The standard of practicality, as used, is inherently a degenerative standard. There is nothing to correct it except suppositions about what the world will be like and what the student will therefore need to know. Because the future is by definition unknown, one person's supposition about the future tends to be as good, or as forceful, as another's. And so the standard of practicality tends to revise itself downward to meet, not the needs, but the desires of the student who, for instance, does not want to learn a science because he *intends* to pursue a career in which he does not *think* a knowledge of science will be necessary.

It could be said that a liberal education has the nature of a bequest, in that it looks upon the student as the potential heir of a cultural birthright, whereas a practical education has the nature of a commodity to be exchanged for position, status, wealth, etc., *in the future*. A liberal education rests on the assumption that nature and human nature do not change very much or very fast and that one therefore needs to understand the past. The practical educators assume that human society itself is the only significant context, that change is therefore fundamental, constant, and necessary, that the future will be wholly unlike the past, that the past is outmoded, irrelevant, and an encumbrance upon the future—the present being only a time for dividing past from future, for getting ready.

But these definitions, based on division and opposition, are too simple. It is easy, accepting the viewpoint of either side, to find fault with the other. But the wrong is on neither side; it is in their division. One of the purposes of this book is to show how the practical, divorced from the discipline of value, tends to be defined by the immediate interests of the practitioner, and so becomes destructive of value, practical and otherwise. But it must not be forgotten that, divorced from the practical, the liberal disciplines lose their sense of use and influence and become attenuated and aimless. The purity of "pure" science is then ritualized as a highly competitive intellectual game without awareness of use, responsibility, or consequence, such as that described in *The Double Helix*, James D. Watson's book about the discovery of the structure of DNA. And the so-called humanities become a world of their own, a collection of "professional" sub-languages, complicated circuitries of abstruse interpretation, feckless exercises of sensibility. Without the balance of historic value, practical education gives us that most absurd of standards: "relevance," based upon the suppositional needs of a theoretical future. But liberal education, divorced from practicality, gives something no less absurd: the specialist professor of one or another of the liberal arts, the custodian of an inheritance he has learned much about, but nothing from.

And in the face of competition from the practical curriculum, the liberal has found it impossible to maintain its own standards and so has become practical—that is, career-oriented—also. It is now widely assumed that the only good reason to study literature or philosophy is to become a teacher of literature or philosophy—in order, that is, to get an income from it. I recently received in the mail a textbook of rhetoric in which the author stated that "there is no need for anyone except a professional linguist to be able to explain language operations specifically and accurately." Maybe so, but how does one escape the implicit absurdity that linguists should study the language only to teach aspiring linguists?

The education of the student of agriculture is almost as absurd, and it is more dangerous: he is taught a course of practical knowledge and procedures for which uses do indeed exist, but these uses lie outside the purview and interest of the school. The colleges of agriculture produce agriculture specialists and "agribusinessmen" as readily as farmers, and they are producing far more of them. Public funds originally voted to provide for "the liberal and practical education" of farmers thus become, by moral default, an educational subsidy given to the farmers' competitors.

THE VAGRANT ARISTOCRACY

But in order to complete an understanding of the modern disconnection between work and value, it is necessary to see how certain "aristocratic" ideas of status and leisure have been institutionalized in this system of education. This is one of the liabilities of the social and political origins not only of our own nation, but of most of the "advanced" nations of the world. Democracy has involved more than the enfranchisement of the lower classes; it has meant also the popularization of the more superficial upper-class values: leisure, etiquette (as opposed to good manners), fashion, everyday dressing up, and a kind of dietary persnicketiness. We have given a highly inflated value to "days off" and to the wearing of a necktie; we pay an exorbitant price for the *looks* of our automobiles; we pay dearly, in both money and health, for our predilection for white bread. We attach much the same values to kinds of profession and levels of income that were once attached to hereditary classes.

It is extremely difficult to exalt the usefulness of any productive discipline *as such* in a society that is at once highly stratified and highly mobile. Both the stratification and the mobility are based upon notions of prestige, which are in turn based upon these reliquary social fashions. Thus doctors are given higher status than farmers, not because they are more necessary, more useful, more able, more talented, or more virtuous, but because they are *thought* to be "better"—one assumes because they talk a learned jargon, wear good clothes all the time, and make a lot of money. And this is true generally of "office people" as opposed to those who work with their hands. Thus an industrial worker does not aspire to become a master craftsman, but rather a foreman or manager. Thus a farmer's son does not usually think to "better" himself by becoming a better farmer than his father, but by becoming, professionally, a better *kind* of man than his father.

It is characteristic of our present society that one does not think to improve oneself by becoming better at what one is doing or by assuming some measure of public responsibility in order to improve local conditions; one thinks to improve oneself by becoming different, by "moving up" to a "place of higher consideration." Thinkable changes, in other words, tend to be quantitative rather than qualitative, and they tend to involve movement that is both social and geographic. The unsettlement at once of population and of values is virtually required by the only generally acceptable forms of aspiration. The typical American "success story" moves from a modest rural beginning to urban affluence, from manual labor to office work.

We must ask, then, what must be the educational effect, the influence, of a farmer's son who believes, with the absolute authorization of his society, that he has mightily improved himself by becoming a professor of agriculture. Has he not improved himself by an "upward" motivation which by its nature avoids the issue of quality —which assumes simply that an agriculture specialist is better than a farmer? And does he not exemplify to his students the proposition that "the way up" leads away from home? How could he, who has "succeeded" by earning a Ph.D. and a nice place in town, advise his best students to go home and farm, or even assume that they might find good reasons for doing so?

I am suggesting that our university-based structures of success, as they have come to be formed upon quantitative measures, virtually require the degeneration of qualitative measures and the disintegration of culture. The university accumulates information at a rate that is literally inconceivable, yet its structure and its self-esteem institutionalize the likelihood that not much of this information will ever be taken *home*. We do not work where we live, and if we are to hold up our heads in the presence of our teachers and classmates, we must not live where we come from.

THE STATUS QUO

So far, in tracing the changes of an American educational ambition, this chapter has necessarily been to some extent conjectural. As elsewhere in this book, I have been writing what my experience has made it possible for me to say—with the understanding that it must then await confirmation, amplification, or contradiction from the experience of other people. I have intentionally placed experience ahead of "proof," feeling that the ordinary visibility of the deterioration of rural life ought to take precedence over statistics and expert testimony.

Nevertheless, the testimony of experts must be taken into account. It seems appropriate that I should conclude this chapter by examining in some detail a prominent expert's justification of the agricultural status quo. The article, "The Agriculture of the U.S.," comes from the September 1976 issue of *Scientific American*. Its author is

Earl O. Heady, Curtiss Distinguished Professor at Iowa State University and director of that university's Center for Agriculture and Rural Development. Professor Heady "was born and raised on a farm in Nebraska" and received his degrees from the University of Nebraska and from Iowa State. He is author or co-author of "17 books and more than 725 journal articles, research bulletins and monographs." He is vice-president of the American Association of Agricultural Economists, vice-president of the Canadian Agricultural Economics Association, and permanent chairman of the East-West Seminars for Agricultural Economists. His biographical note quotes him as follows: "I do a lot of work in developing countries, consulting with planners, evaluating policies for economic and agricultural development and analyzing development in general."

Professor Heady begins his account with this statement: "Over the past 200 years the U.S. has had the best, the most logical and the most successful program of agricultural development anywhere in the world. Other countries would do well to copy it." The occurrence of such an absolute assertion at the *beginning* of a scientific article by an objective scientist can only strike one as remarkable. And a little consideration makes it even more so. Has he forgotten, or did he ever know, for instance, that in 1907, F. H. King, also an American professor of agriculture and chief of Division of Soil Management, United States Department of Agriculture, was traveling in China, Korea, and Japan, studying the ancient agricultural practices of those countries and finding them exemplary? Does Professor Heady know, for that matter, of the work of *any* critic of his assumptions? And who is he trying to convince? Surely not the readers of *Scientific American*, most of whom will at least wish to see his evidence. But, in fact, for the supremacy of American agriculture over that of all other countries, Professor Heady's article offers no evidence whatsoever. And the evidence he does supply leaves the logic and success of the American program very much in doubt.

"At the beginning of the nation's agricultural development," Professor Heady writes, "land was abundant and labor was cheap. Capital inputs such as farm machinery, fertilizer and food for the farmer's family were relatively modest, and most of them were produced on the farm. Farmers created their own power in the form of the physical work of family members and of animals raised on the farm. They also harnessed energy from the sun for that work in the form of crops grown on the farm and eaten by the people or the animals. The farmers generated their own fertilizer by rotating crops and by utilizing the wastes from the animals. The rotation of crops also controlled insects to some extent."

That description is not critical enough. In its general outline it describes the agriculture of many parts of this country as late as World War II. The greatest weakness of that agriculture was undoubtedly its wastefulness of the soil itself, but there were other weaknesses also. It was the knowledge of these weaknesses that sent F. H. King to the Orient, and his discoveries there, had they taken root here, might have made our farmers more solvent and productive, and much kinder in their use of the soil. But Professor Heady's description may be allowed to stand; it does represent accurately enough the possibility of a thrifty, independent, diversified, farm-based agriculture that remained easily within our reach until a generation ago.

That possibility and a virgin continent were the endowment that we started with. In the rest of his article Professor Heady tells what we have done with, and to, that endowment.

In the nineteenth century, he tells us, after the United States had expanded to its westward limits and the public land grants had all been taken up, the government's agricultural policy shifted its emphasis from expansion to productivity. The land-grant college system was created "to encourage research and to extend new technical knowledge to farmers." Science and technology became "an effective substitute for land." As a result, production "approximately doubled" in the period from 1910 to 1970, and "by 1970 the nation was producing its food on considerably fewer acres than it had been in 1910." Rapidly put into use, the new technology "became an effective substitute not only for land but also for labor. The result was that between 1950 and 1955 more than a million workers migrated out of the agricultural sector into other sectors of the economy."

We are asked to accept that our agricultural policy-makers displayed profound wisdom in shifting their emphasis from expansion to productivity—as if, after the possibility of expansion had ended, the choice was difficult. And we are asked to accept productivity as a sufficient criterion; nothing is said, here or elsewhere in Professor Heady's article, about the issues of restoration and maintenance. The displacement of a million workers in five years is cited merely as evidence of the efficacy of technology. One wonders what may have been the social and economic costs of that "migration." Into what "sectors of the economy" did those workers move? And it may not be impertinent in a democracy to ask, Did they want to go?

Next Professor Heady focuses on the period from 1950 to 1970: "Farms became larger and more specialized, handling either crops or livestock instead of both. Farms growing crops greatly increased their utilization of fertilizers, pesticides, farm machinery and other capital items . . . the use of fertilizer increased by 276 percent. . . . The use of powered machines increased by only 30 percent, but in 1972 there were substantially fewer farms than there were in 1950. The result was that farm labor declined by 54 percent over that period as labor productivity quadrupled and total farm output increased by 55 percent."

Again, highly problematic changes are cited solely as evidence of the advance of technology, which we are evidently expected to regard as simply good. And again a massive displacement of "labor" is treated as if people were merely underpowered, slow machines, now happily replaced by machines of a better make.

In 1974 and 1975, Professor Heady tells us, American farmers produced "record" yields, which brought them a "record" income. Records, as we know, are made by champions and are good beyond question. But Professor Heady goes on: "The rapid upward movement in income has put farmers in a highly favorable position with regard to capital assets. Although some farmers took advantage of the opportunity to repay their mortgage before it came due, the majority put their higher earnings into acquiring new farm equipment, upgrading their living facilities and enlarging their farms by buying more land. As a result farm real estate values more than doubled between 1970 and 1973."

This is the second time Professor Heady's article has spoken of the recent increases in the value of farmland to "record levels," as if this is some kind of grand agricultural achievement. But is this increase entirely due to competition among farmers for the land, or do inflation, urban development, and speculation have something to do with it? And are there dangers in these high prices? Although the fact of inflation is rather casually mentioned later in the article, the first question is really neither answered nor asked. The second question is answered later on, but the dangers are not admitted.

Meanwhile, Professor Heady acknowledges the existence of certain other problems: "The change in the very nature of farming, with

163

its higher productivity and greater degree of mechanization, has severely affected rural communities. . . . With the decline in the farm population the demand for the goods and services of businesses in the country has been eroded. Employment and income opportunities in typical rural communities have therefore declined markedly. As people migrated out of the rural communities, there were fewer people left to participate in the services of schools, medical facilities and other institutions. With the lessened demand such services retreated in quantity and quality and advanced in cost.

"Nonfarm groups in the rural communities took large capital losses. . . ."

Professor Heady further acknowledges that "Rapid agricultural development . . . has also had a heavy impact on the environment." The larger and more specialized farms are "depleting the soil of certain specific nutrients and thus requiring larger amounts of fertilizer." This increase in the use of fertilizer has been accompanied by an increased use of pesticides and more intensive (that is, more continuous) cultivation. "The burden placed on streams and lakes by the runoff of silt and farm chemicals has therefore increased."

"On the other hand," he says, "the development of American agriculture has fostered the growth of an entire agricultural industry—'agribusiness'—of which farming is only a small part."

Anyone who cares at all for the welfare of the rural home and rural life and for the good health of the farmland will see the arrogance of that phrase "on the other hand." It is the balancing point of a monstrous equation. Professor Heady has just described a serious impairment of rural life that is social, economic, and ecological, and he has said that it is justified and compensated by the growth of "agribusiness." The sacrifice of many and of much for the enrichment of a few is thus justified as if the Declaration of Independence had never been written.

The "industry" of modern agriculture, according to Professor Heady, has "three major components": "the input-processing industry," "the farm itself," and "the food-processing industry." I will quote, nearly complete, Professor Heady's description of the first and last of these, asking the reader to bear in mind the professor's earlier description of the kind of farming we had at the beginning of our "agricultural development."

"The input-processing industry now supplies many things that were once produced on the farm. Today tractors substitute for draft animals, fossil fuels for animal feeds, chemical fertilizers for manure and nitrogen-fixing crops. Such developments not only have shifted a greater proportion of the agricultural work force from the farms into the input-processing sector but also have increased the cash cost of farming. . . . The greater proportion of cash cost has made farm profits much more vulnerable to price fluctuations than they used to be.

"The food-processing sector has in recent years come to represent a larger proportion of the total agricultural industry than farming itself. In 1975, 42 cents of each consumer dollar spent for food at retail prices went to the farmer and 58 cents went to the food processor. Even the typical commercial farm family now buys frozen, packaged and ready-to-serve foods from the supermarket rather than consuming products raised and prepared on the farm."

So much for the ideal—and the practical values—of independence. If the farmer sells his foodstuff to "agribusiness" at a narrow profit, if any, and buys it back ready-to-serve from "agribusiness" to its great profit, then the cash flow has at that point deftly inserted its tail into its mouth, a wonder of sorts has been accomplished, and a reverent "Golly!" is heard from certain agricultural economists.

And now, sufficiently far from the question, Professor Heady gives us an answer as to the dangers of high land prices: "The change in the nature of agriculture has greatly enhanced the financial position of established farmers with large holdings. . . . The situation is not as favorable for farmers who are starting from scratch. . . . One can therefore expect to see an increasing trend toward more large commercial farms and fewer small ones."

Professor Heady's "therefore" is nearly as irresponsible as his "on the other hand." By various inequities, abuses, and misconceptions, a condition has come to exist in which big farmers thrive by the ruin of smaller ones. And Professor Heady enjoins this condition upon the future by a simple "therefore."

Aside from the urgent social and political questions that are obviously raised by Professor Heady's observation, it raises, in fact, some agricultural and economic questions that are also extremely serious. I shall mention two.

First, if hunger and malnutrition are now in prospect for many of the world's people, as hardly anyone (including Professor Heady) denies, and if productivity is therefore the major issue, can we afford this trend toward bigger and bigger farms? The question rises from the awareness, now shared by many experts, that large farms do not produce as abundantly or efficiently as small ones. Sterling Wortman, for instance, writing in the same issue of *Scientific American*, says that "mechanized agriculture is very productive in terms of output per man-year, but it is not as productive per unit of land as the highly intensive systems are." Why, then, does it not make sense to advocate a return to smaller, family-type farms, on which human and animal labor can be effectively substituted for machines?

Second, if the size of farms continues to increase, and the farm population proportionately decreases, will not that population become at the same time more vulnerable, less surely able to reproduce itself? According to Professor Heady, it is one of the grand achievements of American agriculture that it now employs "only 4.4 percent of the nation's population." But at what level does a population—especially one in precipitous decline—become threatened with extinction? I assume, as perhaps Professor Heady does not, that in order to run our farms productively we will have to have farmers, that a knowledge of farming and of land stewardship are of direct value to those who farm, and that the most obvious and economical way to get farmers with this knowledge is to raise them. By this accounting, the knowledge and interest of the many young farmers who are now being priced off the land amounts to a sizable loss.

According to Professor Heady, American agriculture still has plenty of room to expand: if necessary, in order to increase production, we can plow and plant some hundreds of millions of acres of fallows, pastures, forests, range lands, and wetlands. Land, then, so far as he is concerned, is not an agricultural problem. And he evidently has no doubt that we will continue to have plenty of farmers. His worries come from another direction: "The future of American agriculture will depend on a number of factors in addition to its productive capacity. The two most important factors will be the extent to which recent international conditions continue to prevail and the presence or absence of Government policies affecting output either through future supply-control programs or environmental limits on fertilizers, pesticides and soil erosion." In other words, American agriculture will continue to prosper so long as hunger remains an international threat, so long as "agribusiness" is not restrained, and so long as "established farmers with large holdings" are left free to continue the pollution and soil erosion that are the inevitable by-products of industrial agriculture.

By this "most logical" of developments, then, we have passed from a farm-based, family-based, independent agriculture to an agriculture abjectly dependent upon many kinds of industrial "inputs" and firmly based upon several kinds of disaster. We are producing, at an incalculable waste of topsoil and of human life and energy, and at the cost of destroying communities and poisoning the land and the streams, food to be used against the hungry as a weapon.*

EXPERIENCE AND EXPERIMENT

Having for some years attentively read and listened to the statements of agriculture experts, I cannot have the comfort of looking upon Professor Heady as an anomaly. I am constrained to regard him as representative of that academic upper crust that has provided a species of agricultural vandalism with the prestige of its professorships and the justifications of a bogus intellectuality, incomprehensible to any order of thought, but decked out in statistics, charts, and graphs to silence unspecialized skepticism and astonish gullibility.

In spite of his eagerness to defend what he calls a "logical" program, there is no logic in Professor Heady's defense. His defense is deduction *without* logic, a kind of disordered scholasticism that proceeds merely by flinging statistics at a premise. That his premise is called into serious question—if not disproved—by his "proof" does not cause Professor Heady to hesitate.

If Professor Heady and his kind had not so much power, they would deserve far less attention. But because they do have power, because they belong to that association of industrial conquistadors who would claim our future as their colony, it is important to understand how, and how poorly, they think.

Like most of that association, Professor Heady is a specialist. Within the enclosure of his specialty he is no doubt capable of order and sense of a very formidable kind. But when he tries to justify these in terms of value and to say that they and the assumptions on which they rest are "good," then he produces disorder and nonsense, because the order of his specialty does not comprehend a ground large enough to permit such a justification. The calculations that

*At this point one thinks with some solicitude of the "developing countries" in which Professor Heady does "a lot of work." They are apparently in danger of taking the advice of an agricultural consultant the success of whose policy requires them to get hungry.

prove the efficacy of technology as a "substitute not only for land but also for labor" can do so convincingly only by ignoring the human and ecological contexts of the substitution. It would be possible to calculate the probable monetary cost of the unemployment, community and family breakdown, crime, vandalism, pollution, and soil loss that are the results of overwhelming "inputs" of technology— but apparently an agricultural economist is not expected to look either so widely around or so far ahead. Nor is any other agriculture expert. They are free to argue with the blind determination of fanatics from the premises that they prefer to the conclusions that they desire. It is an irony that would be amusing, were it not so frightening, that the prestigious "positions" that have relieved them of the necessity to use their hands have cost them the use of their heads.

No wonder they look forward so eagerly to the future. *We*, with our awkwardly divergent and valued lives, our bothersome rights and meanings, are not yet there. Only posterity is native there, and they have as yet produced nothing; they have no claim recognizable by an expert. The future is already surveyed and ribboned according to the claims of these people and their clients, the corporate industrialists and big businessmen. It is their New World, and they are its self-elected ruling class.

The expert knowledge of agriculture developed in the universities, like other such knowledges, is typical of the alien order imposed on a conquered land. We can never produce a native economy, much less a native culture, with this knowledge. It can only make us the imperialist invaders of our own country.

The reason is that this knowledge has no cultural depth or complexity whatever. It is concerned only with the most immediate practical (that is, economic and *sometimes* political) results. It has, for instance, never mastered the crucial distinction between experiment and experience. Experience, which is the basis of culture, tends always toward wholeness because it is interested in the *meaning* of what has happened; it is necessarily as interested in what does not work as in what does. It cannot hope or desire without remembering. Its approach to possibility is always conditioned by its remembrance of failure. It is therefore not an "objective" voice, but at once personal and communal. The experimental intelligence, on the other hand, is only interested in what works; what doesn't work is ruled out of consideration. This sort of intelligence tends to be shallow in that it tends to impose upon experience the metaphor of experiment.

It invariably sees innovation, not as adding to, but as replacing what existed or was used before. Thus machine technology is seen as a *substitute* for human or animal labor, requiring the "old way" to be looked upon henceforth with contempt. In technology, as in genetics, the experimental intelligence tends toward radical oversimplification, reducing the number of possibilities. Whereas the voice of experience, of culture, counsels, "Don't put all your eggs in one basket," the experimental intelligence, which behaves strangely like the intelligence of imperialists and religious fanatics, says, "This is the *only* true way."

And this intelligence protects itself from the disruptive memories and questions of experience by building around itself the compartmental structure of the modern university, in which effects and causes need never meet. The experimental intelligence is a tyrant that is saved from the necessity of killing bearers of bad news because it lives at the center of a maze in which the bearers of bad news are lost before they can arrive.

But it is imperative to understand that this sort of intelligence *is* tyrannical. It is at least potentially totalitarian. To think or act without cultural value, and the restraints invariably implicit in cultural value, is simply to wait upon force. This sort of behavior is founded in the cultural disintegration and despair which are also the foundation of political totalitarianism. Whether recognized or not, there is in the workings of agricultural specialization an implicit waiting for the total state power that will permit experimentally derived, technologically pure solutions to be imposed by force.

Woe to those who add house to house
and join field to field
until everywhere belongs to them
and they are the sole inhabitants of the land.

ISAIAH 5:8

. . . it is not too soon to provide by every possible means that as few as possible shall be without a little portion of land. The small landholders are the most precious part of a state. . . .

THOMAS JEFFERSON, LETTER TO REVEREND JAMES MADISON, OCTOBER 28, 1785

CHAPTER NINE

Margins

"AGRIBUSINESS" AS ORTHODOXY

Not all agricultural economists are blind to the human and ecological consequences of "agribusiness" economics. On March 1, 1972, Professor Philip M. Raup, of the University of Minnesota at St. Paul, testified as follows before the Subcommittee on Monopoly of the United States Senate Small Business Committee:

"Only in the past decade has serious attention been given to the fact that the large agricultural firm is . . . able to achieve benefits by externalizing certain costs. The disadvantages of large scale operation fall largely outside the decision-making framework of the large farm firm. Problems of waste disposal, pollution control, added burdens on public services, deterioration of rural social structures, impairment of the tax base, and the political consequences of a concentration of economic power have typically not been considered as costs of large scale, by the firm. They are unquestionably costs to the larger community.

"In theory, large-scale operation should enable the firm to bring a wide range of both benefits and costs within its internal decision-making framework. In practice, the economic and political power that accompanies large size provides a constant temptation to the large firm to take the benefits and pass on the costs.

"The rural community receives the immediate impact of this ability of large farm firms to practice selective internalization of benefits and externalization of costs. One of the most pervasive consequences is that the occupational composition of the population changes. Instead of a large number of small entrepreneurs, combining the functions of manager and laborer, the occupational structure includes a small number of managers and a large number of workers. In rural communities dominated by very large firms, the settlement and housing patterns reflect the increasingly transient nature of the labor force. The symbol of the large corporate farm becomes the trailer house. Community institutions suffer from lack of leadership, and from the lack of a sense of commitment on the part of the labor force to long-run community welfare. Those institutions that survive take on a dependent character, reflecting the paternalistic role of the dominant firms. Income levels may stabilize, but at the expense of a decline in local capacity for risk-taking, decision-making, and investment of family labor in farms and local businesses."

And later in his testimony, Professor Raup spoke of the most ironic of these "externalized" costs: "Farmers who have suceeded in increasing their farm size to a scale that will enable them to achieve almost all of the economics of size in production now find that their capital structure is so large that their sons cannot finance a takeover of the family farm."

Professor Raup's distinction between internal and external accounting is of great usefulness in understanding our problem. It is by internal accounting that the modern American agricultural program may be thought "the best, the most logical and the most successful." External accounting brings us to a very different conclusion. External accounting pushes us back into our moral tradition, which asks us to consider that we are members of the human community and are therefore bound to help or harm it by our behavior. This sort of accounting involves much more than economics. It is broad and difficult, and it eludes quantification.

Modern American agriculture has made itself a "science" and has preserved itself within its grandiose and destructive assumptions by cutting itself off from the moral tradition (as it has done also from the agricultural tradition) and confining its vision and its thought within the bounds of internal accounting. Agriculture experts and "agribusinessmen" are free to believe that their system works because they have accepted a convention which makes "external," and therefore irrelevant, all evidence that it does not work. "External" questions are not asked or heard, much less answered.

But these people are human beings who inherit a community

awareness, to whatever extent it may be suppressed, distorted, or ignored. Many, if not most, of them come from family farms, for which they feel some nostalgia, if no loyalty. And so it must be assumed that the claims of external accounting are still obscurely felt in the backs or the depths of their minds. Some of them may occasionally overhear their critics with a tremor of recognition; from time to time some of them may even come face to face with bad external results of internal purposes and recognize them as such. Internal accounting, then, must cohere under some pressure from the external. This obviously defines the necessary condition for a fierce and self-protective orthodoxy—a science-as-superstition, by which one clings to the assumption of the goodness of one kind of knowledge out of fear of knowledge of another kind. This fear makes the specialist scientist not merely willing to define a possibility, but *desperate* to define the *only* possibility. Only this desperation can explain the venomous contempt with which agricultural establishmentarians dismiss suggestions of other possibilities, old or new. These "objective" scientists exhibit an intense craving to be *right*—a craving hardly diminished by the profitability of their faith.

ORTHODOXY, MARGINS, AND CHANGE

Our history forbids us to be surprised that an orthodoxy of thought should become narrow, rigid, mercenary, morally corrupt, and vengeful against dissenters. This has happened over and over again. It might be thought the maturity of orthodoxy; it is what finally happens to a mind once it has consented to be orthodox. But one may be permitted a little amusement, if not surprise, that this should have befallen a modern science, which was set up, as it never tires of advertising, to *pursue* truth, not *protect* it.

But since what we now have in agriculture—as in several other "objective" disciplines—is a modern scientific orthodoxy as purblind, self-righteous, cocksure, and ill-humored as Cotton Mather's, our history also forbids us to expect it to change from within itself. Like many another orthodoxy, it would rather die than change, and may change only by dying.* This determination is enforced both

*Orthodox agriculture is part of the larger orthodoxy of industrial progress and economic growth, which argues the necessity of pollution, unemployment, war, land spoliation, the exploitation of space, etc. And so the question is: Must we all die with it in order for it to change?

from within and from without. It is enforced from within simply by prosperity: the professors, experts, and executives of the agrifaith do not want agricultural policy to change because they are eating very well off of it as it is. From without, it is enforced by the mistaken conviction of millions of believers that it is the only true way, that they have no choice but to accept the agribusiness philosophy or starve. But it is also enforced by the very nature of orthodoxy: one who presumes to *know* the truth does not *look* for it.

If change is to come, then, it will have to come from the outside. It will have to come from the margins. As an orthodoxy loses its standards, becomes unable to measure itself by what it ought to be, it comes to be measured by what it is not. The margins begin to close in on it, to break down the confidence that supports it, to set up standards clarified by a broadened sense of purpose and necessity, and to demonstrate better possibilities. Though it does not necessarily or always work for the better—though indeed this swing from the center to the margins and back again may be in itself a condemnation—this sort of change is a dominant theme of our tradition, whose "central" figures have often worked their way inward from the margins. It was the desert, not the temple, that gave us the prophets; the colonies, not the motherland, that gave us Adams and Jefferson.

The pattern of orthodoxy in religion, because it is well known, gives us a useful paradigm. The encrusted religious structure is not changed by its institutional dependents—they are part of the crust. It is changed by one who goes alone to the wilderness, where he fasts and prays, and returns with cleansed vision. In going alone, he goes independent of institutions, forswearing orthodoxy ("right opin-ion"). In going to the wilderness he goes to the margin, where he is surrounded by the possibilities—by no means all good—that orthodoxy has excluded. By fasting he disengages his thoughts from the immediate issues of livelihood; his willing hunger takes his mind off the payroll, so to speak. And by praying he acknowledges ignorance; the orthodox presume to *know*, whereas the marginal person is trying to find out. He returns to the community, not necessarily with new truth, but with a new vision of the truth; he sees it more whole than before.

In applying this pattern to agriculture, one is startled to realize that this is the first time it has been necessary, or possible, to do so. Not until recently have we had a widespread orthodoxy of agri-culture in the same sense that we have had widespread orthodoxies of religion—an agriculture, that is to say, which is nearly uniform in technology and in its general assumptions and ambitions over a whole continent, and which, like many religions, aspires to become "universal" by means of a sort of evangelism, proclaiming that "Other countries would do well to copy it."

In agriculture there have always been prevalent patterns of technology, practice, and attitude that may have had the customary force of orthodoxy. But these patterns were local; they varied in response to local conditions. And, unlike orthodoxies, they were not imposed by external authority, but grew as part of a complex relationship between the human community and natural conditions. Until the triumph of the industrial values of the "agribusiness" vision, agriculture was very much a regional affair, a response at once to human need and to regional possibilities and limits, and it was successful and long-lasting in proportion to the sensitivity of that response.

A PRE-INDUSTRIAL EXAMPLE

By looking at an example of a sound pre-industrial agriculture we can get a sense of its ecological and cultural coherence and its geographical responsiveness and also a sense of its careful relationship to its margins. Perhaps no more vivid example exists in our time than that of the native agriculture of the Peruvian Andes. I take the following summary from an unpublished paper by Professor Stephen B. Brush, of the Department of Anthropology at the College of William and Mary.

Professor Brush's study focuses on the village of Uchucmarca in a valley in northern Peru. This valley has "one of the steepest environmental gradients in the world." Like other Andean farmers, the people of Uchucmarca farm in four different climatic zones, requiring four different kinds of agriculture:

"1. a tropical zone . . . which produces fruit (such as oranges and bananas), tropical root plants (such as manioc), chile peppers, and perhaps most importantly *coca* . . .

"2. a middle level mountain zone . . . where maize and wheat are grown . . .

"3. a relatively high mountain zone . . . where the staple of the Andean diet, potatoes, and other Andean tubers are grown . . .

"4. a high mountain zone . . . where llamas, alpacas, sheep, horses, and cattle are grazed on natural pasture . . ."

Within a distance of forty miles the valley rises from "roughly 3,200 feet" to "over 14,700 feet"—thus including a diversity of climates as great as that from west Texas to Alaska. The natives of the valley "recognize and name seven different production zones . . . which are variations on the four major zones."

The agriculture of the valley is based upon a highly evolved awareness of the nature of each of these climatic zones and of the differences among them. It involves a careful balance between the use and the maintenance of productivity. Professor Brush says that "The village economy may be understood as a set of subsistence strategies designed to provision each household with adequate food. . . . One of the most important features of the local economy is that it is able to function as a largely nonmonetized economy. The average family in Uchucmarca needs less than $100 yearly. . ." It is significant that the verb in that last sentence is "needs," where "agribusiness" assumptions would require "has only." The governing concept of the agriculture of these Andean peasants, then, is *enough*, a long-term sufficiency, whereas the governing concept of ours is *profit* or *affluence*, without regard for long-term needs.*

Like most farmers, those of Uchucmarca must cope with the hazards of erosion, frost, too much or too little rain, pests, and diseases. They do this very effectively and without recourse to the industrial technology of machines and chemicals.

"The danger of erosion is avoided in three ways. First, fields are kept small—usually less than one acre. . . . A typical family of four to five persons cultivates between three and four acres, spread among as many fields. The small size of individual plots retards run-off and erosion. Second, each field is surrounded by a hedgerow constructed of rocks, brush, and living plants. Ostensibly built to keep out destructive livestock, these hedgerows effectively limit erosion. Their roots hold the soil, and horizontal plowing behind them tends to build up soil at the lower side of the field. This creates a quasi-terrace or lynchet. . . . Third, field rotation is practiced in the highest and steepest part of the valley where rainfall is heaviest and erosion most likely. Potatoes are cultivated under a regime of shifting cultivation

*In a letter to me, dated February 15, 1977, Professor Brush wrote as follows: ". . . I calculate that with their 'primitive' agriculture, the farmers of Uchucmarca produce 2700 calories and 80 grams of protein (vegetable) per capita per day. A very good diet and a well fed population. The worst malnutrition occurs in cities where people must depend on 'modern' agriculture."

in which fields are only planted for two or three years before being returned to a long fallow of five years or more. By using this method, the amount of soil washed off of fields is limited, and organic material is allowed to reaccumulate."

The people of Uchucmarca cope with climatic variations by "the exploitation of multiple zones and crops," so that if one crop fails they may rely on one of a different kind. "Another way is to plant several different fields of the same crop, hoping that if one field is destroyed, the other will survive. These means are reinforced by systems of economic reciprocity and mutual dependence which rely primarily on the kinship system." Within families, "individual households protect themselves from privation by exchanging land, labor, and goods."

Against insects and diseases, the main weapon of the Andean peasants is genetic diversity: "Botanists estimate that there are well over 2,000 potato varieties in Peru alone. In single villages like Uchucmarca people identify some fifty varieties . . ." And here we arrive at the greatest complexity, versatility, and responsiveness of this agriculture, as well as its most intense sensitivity to place. For these varieties are not used at random, but are delicately fitted into their appropriate ecological niches. "In Uchucmarca, a common practice is to plant fast growing varieties during the drier part of the year so as to avoid late blight which increases during the months of heavy rain. Another practice is to cultivate certain varieties believed to be somewhat frost resistant in flat, bottom areas of the high valley where frost but not late blight is common. Other varieties are chosen for hillside cultivation where late blight but not frost is common." Varieties are also chosen according to how well they do at certain altitudes or according to whether or not they need a soil that drains well. Of course, this description gives only a rough idea of the intricacy of possible adjustments among so many varieties and so many kinds of ground.

Professor Brush's work makes it plain that nearly all the methods of the Andean farmers are based upon the one principle of diversity. In their understanding and use of this principle, they have developed an agriculture much more sophisticated, efficient, and conservative of the soil than our own—and one that is also much more likely to survive a crisis. How finely this agriculture is attuned to the needs and circumstances of the community becomes apparent when Professor Brush describes recent attempts to change it by the introduction of industrial technology and "improved" potato varieties. Such change involves a gross simplification of the agriculture itself as well as a drastic complication of the economy. It requires a cash economy and credit, favors the larger producers, and threatens to destroy both the human community and the ecological viability of a farming system that is "the result of thousands of years of natural and human selection."

But the sophistication and durability of Andean agriculture cannot be fully appreciated until one has understood the way it utilizes—indeed, depends upon—its margins. The fifty potato varieties used in Uchucmarca are not a stable quantity, but rather a sort of genetic vocabulary in a state of continuous revision. Professor Brush says that "new varieties are constantly being created through cross-pollination between cultivated, wild and semidomesticated (weedy) species. . . . These wild and semidomesticated species thrive in the hedgerows around fields, and birds and insects living there assist cross-pollination." Thus, if an Andean farmer loses a crop because of an extremity of the weather or an infestation of insects or disease, he may find a plant of a new variety that has survived the calamity and produced in spite of it. If he finds such a plant, he may add it to his collection of domesticated varieties or substitute it for the one that has failed.

This Andean agriculture, then, does not push its margins back to land unsuitable for farming, as ours does, but incorporates them into the very structure of its farms. The hedgerows are marginal areas, little thoroughfares of wilderness closely crisscrossing the farmland, and in them agriculture is constantly renewing itself in direct response to what threatens it. This network of wilderness threading through the fields serves the Andean farmer as a college of agriculture and experiment station. And in at least one respect it serves him better: whatever is discovered there has already been tested in the circumstances of the farm itself, and its worth or worthlessness proven. The farmer, in whose mind culture and agriculture are wedded, acts as both teacher-researcher and student, both extension agent and client. Set thus in the light of a truly healthy agriculture, our land-grant college complex may be seen less as a symbol of our agricultural success than as a symptom of our failure.

And this integration of Andean farming with its margins may serve us in another way. It offers an example of a sort of reconciliation by which we might escape the endless swinging between center and margins, rigidity and revolt, that has dominated our culture for so long. The remedy is to accommodate the margin within the form, to allow the wilderness or nature to thrive in domesticity, to accommodate diversity within unity. It is surely by this means—this graceful, practical generosity toward the possible and the unexpected, toward time and history—that Andean agriculture has survived for so long, cohering even through the severe disturbances of the Spanish Conquest. By responding competently to whatever has threatened it, and by doing so in the most local and immediate fashion, it has kept its hold on the world, much as life itself has kept its hold. Having understood this reconciliation or integration of the human community with its natural margins, we may see how crude and dangerous are our absolute divisions between city and farmland, farmland and wilderness, by which we seek to exclude from our domestic enclosures everything for which we have foreseen no use or market.

This principle of accommodating the margins, of diversity within unity, underlies our Constitution and Bill of Rights. But we live by this principle only negatively and grudgingly: we *permit* or *tolerate* dissent and divergence because the law requires us to. And the law can do no more than that. To put dissent and divergence to use, to turn a curious eye to the margins, eager to see what may have been tried and proven there, we will need a sounder, saner culture than we have.

MARGINS AND HEALTH

By narrowing itself so fanatically, orthodox agriculture has, in one sense, left its margins extremely wide. For motive power, it has made itself almost exclusively dependent on the internal combustion engine, and its ambition is to become completely so—leaving out of use or consideration the large variety of tools and techniques for the employment of human and animal power. Its earlier dependence on wind and water power—for pumping, milling, etc.—has now been shifted to electricity. It has little interest in on-the-farm collection and use of methane gas or solar energy.

It has greatly reduced regional differences in technology, methods of tillage, soil husbandry, etc. At the same time, it has reduced the variety of production within regions. This is, as Maurice Telleen says, "the regional specialization, that inevitably flows from individual specialization." And, just as dangerously, it has reduced the genetic diversity of both field crops and animals.

It has drawn an ever straighter, stricter line between the domestic and the wild, crowding nature itself into the margins. For the complex biological wilderness of a healthy topsoil it has substituted a simple chemistry. It has plowed up fence rows and roadsides and waterways, bulldozed woodlands, drained and plowed marshes. It has made itself not only inhospitable but dangerous to wild animals, birds, and harmless or beneficial insects.

It has made a margin even of the agricultural past, which is no longer regarded as a resource, a fund of experience, or a lexicon of proven possibilities and understood mistakes, but only as an amusement for the idly curious or, in advertisements, a measure of "how far we have come." Farm-equipment corporations are fond of printing old photographs to show the "drawbacks" of the agricultural past in comparison to the shiny "sophistication" of modern times. But as a working principle, whatever has been displaced or outmoded is simply ignored. About anything "old-fashioned," whatever its worth, the invariable comment is that "You can't go back."

For the principle of diversity, in nature and in earlier agriculture, and for the principle of unity that includes and depends upon diversity, orthodox agriculture has substituted a dull, tight uniformity, not only ignorant of other possibilities, but scared of them, and vengeful in its ignorance.

People who remove their minds from this shadowy twilight of agribigotry find that they are surrounded by an abundance of divergent possibilities—from our own past, from the history and present practice of other peoples, from new technology, from new understandings of biology and ecology. But they soon become aware, especially if their interest in agriculture is personal and practical, that this wide margin is only a margin in the mind, seriously beset by speculations, questions, and doubts. The possibilities obviously do exist as possibilities, but where do they exist in proof? Where are they being enacted by a living farmer on a living farm? Having arrived at these questions, one realizes that as the margin of divergent possibility has widened around orthodox agriculture, the margins of geography and practice have been drastically narrowed. Who are the people who know how to farm in these other—and, one believes, better—ways? And where are they? They are few, as the saying goes, and they are far between.

In the last few years, I have made an effort to do a little traveling along the agricultural margins, to visit farms where unorthodox ways are working, to see for myself what these dissident farmers are doing, and to listen to what they have to say. In telling about them, I wish to respect their privacy, and so I will not give their names or say very specifically where they live.

Nor, except for some merely descriptive figures, will I deal very much in statistics. I have chosen instead to rely on the evidence that I have seen, and that other people can see, too, if they will look carefully. One need not be a specialist to understand the difference between good and bad farming. There is nothing mysterious or abstruse about it. It only requires enough acquaintance with land and people to have some sense of what a prospering farm and a prospering farm community ought to look like and the same acquaintance with the signs of greed, hopelessness, neglect, and abandonment.

The health of a farm is as apparent to the eye as the health of a person. To look at a farm in full health gives the same complex pleasure as looking at a fully healthy person or animal. It will give the same impression of abounding life. What grows on it will be thriving. It will seem to belong where it is; the form of it will be a considerate response to the nature of its place; it will not have the look of an abstract idea of a farm imposed upon an area somewhere or other. It will look cared for—groomed, so to speak—like a healthy person or animal; it will look lived in by people who care where they live. It will show no gullies or galls or other signs of erosion. The waterways and field edges and areas around buildings will be grassed, something that becomes more necessary the steeper the ground is.

The place will look well maintained. Buildings, fences, equipment, etc., will have been kept in good repair, carefully used, protected from the weather. One of the commonest sights associated with orthodox farming is a lot of huge, expensive farm machinery left sitting out in the weather, having, like the economy that produced it, outgrown the possibility of care. Like the land itself, the equipment is used but not protected. This is one of the first and most ironic results of the high costs of industrial agriculture. The farmer is forced to protect his investment at the expense of what he has invested in. He plows out his waterways, abusing the land to get the maximum use of it and his machinery, and then allows the machinery to rust to save the cost of the necessary buildings. Such an economy will make a difference very quickly in the looks of a farm, as it will make a difference in the looks of a person or a nation.

A healthy farm will have trees on it—woodlands, where forest trees are native, but also fruit and nut trees, trees for shade and for windbreaks. Trees will be there for their usefulness: for food, lumber, fence posts, firewood, shade, and shelter. But they will also be there for comfort and pleasure, for the wildlife that they will harbor, and for their beauty. The woodlands bespeak the willingness to let live that keeps wildness flourishing in the settled place. A part of the health of a farm is the farmer's wish to remain there. His long-term good intention toward the place is signified by the presence of trees. A family is married to a farm more by their planting and protecting of trees than by their memories or their knowledge, for the trees stand for their fidelity and kindness to what they do not know. The most revealing sign of the ill health of industrial agriculture—its greed, its short-term ambitions—is its inclination to see trees as obstructions and to strip the land bare of them.

Woodlands, orchards, and shade trees are part of the diversity of life that is another of the prime characteristics of a healthy farm. And this principle will extend to cropland and pasture. The aim of a healthy farm will be to produce as many kinds of plants and animals as it sensibly can. This will be an *ordered* diversity, the various species moving in rotation over the fields. The land will be fenced for livestock, and its aspect will change from field to field.

Related to the principle of diversity is that of carrying capacity: the various crops and animals will be sensibly proportionate to one another; the farm will strive as far as possible toward the balance, the symmetry, of an ecological system; there will not be too much of anything. The fields will not be overcropped; the pastures will not be overgrazed. It will be understood that the plants growing on a farm are not just its produce, but also its protection, and so a row crop will be followed by a cover crop, the cover crop by a sod of grass and clover.

And a healthy farm not only will have the right proportion of plants and animals; it will have the right proportion of people. There will not be so many as to impoverish themselves and the farm, but there will be enough to care for it fully and properly without overwork. On a healthy farm there will be the right proportion between work and rest. Outside the Amish communities I do not know where in American agriculture one can find people and land in healthy balance. As far as I know, the Amish are the only American community to have formed deliberate strategies to keep enough people on the farms. All the non-Amish, full-time working farms that I have seen in this country have showed the need of more human hands.

Finally, a healthy farm will be so far as possible independent and self-sustaining. It is necessary to say "so far as possible," for we are by no means talking here about a "closed system." Simply by selling produce, a farm involves itself with other places both economically and biologically. And unless it encapsulates itself under a glass roof— which is really to become less independent—a farm cannot produce its own weather. Many farms cannot provide their own water. The wild plants, animals, birds, and insects upon which a farm's health depends will not respect its boundaries any more than the rain. And, of course, the people of a farm will belong complexly to a larger human community. Nevertheless, a certain kind and a certain measure of independence is a practicable ambition for a farm, and it is a necessity of agricultural health and longevity.

For one thing, fertility, the major capital of any farm, can be largely renewed and maintained from sources on the farm itself— assuming that all else is in balance. By proper tillage, rotation, the use of legumes, and the return of manure and other organic wastes to the soil, the fields can be kept productive with minimal recourse to fertilizers from outside sources. If the organic or decayable wastes of the cities, which have their source on the farm, could be returned to the farm, that would greatly increase both the health of the land and the independence, if not of the individual farm, at least of agriculture.

Equally important, by the good use of human power, animal power, solar, wind, and water power, methane gas, firewood from its own woodlands, etc., a farm can produce by far the major part of its own energy. This, of course, calls for a revitalization of local skills. But given the skills, these sources of power are possible. They come from the past and/or from new technology.

As a farm measures up in these various ways to the standard of health, its troubles from pests and diseases will radically diminish, and so consequently will its dependence on chemicals. A healthy farm will have no more need for these expensive remedies than a healthy person has for medicine.

Health, then, does not "come from" independence or "lead to" it. Health *is* independence. The healthy farm sustains itself the same way that a healthy tree does: by belonging where it is, by maintaining a proper relationship to the ground. It is by this standard of health or independence that one recognizes the absurdity of a farm absolutely dependent upon a complex of industrial corporations, which are in turn dependent upon the actions of foreign governments and politicians whom the farmer did not vote for or against and cannot influence.

The ultimate good health of a farm is in its ability to produce independently of the ups and downs of the Dow Jones industrial averages or the vagaries of politics. (When I visit a farm I always look to see how many trademarks and brand names are in sight. The orthodox industrial farm is, among other things, an advertising space for any number of corporations.) Those who pride themselves on the "science" that has made agriculture an industry have found this sort of independence simply beneath their notice. But I have watched, in Tuscany, a plowman driving a team of white cattle to a wooden plow, and realized that I was seeing the continuance of a motion and a way and a preoccupation begun before the rise of Rome. It is not nostalgia or sentimentality or wishful thinking to say that that man and his plow and team on the hand-built terrace under the olive trees represented a value, perhaps an immeasurable value, that modern agriculture has superseded but has by no means replaced.

A MARGINAL PLACE

But one's travels should begin at home. Before speaking of my travels on the margins in other places, I would like to say something about the margins I live among. Perhaps that will give an idea of what I have had in my mind as a sort of basis, and of the meanings and possibilities I have been looking for.

Not far from my house there is a hillside whose soil, declivity, and history are fairly representative of much of the hillside land in my part of the country. At one time this hillside was covered with a fine hardwood forest, which was no doubt cut soon after the establishment of the white people's tenure. The logs may have been sawed into lumber, but more likely they were burned simply to rid the land of them. The land was used agriculturally, for both row crops and pasture, with results that will remain visible for many more generations than the land was in use. Around the time of the Second World War, when machines began to replace the horse and mule teams as well as the people, the hillside began to "go back to the bushes." The thicket growth that follows agriculture began to take it over.

It is still "in bushes." In some places the better forest hardwoods have begun to establish themselves again among the weed trees. In other places there are still tangles of briars, cedars, thorns, sumac, box elder, elm. Under the trees are the slowly healing scoops and gullies of old erosion—part of the "investment" in a way of farming unsuited to the place, which no generation's income will ever redeem.

Walking along the contour of the slope, one crosses at intervals a series of natural waterways cut to the rock and running straight down the hill. The plows stopped short of these places by somewhat more than the length of a horse. The land here is whole; one supposes that it is virgin. The trees here are larger, and species grow here that do not grow in the abandoned fields. Beside one of these hollows, high up the slope, there is a big tulip poplar, a loam-loving tree rarely found in the uplands. It is two feet thick at the butt, and its trunk rises thirty or forty feet to the first branch. It is comparatively young, not by many years a survivor of the original forest, but in its proportions and its great health it is a reminder of that forest. It stands there on the edge of the hollow, not just because it has been spared, but because it is growing in excellent soil.

And so on the one hillside you are aware of crossing agricultural margins of two radically different kinds: one that farming damaged and has virtually abandoned and one that farming never came to. The second is not only the indispensable measure of the first, telling us by how much our history here has failed, but it shows us just as exactly what we must aspire to. It is an indispensable example, a little border of health along the edge of bewilderment and defeat.

But what of the abandoned fields, hidden with their scars under the bushes? What are we to think of them? Many people would say that we should not think of them at all, that they are fit only for growing bushes, as they are doing. But I disagree. If we are to have a respectable agriculture we will have to think competently and kindly of lands of all sorts, even the apparently useless. But, in fact, this hillside is not even apparently useless. Its soil, even where badly eroded, is fertile and readily responsive to good treatment. Such hillsides can be made to produce excellent pasture. I know that this is so because I have seen it done and I have done it myself.

And pasture is not all that such slopes are good for. They might, with care, be made to support a kind of mixed or "two-story" agriculture of both pasture (with selectively located hay crops) and trees. Natural stands of walnut trees are already established and thriving on many of these overgrown hillsides. These stands can be managed for their yield of nuts, for timber, or for both. And they could be augmented by planting grafted varieties of walnuts and perhaps of other native nut and fruit trees. If these plantings were done on the contour, perhaps along the backslopes of terraces, they would be perfectly compatible with the use of the land for pasture and hay.

The fertility of these slopes is by no means unknown to local farmers. But at present the use of them is problematic. The almost invariable method of clearing them nowadays is to bulldoze all the forest or thicket growth off the entire hillside at once, occasionally leaving an exceptional walnut or shade tree, and then either pile the brush and burn it or shove it off into the hollows, where much of the topsoil that comes in with it may be washed away and wasted. The cleared land is usually sowed in fescue or a mixture of fescue and clover. Rarely can a farmer afford the time and expense of sowing rye or another quick-growing crop along with the grass. Until a sod is established, the slope is seriously vulnerable to erosion, and soil loss is frequently added to the other expenses of the job. Some farmers mow these cleared fields once a year with tractors and rotary mowers, and so keep the bushes from returning. You can find some hill pastures kept in good shape in this way. But mowing them with a tractor is both dangerous and expensive, and far more time-consuming than the same work on leveler land. And the use of a tractor tends to work against any hospitality the farmer may feel toward trees; a tractor driver on a steep slope will look at a tree as at best an obstacle and at worst a hazard.

Another common practice, used to save time and expense, is simply to bulldoze the trees and bushes off the land, sow it to pasture, and then stock it heavily with cattle. As the pasture becomes stale and overgrazed, the cattle turn to browsing on the sprouts that come up from the old tree roots, and so for a while the bushes are controlled. But the cost of this practice is high, for the hillside suffers serious erosion from the combination of overgrazing and heavy trampling in wet weather and is finally grown over by the thorns and other rough trees that the cattle refuse to eat.

The good use of such land (use that is at once full, efficient, and careful) requires something altogether different and is probably unthinkable in terms of our present agricultural economy and cultural values. Good use calls, first, for great care in clearing, minimal groundbreaking, minimal bulldozing. Clearing probably should be done in narrow strips on the contour, working from the top of the slope downward in successive years. Terracing should be considered, wherever feasible; it seems to me that slowing and retaining the run-off behind terraces might make excellent sense in combination with the planting of tree crops. In some situations, when there is time and when earth does not have to be moved to repair washes, the over-growth may be taken off by sawing; the best thrift would salvage a great quantity of fence posts and firewood from this sort of clearing. The steeper slopes, of course, should not be cleared at all, but should be left in trees for shade and to be selectively logged for posts, fire-wood, or lumber. The rule would be to clear only what can safely be kept clear.

Second, after clearing, the land should be sowed as quickly as possible. This sowing should include as great a diversity of clovers and grasses as makes sense for the location. (I have lately been using both bluegrass and fescue, as well as a clover mixture consisting of red, ladino, and sweet clovers, and Korean lespedeza.) A quick-growing "shelter crop" should be sowed with the pasture mixture to hold the ground until the grass and clover can get established. The seed can be sowed right onto the disturbed ground, which then ought to be passed over with a light harrow to cover the seed a little and to smooth the surface.

Third, such land needs to be managed intensively and in small fields. Steep land requires close attention, thorough understanding, and selfless care. It must be mowed at least once a year to control weeds and bushes, to stimulate new growth, and to encourage uni-form grazing. Stock should be rotated from field to field, both to keep enough growth on the ground to protect it and to prevent the wearing of paths. Grazing such land too closely endangers it, and paths can be disastrous, especially if they run up and down the hill. For these reasons, large numbers of animals are incompatible with the good use of hill land; a big herd can do severe damage to a slope when the animals all must converge daily on the same watering or feeding places, gates, or milking barns. A good hill farm, if it is located where climate and soil permit intensive use, is almost by definition a small farm; and, insofar as it benefits from long-standing knowledge and devoted care, it is almost by definition a family farm. Nothing could be more alien to healthy agriculture than a large, production- or profit-oriented hill farm whose owner or owners do not live on it. In such a situation the balance between use and care is overthrown, and waste is the result. The small differences may be the most important. A family farmer, for instance, will walk his fields out of interest; the industrial farmer or manager only out of necessity.

And, finally, the good use of hill land requires a technology appropriate to it in scale and cost. Here we approach what most of the agriculture specialists and all of the "agribusinessmen" would be quick to describe as nostalgia or fantasy or craziness. They would do this to protect themselves and their assumptions and to disguise their most serious error. For the true measure of agriculture is not the sophistication of its equipment, the size of its income, or even the statistics of its productivity, but the good health of the land. And we are talking here about seriously damaged but potentially useful land, where American agriculture has so far failed. One must assume that if these hills *could* be farmed well with big, expensive, "modern" technology, they *would* be. That they are not suggests both that the technology is ill-suited to the terrain and that the cost cannot be afforded.

What sort of technology might make sense on such land? It will be at least strongly suggestive at this point to quote Thomas P. Cooper, one-time dean and director of the Extension Division of the University of Kentucky College of Agriculture:

"In Kentucky and many other states there are farming areas where work animals are indispensable. Small farms, hillside fields, rolling land and poorly drained areas can be successfully and economically farmed only by the use of horses and mules. The economic advantage of the use of workstock instead of power machinery for farm use is that horses and mules can be raised on farm-produced grasses and grains and maintained, while at work, in the same way. Farmers who own rolling or infertile farms, or who are farming on a subsistence basis are unable to purchase tractors or other power machinery. Such farmers are able to raise horses or mules and to use them to do farm work with the outlay of but little money. . . .

"There is much work on large as well as on small farms that can be done successfully and economically by horses or mules."

That circular is dated November 1937. I would not argue that we ought to "go back" to 1937. That, I am sure, *would* be nostalgic, fantastical, and crazy. But I am not so sure that what was considered "indispensable" in 1937 can be simply dismissed as "out-of-date" in 1977. My doubt is strengthened by the fact that in the intervening forty years, on thousands of acres of such land as I have

188

just described, Dean Cooper's successors have produced, not a better agriculture or even a different one, but virtually none at all. That is, they have removed from consideration a way of farming suited to certain kinds of land and have replaced it merely with neglect and waste. It is notable that Dean Cooper's approach is to look at both the land and the farmer and then to suggest a suitable technology, whereas the approach of his successors has been to focus on the most "up-to-date" technology and expect the land and the farmer to conform to it. They seem to have answered Dean Cooper's argument that horses and mules were indispensable for certain farmers on certain lands by declaring that those farmers and those lands were themselves dispensable. I suggest that in light of the staggering losses of both farmers and land since 1937, and in light of the social problems and food needs of 1977, this assumption may be seen to be what it has always been: an extremely serious error of judgment.

A MARGINAL PERSON

The hillside that I have described, then, represents both a marginal place and a marginal possibility. As such, it is a measure both of local agricultural history and of the capacities and limits of prevailing agricultural technology and practice. But the full force of the necessary judgment will not be felt until I have also described a marginal person.

Some years ago I frequently used to drive past a farm in a creek valley of narrow, scarce bottomlands and hillsides rougher and less fertile than the one I have been talking about. The farm was small, mostly hillside, with a few narrow ridges and a creek bottom that could not have been larger than an acre and a half. In an area of semi-abandoned land, this farm was outstanding, not because of its "improvements," which were old and few, but because it was clearly both well used and well cared for. It was farmed by an old man and woman and a team of Percheron horses.

Everything about the place was neatly kept. House and yard and barn always showed a resident pride. There was an orderly, abundant vegetable garden beside the house. The pastures were mowed every summer. The tiny bottomland where the old man grew his tobacco crop was cut into three or four pieces by waterways which were grassed and bridged. More than anything else, those little timber bridges bespoke the old man's care; the usual thing would have been to drive regardlessly across such shallow drains and so wear the banks away. In addition to the team of horses, the pastures were stocked with a little herd of excellent beef cows.

This place interested me because it was a *good* marginal farm and because it was obviously a relic, the lone survivor within hundreds of square miles of a kind of farm that had been commonplace only thirty or thirty-five years ago. And finally it, too, went the way of the rest of them.

As I watched the old man's farm, driving by it at intervals, I saw it suddenly begin to change. The yard began to look unkept. Disorder began to spread around the house. The team of horses disappeared. I learned a little of the story. The old man had died. His wife had moved to town to live with her children. The house had been rented to people who, though they had technically become its residents, clearly did not *live* there. The farm also had begun to be used by someone who did not belong to it.

I had stopped once and talked a while with the old man. He was busy fixing a fence at the time, and though he received me courteously enough, he did not permit himself to be much interrupted. I told him that I admired his farm. He thanked me, but without enthusiasm, obviously having spent little time yearning to be complimented by strangers. I said his team of horses looked like a good one. He said that they did very well.

One morning after I had learned of his death, I stopped at the farm again—in his honor, maybe, or in honor of my own sense of loss. It was a gray, wintery day. The place looked and felt forgotten. It had gone out of mind. Absence was in it like a force. The barn was closed, empty, the doors tied shut by someone who did not intend to come back very soon. Peering in through a crack, I found that I was looking into a milking room with homemade wooden stanchions, unused for years. I knew why: it had become impossible to be a *small* dairyman. I spent some time looking at the old man's horse-drawn equipment. Some antique collector had taken the metal seats off several of the machines; these had become bar stools, perhaps, in somebody's suburban ranch house. For the rest apparently nobody now had a use. Examining the pieces of equipment, I saw that they were nearly completely worn out, patched and wired together like the fences and buildings, made to do—the forlorn tools of a man who had heirs, but no successors.

By the standards of orthodox agriculture, as well as by those of the present economy and culture, this old man and his farm were merely anachronisms, leftovers. The possibility of their existence would seem contemptible, not just to the majority of agriculture experts, but to the majority of influential people of other kinds. And yet we must ask *why*. And we must be careful not to accept too hasty or easy an answer. For no matter what may be said by the current standards of economics or technology or cultural fashion about this old man's life, there is still no legitimate way of withholding respect from him. In a time when millions of people, including very able and expensively educated young people, are finding it easy to accept a dependence on welfare or unemployment, and when millions more are dependent on social security and other public means of support, here was a man who worked until he died, taking care of himself and of his part of the earth.

The curious thing is that many agriculture specialists and "agribusinessmen" see themselves as conservatives. They look with contempt upon governmental "indulgence" of those who have no more "moral fiber" than to accept "handouts" from the public treasury— but they look with equal contempt upon the most traditional and appropriate means of independence. What do such conservatives wish to conserve? Evidently nothing less than the great corporate blocks of wealth and power, in whose every interest is implied the moral degeneracy and economic dependence of the people. They do not esteem the possibility of a prospering, independent class of small owners because they are, in fact, not conservatives at all, but the most doctrinaire and disruptive of revolutionaries.

Nevertheless, the old man and his farm together made a sort of cultural unit, recognized and valued in this country from colonial times. And it is still a perfectly respectable human possibility. All it requires is the proper humanity.

TRADITION AND EXPERIENCE

It is of great importance to understand that the marginal possibility, the marginal place, and the marginal humanity that I have been describing are reinforced by a marginal way of thinking—until now a sort of counter-theme in our history, so far always subordinate to the theme of exploitation, but unbroken and still alive. This is the theme of settlement, of kindness to the ground, of nurture.

To exhibit this theme, in both its articulateness and its commonness, I offer the following quotations from the *Farmers Home Journal*, a regional farm magazine once published in Louisville, Kentucky. The quotations are taken from the issue of January 2, 1892.

One correspondent writes "to urge every man in Kentucky to set out nut-bearing trees." And this purpose is urged upon the writer by his sense of the necessity of *settling* on the land: "The first thing a young man should do is to get him a home; the next thing get him a wife, and next set him an orchard, but do not think an orchard complete till you have set a few nut-bearing trees."

Another writes that "No man . . . should spend his labor and time over so large an acreage as to fail in making a first class garden." (The reader should be reminded here that the agricultural orthodoxy boasts that farm families have become patrons of the supermarkets.)

Even as early as 1892, we meet industrial arrogance, already fully inflated: "That farmers do not apply more commercial manures to their gardens is mainly because they do not think."

But we also have an example of such not-thinking in a letter from "W. C." of Rural Neck, Kentucky, a place no longer on the map. W. C.'s letter is an exuberant essay on the economy of the soil, and he makes a direct connection between that economy and the economy of money. He recommends the use, as fertilizer, of manure fresh from the barn, and also of scrapings from the barn lot, rotten straw from last year's threshing, old piles of chips and ashes, anything that will rot. "Yes, rot is the word. Rot means death, and without death and rot there can be no new life." He says that one can even use bone dust or superphosphate. "But it won't do for a farmer to go in debt for special or commercial fertilizers, as a rule. You can more safely go in debt for a good stable manure. . . . Nature never loses anything: she preserves and protects herself. It is only a fool man who squanders his substance and makes himself poor, and everybody around him, and the land that he lives on too." He follows this with an attack on soil erosion and praise for manure, industry, and brains. And he concludes: "When people learn to preserve the richness of the land that God has given them, and the rights to enjoy the fruits of their own labors, then will be the time when all shall have meat in the smokehouse, corn in the crib and time to go to the election."

It is a remarkable letter. W. C.'s argument is the one we get— howbeit with greatly increased scientific authority—from Sir Albert Howard, but W. C. is stating it plainly enough fifty years before

Howard's books were published. "Rot means death, and without death and rot there can be no new life." This is a principle as new and common as biology, as old and exalted as the Bible: "Except a corn of wheat fall into the ground and die, it abideth alone: but if it die, it bringeth forth much fruit." And W. C.'s voice is seamlessly joined to those of his fellow correspondents who were insisting on the importance of home, household and family, orchard and garden.

What are we to make of these undistinguished men from out-of-the-way places, who pled their cause with the eloquence of good sense and the exuberance of conviction? Jefferson spoke for them in politics. Albert Howard would speak for them, later on, in science. But they speak out of a much more particular engagement with the life of farming than Jefferson ever did. And Howard was still half a century ahead of them. We have to conclude, I think, that they were speaking out of tradition (the yeoman's or the agrarian tradition, which grew out of a peasant tradition still older) and out of experience—out of tradition proved and upheld by experience. This association of tradition and experience in the intelligence of a living person is humanly broad and deep. It is biologically, agriculturally, economically, politically, and culturally sound. It is deeply founded, solid enough to build a civilization upon, whereas the orthodox agriculture can support nothing but the shallow expansion of a book-keeper's economy.

ORGANIC FARMS

The attitudes and values of traditional agriculture still survive in our time and are supported by the experience of our time. Their survival is marginal and is mostly ignored both by the colleges of agriculture and by the agricultural press, which, if they acknowledge it at all, do so in order to treat it with contempt. But survivors do exist. They are connected by a sort of network that one travels by hearsay and friendship. By now I have encountered a good many of them, and have been impressed as often by the excellence of their characters as by the excellence of their farms. They are people of principle, both stubborn and adventurous, independent enough to trust their own experience and strong enough to hold in considerable isolation to truths not officially or popularly favored. Their farms stand for their principles and prove them; one has only to notice their example, or their examples, to understand that the orthodox agriculture has founded its "scientific proofs" upon shallow assumptions.

In spite of some public notice in the last year or two, it probably still is not generally known that there are a number of large-scale, highly mechanized farms that do not use chemical fertilizers or pesticides. When I first began my search for examples of healthy agriculture, I did not realize how compatible organic soil management could be with a large scale of operation. And then in the spring of 1974, I visited a 900-acre organic farm in Iowa. This farm made extensive use of a commercial organic fertilizer. But that seemed to me probably the least important element of the farming there. More important, I thought, were a careful plan of crop rotation (corn for a year or two, oats, soybeans, and then two years of pasture), the use of animal manure on corn ground every year, and the use of a chisel plow rather than the conventional turning plow for the preparation of crop ground.

This system was said to have the following advantages: within the first year or two of its use, earthworms and other forms of life had again become abundant in the soil; the ground had become darker, looser, easier to work each year; crops could be planted earlier because the increased humus in the soil permitted it to dry more quickly; stock feed went farther every year, because as it became more palatable and nutritious it took less to satisfy the cattle; the farm had no insecticide program at all, either for crops or stock.

In its machinery, buildings, etc., this farm was as "modern" as any other of comparable size. Even though it was far more diversified than most large farms of these times, and did not use chemical short-cuts, it required only four full-time workers. Late in 1975 I visited another highly mechanized organic farm—this one a 700-acre farm in Nebraska—another extremely impressive example of organic farming on a large scale. The existence of such farms as these, on which crops, animals, and the farmers themselves are obviously thriving, invalidates out-of-hand the contempt of orthodox agriculturists and suggests strongly that their contempt must rest on ignorance or fright.

If all the farms in the country were managed organically, both our people and our land would undoubtedly be healthier and there would be a considerable ramification of the benefits. And yet the 700- or 900-acre organic farm equipped with up-to-the-minute machine technology cannot be considered the solution to all of our agricultural problems, or to the problems that grow out of our agricultural problems. If we accept this as a solution, we forswear, for one thing, any further discussion of the cultural and political importance of the small landowner.

Much more suggestive, in this light, was another Iowa farm that I visited, this one a family-size holding of 175 acres. Of this, 50 acres were in permanent hillside pasture for twenty-eight Charolais cows. On the remaining 125 acres, the farmer grew corn, oats, wheat, soybeans, and hay. In addition to his cow herd, he kept twelve brood sows and a laying flock of 200 hens.

This farm had been under a completely organic system of soil management for eleven years at the time I saw it in 1974. Here again some commercial organic fertilizer was used to supplement a careful plan of soil husbandry. The cycle of crop rotation was as follows: oats and/or wheat, legumes for hay, soybeans, corn. The application of animal manure was estimated (conservatively) at two tons per acre, and this was put on the bean ground before planting it in corn. The expenditure for commercial fertilizer, which was used only on the corn ground, came to twelve dollars per acre. Every three years or so the pastures were dressed with 300 pounds per acre of a natural mineral fertilizer.

The farmer here was a man of impressive intelligence and judgment and impressively independent in both. Prescribed measures had been altered as he felt necessary to fit his place and his needs. The secretary of agriculture had called for all-out production that year, and on many farms the plowlands had begun to edge out dangerously into waterways and hillside pastures. I asked this farmer if the secretary's recommendation had affected his program. He answered that it had not done so in the least.

On this farm I first had a chance to watch a chisel plow at work and to see the ground it had prepared. This is a favorite tool of many mechanized organic farmers, who give it enthusiastic praise. I could see why. To begin with, it does all the work of seed-bed preparation, replacing both turning plow and harrow. But its great advantage is that it leaves the top layer of soil on top, which is where it belongs. Loosely stirred into this top layer, animal manures and plant residues decompose aerobically. The resulting high content of organic matter causes the surface of the field to act as a sponge, readily absorbing and retaining water and also allowing it to percolate downward into the lower layers. Another advantage of this plow is that it does not cause a hardpan; it does not interfere with the downward course of water through the pores of the soil, worm holes, and old root channels deep into the subsoil. The result is that the soil becomes at once less drouthy and less subject to erosion. It also becomes looser, easier, and cheaper to work, and so operating money goes farther and machinery lasts longer. On this farm, sod ground to be broken is plowed once with the straight chisels in the fall and is then plowed twice again with sixteen-inch sweeps in the spring before planting. These sweeps are very good for destroying deep-rooted weeds.

This farmer used no herbicides. The reason he gave was that he did not want to contaminate the streams. But he also appeared to have no great need for such chemicals. He tried to plant in the latter part of the planting season so as to allow more weeds to germinate and be killed in the preparation of the ground. He cultivated his row crops to remove large-stemmed weeds, and he found that taking three cuttings a year from his hay fields helped considerably to control weeds in the row crops that followed.

As for crop yields on this farm, I quote the following from a letter that the farmer wrote to me several months after my visit: "I would say our soy beans average 40 or more bu. per acre in an average year. The state average is 30 to 33 bu. Our corn has been yielding 90 to 100 bu. the past 5 years. Neighbors' yields are about the same for the same soil type and lay of land. Our wheat yielded over 25 bu. per acre which we feel is very good for this area. . . . Our oats have been 60 bu. on the average."

The cow herd on this farm was given a balanced mineral mixture as a supplement but was wintered on hay alone, without grain. No insecticides were used on the cattle. The farmer wrote that although his cattle have flies on them in the summertime, they do not have pinkeye or other eye problems usually associated with flies. He attributed this to their extraordinary good health. In December of 1974, he wrote me that the twenty-three March and April calves off this herd weighed variously from 400 to 700 pounds per head. These calves were in robust health, without pinkeye or any other disease.

Another mechanized organic farm is the new experimental farm belonging to Rodale Press, publisher of *Organic Gardening and Farming*. In 1972, 290 acres of this farm were rented to an excellent Mennonite farmer, who agreed to operate it according to strict organic principles. A five-year rotation cycle was set up (corn to rye to barley to wheat to timothy and clover), with twelve tons of manure per acre to be applied to the corn ground. The crops were planted in strips on the contour. Before 1972 this farm was cropped in the orthodox fashion, using heavy applications of chemicals, and the following corn-production figures are especially interesting for that reason. (Figures are available only for corn.) In the first year the yield was 40 bushels per acre; in the second year, 60; in the third year, 80; in the fourth year, 140. In that fourth year the top yield in the same county was 157 bushels per acre—obtained with an application of 190 pounds of nitrogen, 230 pounds of phosphorus, and 673 pounds of potassium.

DR. COMMONER'S ARGUMENT

There is, then, no way to deny that crops and animals can be produced in respectable yields by the methods generally designated as "organic." These methods work on large farms and on small ones. Available evidence indicates that they work at least as well as orthodox methods within the economy of the individual farm, and they will undoubtedly work better as the costs of chemical fertilizers, pesticides, and herbicides rise with the cost of petroleum. But perhaps the greatest benefits from the widespread adoption of organic methods of soil management would go to the general public—in greatly reduced soil and water pollution, in reduced public expenditures for pollution control, in better health, and at least eventually in cheaper food.

The abounding good health of the farms I have described is dramatically evident to an experienced observer. I believe that it would be just as evident to an inexperienced observer who would spend a few hours looking closely and comparing. But in support of the visual impression we now have some evidence from the Center for the Biology of Natural Systems at Washington University—a report published in 1975 and entitled *A Comparison of the Production, Economic Returns, and Energy Intensiveness of Corn Belt Farms That Do and Do Not Use Inorganic Fertilizers and Pesticides*. In *The Poverty of Power*, Barry Commoner makes this study the fulcrum of a powerful argument for organic soil management. I am going to make extensive reference to Dr. Commoner's argument both because it supports and completes my own and because I want to take issue, a little further on, with one of his assumptions.

Dr. Commoner begins by going over some ground often traversed by the specialists and apologists of orthodox agriculture, but he goes further and sees much more clearly. From 1950 to 1970, he acknowledges, American agriculture made some impressive increases in productivity: corn production per acre tripled; "a broiler chicken gained nearly 50 percent more weight from its feed"; egg production increased by twenty-five percent; overall farm production "increased by 40 percent." *But* during that period the real farm income "*decreased* from about $18 billion in 1950 to $13 billion in 1971. . . . Because the number of farms also decreased by 50 percent, the income per farm rose by 46 percent. . . . However . . . the average increase in the family income of *all* U. S. families in that period [was] 76 percent. Meanwhile, the total mortgage debt of U. S. farms rose from about $8 billion in 1950 to $24 billion in 1971." During this time there was also a massive shift from diversified farming to monoculture, which reduced the time that the farmland was covered with plant growth, which in turn reduced the amount of solar energy put to use on the farm. The removal of animals from farms growing crops in monocultures reduced the amount of organic waste returned to the fields. And there was a shift from the use of nitrogen-fixing legumes to the use of commercial nitrogen fertilizers. From 1959 to 1973 there was a sixty-percent decrease in the production of legume seed. By these and other changes, "The farm's link to the sun has been weakened, replaced by a new and . . . dangerous liaison with industry." And this dependence on sources of energy off the farm explains the decline of farm income. The net farm income decreased from 1950 to 1970, not in spite of, but *because of* the new technology of machines and chemicals. Dr. Commoner concludes his analysis of the effects of this technology with the following indictment:

"One can almost admire the enterprise and clever salesmanship of the petrochemical industry. Somehow it has managed to convince the farmer that he should give up the free solar energy that drives the natural cycles and, instead, buy the needed energy—in the form of fertilizer and fuel—from the petrochemical industry. Not content with that commercial coup, these industrial giants have completed their conquest of the farmer by going into competition with what the farm produces. They have introduced into the market a series of competing synthetics: synthetic fiber, which competes with cotton and wool; detergents, which compete with soap made of natural oils and fat; plastics, which compete with wood; and pesticides that compete with birds and ladybugs, which used to be free.

"The giant corporations have made a colony out of rural America."

Dr. Commoner then turns to the organic farmers studied by the

Washington University research group, of which he was a member. He sees in the methods of these farmers the obvious solution to the problem:

"The group analyzed the production of these farms for the 1974 season. The market value of the crops produced by the conventional farms was an average of $179 per acre, while the average value for the organic farm was $165 per acre. However, the operating costs of the conventional farms averaged $47 per acre, and those of the organic farms $31 per acre (the difference is largely due to the cost of the nitrogen fertilizer and pesticides used by the conventional farmers). As a result, the net income per acre of crop for the two types of farms is essentially the same. . . . The yields of different crops obtained by the two groups of farms are about equal, except for a small excess (12 percent) of corn yields on conventional farms as compared with organic farms.

"The organic farms used only 6800 BTU of energy to produce a dollar of output, while the conventional farms used 18,400 BTU. Thus, organic farms appear to yield about the same economic returns as the conventional ones, but do so by using about one-third as much energy."

THE USE OF DRAFT ANIMALS

Because "U.S. agriculture now consumes only about 4 percent of the total national energy budget," Dr. Commoner correctly perceives that the overriding issue here is not that of energy conservation, or even that of pollution resulting from farm use of fossil fuel energy. The overriding issue is economic: the colonization of the farmland by the petrochemical industry. But it seems to me that this perception is not carried far enough. Speaking of the adverse energy economy of the conventional farm, Dr. Commoner says that "when a farmer uses commercial nitrogen fertilizer, the amount of thermodynamic work expended to produce it is seven times greater than the minimum amount of work that is needed to accomplish the same result by planting vetch. But the external energy required to grow vetch *could* after all be reduced to essentially zero (for example, by using a horse fed on farm grown corn). On this albeit impractical standard, the fertilizer's thermodynamic efficiency is zero."

It is the qualifier in that last sentence that concerns me. Dr. Commoner is saying that he is willing to advocate only half the remedy that is called for by his argument. That is, he wishes to do away with agriculture's dependence on petroleum-derived fertilizers, pesticides, and herbicides, but he will not contemplate the reduction of its dependence on petroleum fuels. In the midst of an argument everywhere else incisively intelligent, he suddenly makes this perfunctory bow before the golden calf of "agribusiness"—this spurious standard of "practicality" by which any unorthodox technology may be loftily waved away. To suggest that anything besides a tractor could be used for motive power on the farm is like setting fire to the church—the righteous not only do not *do* it, they do not *think* about it.

But Dr. Commoner's routine refusal to defile the sanctuary is mild indeed in comparison to the official reaction to the same idea. In August of 1975, the *Farm Index*, a publication of the United States Department of Agriculture, carried an article entitled "Wanted[:] 61,000,000 Horses & Mules[,] 31,000,000 Farm Workers." This by now widely circulated article is "based on" a speech delivered by Earle E. Gavett of the National Resource Economics Division.

Mr. Gavett's purpose is to confound "some critics of today's farming practices" who, the article says, have advocated "an anti-technological revolution" involving an immediate and complete return to the use of horse and mule teams on American farms. This alleged proposal, the article is relieved to note, has "some serious—if not insurmountable—drawbacks" in that it requires sixty-one million horses and mules, of which there were only three million in the United States in 1975, and thirty-one million farm workers, of whom only four million were available. These figures were derived in the following way:

"The 1967 index was the yardstick. The 1918 crop had an index of 48—that is, 48 percent as large as the 1967 crop—compared with 109 in 1974. Thus 1974 production was about 2¼ times greater.

"As a peak year of nonmechanized farming, 1918 is an ideal choice in the comparison.

"A straight projection of 1918 resources to meet 1974 production can be made by simply multiplying the 26.7 million mules and horses and the 13½ million farm workers carrying on farming in 1918 by the 2.27 times larger output in 1974."

The article concedes that this is "only a guideline projection. Obviously, nonmechanical and nonchemical technology improvements . . . since 1918, such as hybrid seeds, would lessen the manpower and horsepower requirements by allowing greater yields for less work.

"But agricultural economists quickly emphasize that the point of the projection is valid: a complete abandonment of mechanized technology is a biologically impossible and sociologically impractical idea."

The necessary animals could not be produced, the article continues, before 1992 or 1993. To grow feed for these animals would require "180 million acres of prime farmland." And there would be "questions over feeding so many horses in this country while people abroad are starving."* Moreover, the necessary people are also in short supply, and "A movement of 26 million workers from city to farm would provide mind-boggling problems."

That gives the main line of the argument, which gets considerably more elaborate without ever becoming more intelligent. Like many another, this document would merit no more attention than it merits respect if it were not for its influence. It happens, however, that this argument was given the status of official policy of the United States Department of Agriculture in a speech by no other than former Secretary Butz himself. And so we have before us one of the characteristic political necessities of our time: to take seriously what we cannot respect.

The chief objection to this argument is that there was never a reason or an occasion for it. There are simply no serious critics of conventional agriculture who have advocated "a complete abandonment of mechanized technology." As the *Draft Horse Journal* noted in an editorial, "Most of the critics of today's agriculture . . . don't talk about any such complete anything, but rather a picking and choosing of techniques and tools to get the job done in the most energy conserving way possible." The key phrase here is "picking and choosing." There are indeed critics who believe that a much larger range of technological choices and alternatives ought to be available, that we will have neither a healthy agriculture nor a dependable food supply until such choices and alternatives are available—that, in short, the strength of agriculture is in diversity, of technology as of other things, and that the present agricultural orthodoxy ignores the principle of diversity altogether. A few of

*It is fascinating to observe the agriculture specialists' flexible mindfulness of the hungry, who are, according to the argument at hand, either to be compassionately fed or starved into compliance. Either way, their fate is directly bound to the ambitions of the "agribusiness" corporations, who have thus added an enlightened versatility to the originally narrow and primitive Christian concept of charity.

these critics have published articles in such magazines as *Organic Gardening and Farming, Mother Earth News*, and the *Draft Horse Journal*, in which they have pointed out that there are presently places in agriculture and forestry that can be competently and economically filled by horses or mules. Some have said that, given our difficult economies of both energy and money, much wider use might reasonably be made of draft animals in the future. No one, as far as I know, has *ever* proposed that such a change could, or should, be either complete or rapid.

That this small advocacy of a small diversity should have drawn a full-scale attack from the Department of Agriculture bespeaks both the totalitarianism and the paranoia of the "agribusiness" mentality. What can be the excuse for all this carrying on? If these critics are right, then as scientists, the agriculture experts might be expected simply to agree. If the critics are wrong, then it appears that they might safely be ignored, for orthodox farming is far too widely accepted to be seriously threatened by a bad idea. The truth is that these critics have offended, not by being either right or wrong, but by being *different*.

Even if we could grant that we are indeed threatened with "an anti-technological revolution," the competence of Mr. Gavett's argument is still in question. As the *Draft Horse Journal* pointed out, the arithmetic of his "projection" is far too simple, assuming, as it does, "that it takes three times as many horses and mules to cultivate corn yielding 120 to 150 bushels to the acre as corn yielding 40 to 60." And of his assertion that it would require three acres of "prime farmland" to feed one horse, it can only be said that he does not know what he is talking about. By my figures, using the rations recommended in the twentieth edition of Morrison's *Feeds and Feeding*, a ton horse doing medium to heavy work every day of the year would require 104 bushels of ear corn and 7300 pounds (about 209 thirty-five-pound bales) of hay. Assuming that the hay is of grass and alfalfa, this much feed could be produced on less than two acres at today's yields. But not all draft horses would or should weigh a ton—1300 to 1800 pounds would be a realistic range. And very few indeed would work every day the year around. The above figures do not consider the horse's off-time subsistence on pasture alone or on a maintenance ration mostly of hay, and they do not consider his ability to utilize roughages such as cornstalks, now seldom used as feed. A more realistic accounting might be that of the *Draft Horse*

Journal's editorial, which states that a horse eats "the energy equivalent of 70 bushels" of corn.

One also notes this article's easy assumption that *all* of the thirty-one million needed people would be "workers" and not farmers. And that the mind that is "boggled" by the problems of "a movement of 26 million workers from city to farm" is apparently not boggled at all by the continuing and appalling problems of the recent movement of many more than that from farm to city. If there were any suspicion that such a reverse migration might be profitable to "agribusiness," we may be sure that there would be an unhesitating effort to bring it about. This is a kind of mind that is boggled only at its convenience.

The same is true of the "questions over feeding so many horses in this country while people abroad are starving." This serviceable charity is not at all troubled by work now being done at the University of Nebraska on the possibility of using grain alcohol as a motor fuel. It is morally questionable to feed grain to a work horse; but if the grain is to be consumed by engines to the profit of energy corporations and the machinery and automobile manufacturers, then the starving are forgotten. Nor do the people who attack the use of horses for farm work ever say a word against their use for racing, show competition, and other frivolous purposes.

"Horses," the *Draft Horse Journal* said, ". . . are no more anti-technological than legs on humans." They are simply a technological possibility that we have almost ceased to consider. We must learn to consider it again, for until we do we cannot complete the logic of Dr. Commoner's argument, nor can we answer the questions raised by the existence of, and the potential need for, such "marginal" lands as I described earlier. There are certain problems for which the use of horses is the appropriate solution—or for which we have so far found no more appropriate solution. There is also the possibility that a revival of the lapsed technology of horse-powered agriculture is necessary to complete our agricultural intelligence and judgment— to give us the diversity of choices required for the subsistence of intelligence and judgment.

The issue of economics merges finally into the much larger issue of health, just as the issue of the health of any one creature merges into that of the health of Creation. In the context of that issue, Dr. Commoner's "impractical standard" of near-perfect thermodynamic efficiency becomes not just thinkable but indispensable. It is no more impractical than the standard of perfect health, which we all apply to our bodies. We desire—our bodies desire—to be perfectly healthy. That is what we hope and strive for. And it is the way we understand our effort; without the ideal of perfect health, we could not know how healthy we are. To be three-quarters or seven-eighths healthy is not an ambition that ever occurs to us.

There is no point in saying that perfection of health, as of all else, is not attainable by humans. The point is that we must have the vision of perfection, we must strive for it, we must sense the possibility of approaching it, or we cannot live. Jesus enjoined his followers to be perfect—not, I think, because they could hope for perfection, but because perfection is the necessary standard. People cannot understand themselves, or live fully and humanly, without it. To reconcile ourselves to imperfection, to place great practical barriers in our own way, is brutish. It condemns us immediately to great suffering of the spirit and undoubtedly, in the long run, of the body as well. Common sense alone requires us to consider well any technology that might bring us nearer the vision of perfect health. To repudiate such technology on the ground that it is "old-fashioned" is madness.

It is hard to overestimate the importance of applying the correct standard to agricultural performance. I do not see how a stable, abundant, long-term agriculture can be built up and maintained by any standard less comprehensive than that of the perfect health of individual human bodies, of the community, and of the community's sources and supports in the natural world—whereas the standards of orthodox agriculture tend to be extremely simple and exclusive: productivity (as determined by "records" and by the equation between the number of eaters and the amount of food) and the financial prosperity of "agribusiness."

It is easy to say, as former Secretary Butz said in his own fatuous attack on the "anti-technological revolution," that "To return to the 'good old days' in agriculture, or indeed just to cling stubbornly to the farming methods of today, would be to condemn hundreds of millions of people to a lingering death by malnutrition and starvation in the years ahead." But that is simply the oldest—and the most profitable—cliché of the industrial revolution, supported only by a thoughtless obeisance to "progress." We must look beyond that to what is assumed. So far as I can make out, Mr. Butz's statement rests upon two main assumptions, both suspect: that the health of humans may be safely distinguished from the health of the rest of Creation and that there is no distinction between affluence and survival.

People who argue for ways of farming that are ecologically sound, says Mr. Butz, are "placing the needs of man second to the needs of all other creatures." Man, he says, is "as much a 'part of nature'" as the other creatures. But what he means is that human needs must be put *ahead* of the needs of all other creatures, as we see when he equates a hydroelectric or an irrigation dam with a beaver dam. His solution to the problem of hunger is therefore remarkably unencumbered by moral, cultural, or ecological considerations: "We'll turn to science and technology for the answer—we'll modify the environment." Thus, with a shrug, he sets agriculture free of ecology. But we are left with an awesome ecological question: How can humans, who are creatures, hope to survive in a world in which other creatures perish? Or how much can we "modify" the environment before we fatally "modify" ourselves? Here is Mr. Butz's answer: "The challenge to agriculture and science is to find the right application of technology to modify the environment in a way that will benefit both man and the rest of nature." One can only agree, pointing out, however, that the applications of technology so far advocated and defended by Mr. Butz have notoriously failed to do so and that his colleagues and constituents in the "agribusiness" system have so far failed notoriously even to consider the advisability of doing so.

The second assumption is, of course, closely related to the first. Mr. Butz begins with the term "survival" and a most dramatic issue he makes of it: "Backed in a corner with no job, no income, and an empty stomach churning from hunger, the most dedicated environmentalist will forget his fight for the seagull or the walrus. He will get down and scrap for survival like any other creature . . ." Of course he will—though he may even then remember that he and the sea gull and the walrus are all scrapping for survival in the same world and against the same abuses. But by the end of Mr. Butz's speech, without transition or warning, the term has changed: ". . . there can be little hope for mankind's continued *affluence* [my emphasis] unless we face up to the moral question of the need to limit our numbers. In the meantime, science and agriculture will have to buy the time for us to reach that solution." And with this shift of terms, "science and agriculture" have been nominated to do the work that can be done safely and adequately only by complex cultural changes leading to restraint of consumption and competent care of the earth. It is exactly this refusal to consider survival except as "continued affluence" that has brought our survival into doubt. There is, anyhow, only a fanciful connection between affluence and survival; we do not have to be as comfortable and extravagant as we are in order to survive. And there is no connection between affluence, as we understand it, and civilization. All that civilization requires is enough; it does not require extravagance. Until these distinctions are made, we cannot even begin to talk sensibly about the problem of hunger.

The fact is that Mr. Butz and his colleagues in the corporations and the universities do not know whether unorthodox technologies and methods will produce more food or less. The only information that they have, or that they acknowledge, is that which "proves" the efficacy of "agribusiness" technology. Where are the control plots which test the various organic systems of soil management? Where are the performance figures for present-day small farms using draft animals, small-scale machine technologies, and alternative energy sources? Where are the plots kept free of agricultural chemicals? If these exist, then they are the best-kept secrets of our time. But if they do not exist, whence comes the scientific authority of orthodox agriculture? Without appropriate controls, one has no proof; one does not, in any respectable sense, have an experiment.

HORSE-POWERED FARMS

Mr. Gavett, followed by Mr. Butz and others, bases an amazingly bitter attack against the use of horses upon a "projection." There was no need for so speculative a maneuver, for a number of horse-powered farms presently exist—not experiments or controls, but living examples, requiring only to be carefully observed. I have visited a number of farms powered either partially or exclusively by draft horses. I can offer only a few random figures having to do with these farms, and so what I have to say is offered as proof of nothing except their possibility. But the fact of their possibility suggests strongly that we ought to have thorough studies of their ecological and economic performance.

In the early spring of 1975 I visited three good Iowa farms, all of which made extensive use of horses. All three were farmed by older men, working for the most part alone, who farmed this way by conviction; who were thoughtful, indeed passionate, holdouts against the capital-intensive, highly mechanized farming of their neighbors; and who lived in the isolation of those who are "different." Of their financial condition, I can say only that from all visible signs they were better than solvent. Their homes were comfortable, their farm buildings well kept up, etc.

The first of these men farmed 120 acres. He had two teams, one of which was a young pair he was breaking for another horseman. He owned two thirty-year-old H Farmall tractors that he used mainly for the heavy work of plowing and disking; the rest of his work he did with the horses. Aside from the manure from his barn, he used no fertilizer. He did not use insecticides. Herbicides he used only selectively, for the control of thistles. In addition to the considerable saving of fuel, he mentioned two other benefits from his way of farming: he believed that he had less erosion than his neighbors and that his ground worked easier. His corn yielded an average of seventy bushels per acre.

The second of these farmers had 300 acres of excellent land surrounded by cash-grain farm "businesses" of the orthodox make. He did most of the farming with horses, keeping an ancient Farmall tractor to do only the heaviest field work and to provide stationary power. Except for plowing down "a little" fertilizer, he used no chemicals. His fields were fertilized with manure, and tilled in rotation from corn to beans to corn again to oats to hay. His corn yield ran to about seventy-five bushels to the acre. The economy of this farm was carefully diversified. Among his other enterprises, the farmer had a dairy herd of six cows, which he milked by hand.

The third farm was similar to the second in size and in the combination of horse power with an old tractor (a 1946 WD Allis-Chalmer) used for power-takeoff work and for the heaviest work in the field. This farmer said that he had "never used a pound of fertilizer." He owned twelve horses, one a Percheron stud. The income from this horse-breeding operation was paying *all* the operating expenses of the farm. I neglected to ask this farmer what his corn yield was. But I did ask him how his economic situation compared to that of his neighbors. He said that he couldn't say, but that they often called him over "to buy something that they ought to keep."

My visits to these farms involved long distance and short time, and so were necessarily far too hasty. And it was too early in the season to get a fair look at the condition of the fields. For those reasons my information is not nearly so complete as I now wish it were. I am able to fill out the impression somewhat by quoting a letter from an Iowa agriculture student who spent much more time on the second of these farms than I did. His visit, like mine, was before the growing season, and again the facts are scanty. But his description is much more detailed than mine, and a context is given in which the *meaning* of such a farm is made plain.

"At this time of the year 95% of the land has either been cut (soybeans) or plowed up (corn). The few guys who have any livestock at all have it on an enormous scale and they are among the few who have let fences remain. So the majority don't plow to the fence row; they plow to the culvert's edge. Row crop cultivation is done on such a large scale here that they must fall plow so that they can be timely in planting the vast acreages come spring. But what I saw on the south and west sides of fields in the culverts were snow drifts that were black to dark grey—each layer of snow has a layer of topsoil on top. You see this beside every field without exception that has been fall plowed. There's no protection from the wind in this flat country and if they don't get early freezes with heavy snow the land is vulnerable. There are many abandoned farm buildings with the ground cultivated within a few feet of them. I often saw good stock barns, the likes of which you rarely see in the southeast, with the south or east end cut out, and all they hold are large tractors and implements. You don't have to travel far to see whole square miles of land with no farm houses or outbuildings, plowed up north to south and east to west—right up to the culverts. And in the midst of this land, where farmers are no less dependent on Shell Oil Co. and John Deere than they are on the weather, stands _____'s place; honestly, to see it is to believe that it's an oasis in the midst of a desert. I knew from a mile and a half down the road that it was his place. His milking shorthorns were out gleaning corn. The fields were well fenced, the buildings being used for the purposes intended. His rotation is the old Iowa standard: 60 acres of corn (and some sorghum), 30 of oats, 30 of hay (clover), 30 of soybeans all on the home place. He has another 120 acres on a neighboring section. He keeps 40 shorthorns, five* of which he milks by hand. He fattens about twenty hogs, keeps 200 chickens by which he's able to sell eggs to his neighbors."

It will be observed that the use of horses is not just a means of doing work, a kind of power added to a farm from outside as petroleum or electricity is added to it. The use of horses is a means that

*One had evidently been turned dry since my visit.

belongs to the farm; it is a way of farming; it is, as Maurice Telleen points out, invariably accompanied or followed by a set of practices that belong together. If made to belong to the land by good care and good sense, horses tend to preserve its health. With horses come pastures and hay fields, because the horses must eat. And if one is going to grow forage for horses, then one finds it natural and economical to grow it also for other animals. From the growing of forage and the diversification of animal species, there follow naturally the principles of diversification and rotation of field crops. Having animals, one has manure, and so manure is used instead of commercial chemical fertilizers. And the use of manure, the conservation of humus, and the practices of rotation and diversification tend to work against diseases, insects, and weeds, and so one uses few or no pesticides. It is a way of farming that involves year-round use of the land by animals, plants, and the farm people—in contrast to the "corn, beans, and Florida" rotation of orthodox cash-grain farmers. Moreover, the farmer who farms with horses is not likely to be an expander. His way of farming tends to confine him to a limited acreage near home. He therefore concentrates his attention and, instead of getting more, takes good care of what he has—sows cover crops, guards against erosion, etc.

What we have here is a description of a permanent, settled, careful, largely independent agriculture that uses the land more efficiently, at least in the sense that it uses it more months in the year and more conservatively, than the orthodox agriculture. The defenders of the orthodoxy will immediately point out that the corn yields I have cited are extremely low and that we would run great risks should we reduce all yields to that level. This point must be taken seriously—not just by people on my side of the argument, but by all students and scholars of agriculture, for what is required is a definitive, scientifically sound answer. In the absence of such an answer, there are still a couple of points that need to be made.

First, it must be emphasized that all three of these farmers are older men whose children have left the farm and who are working for the most part alone. We must therefore consider that they may lack the energy, help, and motivation to push themselves and their fields toward maximum production. Second, these farms are survivals of an old way—a good way, when well followed, but not necessarily the best. The pressures of surviving, of keeping their inherited values intact in an increasingly alien atmosphere, have undoubtedly kept these farmers from being as innovative as they might have been in kinder circumstances. Particularly suggestive is the possibility of grafting the soil management methods of the more advanced organic farmers upon the traditional structures and skills of the old horse-powered farming.

But offsetting the smallness of these yields is their relative independence of economic and political conditions. Such yields are attainable on these farms year after year, *whatever* the availability of credit or of petroleum products—something that cannot be said of the much larger yields of orthodox farms, which depend absolutely on credit and on "purchased inputs" from the oil industries. The horse teams will go to the fields no matter what is happening on Wall Street or in the capitals of the Middle East. Seventy bushels of corn per acre is only half as good a yield as 140 bushels, true enough. But then it is infinitely preferable to no bushels at all.

THE AMISH

My final example of an exemplary marginal agriculture is that of the Amish. Nothing, I think, is more peculiarly characteristic of the agricultural orthodoxy—as of American society in general—than its inability to see the Amish for what they are. Oh, it *sees* them, all right. It sees them as quaint, picturesque, old-fashioned, backward, unprogressive, strange, extreme, different, perhaps slightly subversive. And that "sight" is perfect blindness. What is not seen is that the Amish are a community in the full sense of the word; they may well be the last surviving white community of any considerable size in this country. And for this there are reasons. It is especially the reasons that we do not want to see, for these reasons invalidate most of the assumptions and ambitions by which we proudly characterize ourselves as "modern."

My knowledge of the Amish, as of the other farmers I have discussed, is by no means thorough or detailed enough to satisfy the demands of strict scholarship. And I shall not pretend to be "objective" about them. I admire and respect them deeply, with few reservations; in many ways I envy them. In addition to reading several published accounts of Amish culture and agriculture, I am able to speak to some extent from experience. I have looked carefully at Amish farming in Iowa, Pennsylvania, Indiana, and Ohio, and these travels have involved some personal contacts.

What, then, are the reasons that the Amish have been able to survive as a community—or, it might be more correct to say, as a closely bound fellowship of many communities? I think that there are three primary reasons, from which spring many others.

First, the Amish communities are, at their center, religious. They are bound together not just by various worldly necessities, but by spiritual authority. Theirs is, moreover, a religion unusually attentive to its effects and obligations in this world. Whereas most contemporary sects of Christianity have tended to specialize in the interests of the spirit, leaving aside the issues of the use of the world, the Amish have not secularized their earthly life. They have not hesitated to see communal and agricultural implications in their religious principles, and these implications directly influence their behavior. The "goal" of Amish culture is not just the welfare of the spirit, but a larger harmony "among God, nature, family, and community."*

Second, the Amish have severely restricted the growth of institutions among themselves, and so they are not victimized, as we so frequently are, by organizations set up ostensibly to "serve" them. Though they pay the required deferences to our institutions, they accept few of the benefits, and so remain, in perhaps the most important respects, free of them. They do not become dependent on them and so maintain their integrity. As far as I know, the only institutions in our sense that the Amish have started are their schools—and this, by our standards, for a strange reason: to *keep* the responsibility for educating their children and so, in consequence, to keep their children. Amish ministers and bishops are chosen by lot, after fasting and prayer (as Mathias was chosen), and so they do not have a professional, a paid, an economically dependent, or an ambitious clergy. Their religious services are held in barns or homes; their charities are not organized or abstract but are usually in direct response to observed needs. And so they do not have a church building or a building fund or church functionaries or administrators. There is little distinction between the church and its members.

*The Amish have two considerable problems, now, which trouble this ideal of harmony. They are having more children than, in present economic conditions, they can provide farms for, and so some of their young people are taking town jobs. And where coal underlies their land, some are permitting the strip-miners to come in. Reclamation was better than usual on the Amish farms I saw that had been stripped, and the land was going back into pasture. Some Amishmen nevertheless feel the practice to be wrong.

There are, one may as well say, only two Amish institutions: the family and the community. And these institutions fulfill directly, humanly, simply, and quietly nearly all the functions that we have delegated to our obtrusive, inhuman, indifferent, clumsy, expensive institutions. Family and community serve as insurance, welfare, social security, public safety. Indeed, they serve as, and replace, government. The simple living together of relatives and neighbors makes unnecessary to them our obsession with "security."

Third, the Amish are the truest geniuses of technology, for they understand the necessity of limiting it, and they know *how* to limit it. They have refused to see "technological innovation as an end in itself." And so their "religiously enforced family and community values are safeguarded against the social costs of changes which in their estimation did more harm than good to the community as a whole." Whereas our society tends to conceive of community as a loose political-economic mechanism of mutually competing producers, suppliers, and consumers, the Amish think of "the community as a whole"—that is, as all of the people, or perhaps, considering the excellence both of their neighborliness and their husbandry, as all the people and their land together. If the community is whole, then it is healthy, at once earthly and holy. The wholeness or health of the community is their standard. And by this standard they have been required to limit their technology.

By living well without such "necessities" as automobiles, tractors, electrical power, and telephones, the Amish prove them unnecessary and so give the lie to our "economy." And by these restraints they have kept their health, for by them they have kept themselves at home and have, for the most part, kept their children at home. They have not the knowledge of experts, which is by definition a homeless or rootless knowledge—the knowledge, in Sir Albert Howard's words, of people who cannot "take their own advice before offering it to other people"—and which is, as such, dangerous. They do not use knowledge to prey upon one another.

The healthy results of these restraints are readily visible to anyone who so much as drives an automobile through an Amish community. Unlike so much of the best farmland, which has become a kind of agricultural desert, the Amish landscape is vibrantly populated with both people and animals. Busy people are seen everywhere. All the houses are lived in. All the buildings are in use. Fences and buildings are in excellent repair. And there are signs of a thriving and thrifty home life: vegetable gardens, flower gardens, fruit trees, grape arbors, berry vines, beehives, bird houses. People are making careful, comely, dignified work of the essential tasks defined by modern values as "drudgery." And because they have thought of the well-being of all the people, all are busy. There is a use for everyone. The Amish do not have the abandoned children, cast-off old people, criminals, indigents, and vagrants whom we have "freed from drudgery."

And these people practice a way of farming capable of taking exquisite care of the land. In the fall of 1976 I stood on a hillside that had been used and cared for by three generations of Amish farmers. It was steep land of the sort more often than not worn out under the old American agriculture and simply unusable by the new. This hillside had been cropped in alternating strips of corn and sod. The corn crop, which was excellent, had been cut with a binder and shocked. The farmer and his sons had carried the bundles off the plowed ground—eight rows up the hill, eight rows down—and shocked them on the sod strips, so as to get the cover crop sowed as soon as possible. By orthodox standards, this work was demeaning drudgery. By the standard of the health of the field, it was simply necessary, and so it had been done. When I was there the cover crop was coming up to safeguard the ground over the winter. I looked for marks of erosion. There were none. It is possible, I think, to say that this is a Christian agriculture, formed upon the understanding that it is sinful for people to misuse or destroy what they did not make. The Creation is a unique, irreplaceable gift, therefore to be used with humility, respect, and skill.

And so, though Amish agriculture is not modern or progressive, it is by no means ignorant or unintelligent. By the correct standard, it is much more sophisticated than orthodox agriculture. The Amish were among the first to understand the uses of rotation, manure, and legumes. They keep a balance between livestock and crops. They benefit from exchanges of labor and other forms of neighborliness. In lieu of massive consumption of fossil fuels and electricity, they make the fullest possible use of energies available on the farm—of the wind, of draft animals, and, of course, of their own bodies. Their technological restraints are balanced, quite naturally, by inventiveness. The Amish are good mechanics, and they have displayed much ingenuity in, among other things, the adaptation of tractor implements for use with teams of two to eight or more horses.

Another observer of Amish farming wrote a letter to the editor of the *Draft Horse Journal*, who published exerpts in the issue of Autumn 1976. The editor noted that "the writer of this letter owns no horses, has no vested interest in the horse business, that I know of." The following paragraphs are taken from that letter.

"My farming consists of just under a hundred acres of rather heavy, low lying land. At one time our family did something or other on three farms, of which one has gotten completely covered by houses and another has been sold to an Old Order Amishman. We still call the third one home.

"When the one farm was sold to the Amishman I forgot to tell him that one particular field was too heavy and low to grow alfalfa. By experience, I knew it wouldn't work. For a couple of years he had it in other crops, then he went to alfalfa. This embarrassed me because I knew I should have cautioned him on this. But he had a marvelous stand and a very heavy yield. It was puzzling. I puzzled over it for years but am now very persuaded of the why and wherefore.

"With our tractors we kept the soil rather permanently compacted because it was necessary to get on the land as soon as surface moisture conditions permitted. And the tire patterns pretty well rolled the entire area in the course of repeated passage. With his horses, this just didn't happen. And in the course of a couple of winters the deep frost had corrected my tractor compaction mistakes. Soil structure improved. Root penetration was facilitated. Water holding capacity as well as internal drainage both benefited, and the alfalfa flourished.

"The Amish will not argue the point because they don't think anyone is interested, but will say that a farm "works" easier after a couple of years of horse farming. This compaction problem has to be the explanation. The resulting improved soil structure, allowing for better root penetration, is probably the reason they can get similar yields with less chemical fertilizer than their mechanized neighbors.

"But back to that heavy land alfalfa for a moment. The crop was disgustingly rank and lodged. Mowing it would be a problem. So I paid a visit, and . . . was flabbergasted to notice the farmer slowed down and mowed right through. . . . Then I realized that something very nice was being demonstrated; since the sickle drive was independent from ground travel (his horse drawn mower was equipped with an engine to drive the sickle . . .) this 'horse farmer' had sickle-cycle-to-ground-speed control that no tractor farmer could have unless he had a hydrostatic drive tractor! It gave him a control flexibility that I had never experienced and left me feeling sort of humble. I came away wondering which of us had the better technology . . . and I'm still not sure."

And then this writer addresses himself to the standard orthodox argument that we cannot feed draft horses without starving humans.

"Of course you have to feed draft animals. But this does not necessarily mean you'll have less to sell per acre farmed. In my observation, good horse farmers seem to have about as much to market per acre as the rest of us. Certainly they manage to nourish their animals very well, too. Closer examination would probably show the animals are at least partly nourished on what is wasted on fully mechanized farms. I'm not speaking just of corn fodder, either. Who else hand gathers the ears the picker missed now-a-days ? . . . Does the man with the 4 row combine? And could he gather the shelling loss if he would? Hardly.

"Well, I'm not very impressed by the statistics that prove we'd starve if farming went back to animal power. In many sections of the country that is exactly what happens when a farm, or a group of farms, comes into the hands of an Amishman. The farming has gone from tractors back to horses on hundreds of farms in my part of the United States without any noticeable reduction in agricultural output. Any suggestion that our county produces less now than 20 years ago would seem outrageous to all the people I know."

In support of these impressions of the general good health of Amish agriculture, some more specific information is available in an article entitled "Agricultural Alternatives" in the March–April 1972 issue of *CBNS Notes*, published by the Center for the Biology of Natural Systems. I take the following quotations from that article:

"Amish attitudes toward fertility maintenance are amazingly varied. . . . Preliminary analysis of the data shows three distinct patterns. The traditional pattern consists of crop rotation which includes nitrogen-fixing legumes, heavy application of manure to at least 1/5 of the farm in any growing season and lime and rock phosphate to one of the fields in the rotation every year. With the aid of hybrid seed corn some farmers estimate their yields at 90 to 100 bushels per acre although some estimates fall as low as 70.

"A second pattern is the conventional with Amish modifications. The soil will be tested for its acidity and for its phosphorous and potash balance. A county agent or a fertilizer dealer will then make a recommendation for lime and fertilizer application in relation to specific cropping plans. This can include the use of anhydrous ammonia as a cheap source of nitrogen for corn. It is observed that Amish operators who follow this pattern 'factor in' the effects of their crop rotation and the availability of manure and thus apply fertilizer less heavily per acre. . . .

"The third pattern is the use of organic fertilizers. . . . Some of them tend to be costly in terms of additional yield per acre but a minority of the Amish farm operators are very enthusiastic users. The appeal is on the basis of a claim to a more nutritious quality of feed grain which in turn leads to healthier livestock, healthier soil and eventually healthier humans. Interestingly, several of the operators interviewed adopted a program of organic fertility maintenance after having been on a conventional program of commercial fertilizer for several years."

As for the effects of this agriculture, the article offers evidence which suggests that, ecologically and economically, the Amish methods are sounder than the orthodox. Water pollution from Amish fields was far less: "One of the comparative samples taken in March, 1971 showed concentrations of nitrate nitrogen of 12.1 ppm and 8.9 in the tile of conventional farms in Douglas County [Illinois]. The Amish tile had a concentration of 4.6 ppm (corn). A comparison in May showed a concentration of 26.6 ppm (corn) and 10.9 ppm (beans) in the conventional farms and 4.6 ppm in the tiles of the Amish farmer."

And the Amish, whose farms in 1965 averaged only 76.55 acres, were prospering financially during a time when many of the smaller orthodox farmers (with far larger holdings) were being "squeezed out": "Our best single indicator of economic viability is bank data which compares 88 Amish bank accounts in 1964 with those same accounts in 1971. During these years the Amish accounts showed an increase in net worth from $2,379,000 to $4,045,000."

Since the Amish are manifestly excellent farmers, and are so complexly successful in other ways, one wonders why they have been ignored by the officials and the scholars of agriculture—especially since their technology and methods are so well suited to land not even farmable by orthodox methods and to farmers not able to survive in the orthodox economy. I have been able to think of only two answers, aside from the conventional contempt for anything small: first, the Amish are a thrifty people, hence poor consumers of "purchased inputs" from the "agribusiness" industries; and, second, they are living disproof of some of the fundamental assumptions of the orthodoxy.

PRODUCTION AND REPRODUCTION

To these exemplary forms of unorthodox agriculture, we may add the new work in urban homesteading, aquaculture, solar greenhouses, alternative energy sources, small technology, organic pest control, etc., by the New Alchemy Institute, the Farallones Institute, Rodale Press, and others, as well as the various farmers' and consumers' cooperatives that have been started in the past few years both as strategies of health and as protests against the "agribusiness" juggernaut. Together, these have restored a sense of possibility, both cultural and agricultural, that has been nearly obliterated by the ambitions of agriculture specialists and businessmen. They make possible a vision of an agriculture many times more versatile and diverse than the orthodox, hence many times more responsive to the demands of good husbandry, to local conditions, and to human needs.

For the orthodox obsession with production, profit, and expansion, this healthier agriculture would substitute a more complex consciousness, the terms of which would be ecological integrity, nutrition, technological appropriateness, social stability, skill, quality, thrift, diversity, decentralization, independence, usufruct. Or, put more simply, it would replace the concern for production with a concern for reproduction. Production, some would say, is the male principle in isolation from the female principle. Thus isolated, the male principle wants to exert itself absolutely; it wants to "do everything at once"—which is, of course, what doomsday will do. But reproduction, which is the male and the female principles in union, is nurturing, patient, resigned to the pace of seasons and lives, respectful of the nature of things. Production's tendency is to go "all out"; it always aims to set a new record. Reproduction is more conservative and more modest; its aim is not to happen once, but to happen again and again and again, and so it seeks a balance between saving and spending. At their best, farmers have always had this ancient purpose of reproduction. Without it, they make their art as sterile as mining.

There would, of course, be no need for a different vision of agriculture if the one we had were demonstrably working in the best long-term interests of the people and the land, or even if it were generally believed to be doing so. In fact, there are a great many people who do *not* believe that it is doing so, and their number is growing. And so the last agricultural margin remaining to be noticed is a political one: the people who feel that they are being victimized by orthodox agriculture and whose dissatisfaction is either ignored or held in contempt.

There are, first, many people—ex-farmers, heirs of farmers, and would-be farmers—who want to farm but are prevented from doing so by high land costs, taxes, inheritance taxes, and interest rates. And these economic barriers, which exclude the small operator, directly favor not just the survival, but also the expansion, of the big operator. This is not a necessary result of "the way things are." It is the calculated effect of a deliberate policy to allow the big to grow bigger at the expense of the small. In addition, there are many farmers of the same kinds who are presently farming, but whose survival is in doubt for the same reasons.

Second, there is a rapidly increasing number of consumers who wish to buy food that is nutritionally whole and uncontaminated by pesticides and other toxic chemical residues. And these people would prefer not to pay the exorbitant food prices required by long-distance transportation, processing, packaging, and advertising, all of which result from "agribusiness" control of food.

PUBLIC REMEDIES

And so we come to the question of what, in a public or governmental sense, ought to be done. Any criticism of an established way, if it is to be valid, must have as its standard not only a need, but a better way. It must show that a better way is desirable, and it must give examples to show that it is possible. I have produced the argument and the examples—not definitively, I am sure, but sufficiently to provide an agenda for the further work that is necessary.

It remains for me to suggest public changes that are necessary to bring the better way to realization. This is the most fearful part of my task, for what I have described at such length here is a big problem, and it is the overwhelming tendency of our time to assume that a big problem calls for a big solution. I do not believe in the efficacy of big solutions. I believe that they not only tend to prolong and complicate the problems they are meant to solve, but that they cause new problems. On the other hand, if the solution is small, obvious, simple, and cheap, then it may quickly and permanently solve the immediate problem and many others as well. For example, if a city-dweller walks or rides a bicycle to work, he has found the simplest solution to his transportation problem—and at the same time he is reducing pollution, reducing the waste of natural resources, reducing the public expenditure for traffic control, saving his money, and improving his health. The same ramifying pattern of solutions attends all skills and strategies of economic independence: gardening, cooking, household maintenance, etc. To turn an agricultural problem over to the developers, promoters, and salesmen of industrial technology is not to ask for a solution; it is to ask for more industrial technology and for a bigger bureaucracy to handle the resulting problems of social upset, unemployment, ill health, urban sprawl, and overcrowding. Whatever their claims to "objectivity," these people will not examine the problem and apply the most fitting solution; they will reverse that procedure and define the problem to fit the solution in which their ambitions and their livelihoods have been invested. They are thriving on the problem and so can have little interest in solving it.

And so the first necessary public change is simply a withdrawal of confidence from the league of specialists, officials, and corporation executives who for at least a generation have had almost exclusive charge of the problem and who have enormously enriched and empowered themselves by making it worse.

Second, as a people, we must learn again to think of human energy, *our* energy, not as something to be saved, but as something to be used and to be enjoyed in use. We must understand that our strength is, first of all, strength of body, and that this strength cannot thrive except in useful, decent, satisfying, comely work. There is no such thing as a reservoir of bodily energy. By saving it—as our ideals of labor-saving and luxury bid us to do—we simply waste it, and waste much else along with it.

Third, we must see again, as I think the founders of our government saw, that the most appropriate governmental powers are negative—those, that is, that protect the small and weak from the great and powerful, *not* those by which the government becomes the profligate, ineffectual parent of the small and weak after it has permitted the great and powerful to make them helpless. The governmental power that can be used most effectively to assure an equitable distribution of property, which alone can give some measure of strength and independence to ordinary citizens, is that of taxation. As our present economy clearly shows, the small can survive only if the great are restrained. And there is nothing undemocratic or anti-libertarian about restraining them. To assume that ordinary citizens can compete successfully with people of wealth and with corporations, as our government presently tends to do, is simply to abandon the ordinary citizens. Restraint by taxation is the smallest, most obvious, simplest, and cheapest answer. This is not my idea. It is Thomas Jefferson's. Writing to Reverend James Madison on October 28, 1785, Jefferson spoke of the desirability of freehold tenure of property. And then he said: "Another means of silently lessening the inequality of property is to exempt all from taxation below a certain point, and to tax the higher portions of property in geometric progression as they rise. The earth is given as a common stock for man to labor and live on. If for the encouragement of industry [he means, of course, mainly agriculture] we allow it to be appropriated, we must take care that employment be provided to those excluded from the appropriation. If we do not, the fundamental right to labor the earth returns to the unemployed . . . it is not too soon to provide by every possible means that as few as possible shall be without a little portion of land. The small landholders are the most precious part of a state. . . ." It would, of course, be necessary to consider how much land in any region ought to constitute a living for a family.

Fourth, considering that the price of farmland has now been driven up by urban pressures and speculation until farmers often cannot afford to own it, low-interest loans ought to be made available to people wishing to buy family-size farms. This would probably need to be only a temporary or transitional measure.

Fifth, there should be a system of production and price controls that would tend to adjust production both to need and to the carrying capacities of farms. One purpose of this would be to curb the extreme fluctuations of supply, which work in the long run to the disadvantage of small producers. Another would be the elimination of the phenomenon of "harvest-time depressed prices"—which, in practice, means that the price of grain is low when it is in the hands of the wrong people (small farmers who cannot afford storage) and high when it is in the hands of the right people (big farmers and "agribusiness" corporations).

Sixth, there should be a program to promote local self-sufficiency in food. The cheapest, freshest food is that which is produced closest to home and is not delayed for processing. This should work toward the most direct dealing between farmers and merchants and farmers and consumers. Much might be done by the promotion of growers' and consumers' cooperatives.

Seventh, every town and city should be required to operate an organic-waste depot where sewage, garbage, waste paper, and the like would be composted and given or sold at cost to farmers. Every truck bringing a load of produce to town should go home with a load of compost. This would greatly improve the health of both the rivers and the fields and it would lower the cost of food.

Eighth, there should be a strenuous review of all sanitation laws governing the production of food, and those that are unnecessary should be eliminated. Sanitation laws have almost invariably worked against the small producer, destroying his markets or prohibitively increasing the cost of production. If we are as technologically adept as we claim to be, then it is inexcusable that we do not have, for instance, an acceptable, inexpensive technology for small dairies. And there is no reason, given the necessary collecting points, that we should not have markets for small quantities of other foods. If we are serious about increasing food production, then we must make room for the small producer. Moreover, decency and common sense require us to learn if it is necessary for cleanliness invariably to be expensive.

Ninth, we should encourage the greatest possible technological and genetic diversity, in conformation to local need, as opposed to the present dangerous uniformity in both categories. This diversity should be the primary goal of the land-grant schools. To this end, they should be *required*, as the Hatch Act instructs, "to assure agriculture a position in research equal to that of industry." These schools, and their professors individually, should be forbidden to accept work on assignment from any corporation or other outside interest that might wish to market any resulting product. (This, of course, would not apply to professors working on their own time outside the university.)

Tenth, to de-specialize the interests of the colleges of agriculture—that is, to shift their loyalty from "agribusiness" and industry back to the farmers—two other measures might be useful: (1) The faculties should be opened, on a part-time basis, to farmers, just as faculties of medicine and law are opened to doctors and lawyers; and (2) faculty members could be paid half their salary in cash and given the use of a boundary of college farmland the potential annual income from which would be equivalent to the other half. In both instances, the professor would be in a position to "take his own advice before offering it to other people." And much good might be expected from that. Professors might again become people of experience rather than experts. They might again be able to apply their learning to the small problems of ordinary people and to recommend means and methods not profitable to the suppliers of "purchased inputs."

Eleventh, we must address ourselves seriously, and not a little fearfully, to the problem of human scale. What is it? How do we stay within it? What sort of technology enhances our humanity? What sort reduces it? The reason is simply that we cannot live except within limits, and these limits are of many kinds: spatial, material, moral, spiritual. The world has room for many people who are content to live as humans, but only for a relative few intent upon living as giants or as gods.

Twelfth, having exploited "relativism" until, as a people, we have no deeply believed reasons for doing anything, we must now ask ourselves if there is not, after all, an absolute good by which we must measure ourselves and for which we must work. That absolute good, I think, is health—not in the merely hygienic sense of personal health, but the health, the wholeness, finally the holiness, of Creation, of which our personal health is only a share.

THE NECESSITY OF MARGINS

In Michigan in the fall of 1975, a fire-retarding chemical known as PBB was mistaken for a trace mineral and mixed into a large order of livestock feed. This feed was sent to four Michigan mills run by the Farm Bureau, and from there it went to farms and to the stock troughs. The resulting contamination of meat, milk, and eggs produced a disaster which is still continuing after three-and-a-half years and the limits of which are not known. The immediate and most noticeable result was a state program to destroy contaminated animals and food products. This did away with "about 1.5 million chickens, 29,000 head of cattle, 5,920 hogs, 1,470 sheep, 2,600 lb. of butter, 18,000 lb. of cheese, 34,000 lb. of dry milk products, and 5 million eggs." But many people were also affected, some seriously, and the long-term effects on human health are not known.

This was a tragedy—personal and economic, private and public—caused by one error that "may have been as simple as pulling the wrong lever." And we must recognize that, both in its carelessness and in its magnitude, this tragedy is characteristic of an agriculture, indeed of a culture, without margins. In a highly centralized and industrialized food-supply system there can be no small disaster. Whether it be a production "error" or a corn blight, the disaster is not foreseen until it exists; it is not recognized until it is widespread. By contrast, a highly diversified, small-farm agriculture combined with local marketing is literally crisscrossed with margins, and these margins work both to allow and encourage care and to contain damage.

But such an agriculture would do more than provide us with protective margins. In reducing industrial uniformity it would give us a new sense of our real unity, our common sharing in the good of health. It is a rule, apparently, that whatever is divided must compete. We have been wrong to believe that competition invariably results in the triumph of the best. Divided, body and soul, man and woman, producer and consumer, nature and technology, city and country are thrown into competition with one another. And none of these competitions is ever resolved in the triumph of one competitor, but only in the exhaustion of both.

For our healing we have on our side one great force: the power of Creation, with good care, with kindly use, to heal itself.

Notes

Reference is made to the page of this book on which the material quoted appears.

PREFACE

Page vii. "Surplus of People Called Biggest Farm Problem," *Louisville Courier-Journal*, July 24, 1967.

CHAPTER I

Page 2. Montaigne, *Essays*, translated by John Florio (London: Everyman's Library, 1965), p. 144.

Page 6. Bernard DeVoto, *The Course of Empire* (Boston, 1952), pp. 92-93.

Page 6. *Ibid.*, p. 133.

Page 6. *Ibid.*, pp. 137-138.

Page 8. Harry Weinstein, New York Times News Service, "CIA Report sees power for U.S. in grain shortages," *Minneapolis Tribune*, March 17, 1975. But see also Secretary Butz's speech to the Advertising Council, Washington, D.C., June 24, 1974: ". . . food was . . . a major weapon in achieving an honorable peace in Vietnam."

Page 9. Edwin Muir, "The Island," *Collected Poems* (New York, 1965), p. 249.

Page 11. Roy Reed, New York Times News Service, " 'Paper Rich'—The Farmer's Plaint," *Louisville Courier-Journal*, February 18, 1976.

Page 11. *Ibid.*

Page 11. Ezra Pound, *The Cantos* (London, 1964), p. 63.

Page 14. Thomas Hardy, *Collected Poems*, Eleventh Printing (New York, 1966), p. 511.

CHAPTER II

Page 16. Confucius, *The Great Digest and the Unwobbling Pivot*, translated by Ezra Pound (New York, 1951), p. 31.

Page 17. William Rood, "Environment Groups Invest in the Polluters," *Los Angeles Times*, July 20, 1975.

Page 19. Ivan Illich, *Tools for Conviviality* (New York, 1973), pp. 7-8.

CHAPTER III

Page 30. Sir Albert Howard, *An Agricultural Testament*, Seventh Impression (London, 1956), pp. 1-4.

Page 32. Richard E. Bell, "Meeting World Food Needs," speech to the Fertilizer Institute Annual Meeting, Chicago, February 3, 1976.

Page 32. *Ibid.*

Page 32. *Ibid.*

Page 32. Earl L. Butz, "Agriculture—200 Years After," speech to the National Council of Farmer Cooperatives Annual Meeting, Washington, D.C., January 15, 1976.

Page 33. *Ibid.*

Page 35. Richard E. Bell, Assistant Secretary of Agriculture for International Affairs and Commodity Programs, speech at the Fall Convention of the National Farm Broadcasters Association, Kansas City, Kansas, November 15, 1975.

THE UNSETTLING OF AMERICA

CHAPTER IV

Page 40. Maurice Telleen, in conversation.

Page 42. James R. Russell, "Dairy farming in Kentucky registers sharp decline," *Louisville Courier-Journal*, April 22, 1974.

Page 46. Sir Albert Howard, *The Soil and Health*, Schocken Paperback edition (1972), pp. 1 and 72.

Page 46. *Ibid.*, p. 77.

Page 46. *Ibid.*, pp. 77-78.

Page 46. *Ibid.*, p. 1.

Page 46. *Ibid.*, p. 1.

Page 46. *Ibid.*, p. 11.

Page 46. *Ibid.*, p. 18.

CHAPTER V

Page 50. C. S. Lewis, *That Hideous Strength*, Macmillan paperback edition (1976), p. 203.

Page 54. Carl O. Sauer, *Northern Mists*, Turtle Island Paperback (1973), p. 55.

Page 59. "The Revolution in American Agriculture," *National Geographic*, February, 1970, pp. 147-185.

Page 68. *American Farmer*, October, 1974, p. 3.

Page 77. F. M. Esfandiary, "Homo sapiens, the manna maker," *Louisville Courier-Journal*, August 15, 1975.

Page 78. Matthew 4:9. King James Version.

CHAPTER VI

Page 81. William Blake, *Complete Writings*, edited by Geoffrey Keynes (London, 1966), p. 149.

Page 81. *Ibid.*

Page 82. F. H. King, *Farmers of Forty Centuries* (Emmaus, Pennsylvania, 1972).

Page 88. Lauren Soth, *The Nation*, October 26, 1974, p. 398.

Page 95. Ivan Illich, *Energy and Equity* (New York, 1974), pp. 53-54.

CHAPTER VII

Page 96. James E. Bostic, Jr., "Rural America: Where the Action Is," speech to the Farmers Home Administration State Conference, Raleigh, North Carolina, April 16, 1976.

Page 96. Richard Deats, "A Conversation with Lanza del Vasto," *Fellowship*, September, 1975, p. 14.

Page 98. *King Lear*, act 4, scene 6, lines 13-20.

Page 99. *Ibid.*, act 4, scene 6, lines 221-223.

Page 99. *Ibid.*, act 5, scene 3, line 198.

Page 101. Hart Crane, *The Collected Poems*, edited with an Introduction by Waldo Frank (New York, 1946), p. 3.

Page 103. Blake, *op. cit.*, p. 149.

Page 105. *The Major Plays and the Sonnets*, edited by G. B. Harrison (New York, 1948), p. 1062.

Page 109. Proverbs 24:30-34. King James Version.

Page 122. William Butler Yeats, "Solomon and the Witch," *Collected Poems* (New York, 1954), p. 175.

Page 125. Homer, *The Odyssey*, translated by Robert Fitzgerald (New York, 1961), p. 99.

Page 126. *The Odyssey of Homer*, translated by Richmond Lattimore (New York, 1967), p. 17.

Page 127. Fitzgerald, *op. cit.*, p. 447.

Page 127. *Ibid.*, p. 448.

Page 128. *The Great Digest and the Unwobbling Pivot*, translated by Ezra Pound (New York, 1951), p. 65.

Page 128. Fitzgerald, *op. cit.*, p. 464.

Page 129. Isaiah 2-4. King James Version.

Page 129. Fitzgerald, *op. cit.*, p. 201.

Page 132. Millen Brand, "The Danger," *Local Lives* (New York, 1975), p. 6.

Page 133. Sabrina Michaud, *National Geographic*, November, 1975, p. 664.

Page 139. George Ewart Evans, *The Horse in the Furrow* (London, 1960), pp. 40-41.

CHAPTER VIII

Page 142. Sir Albert Howard, *The Soil and Health*, Schocken Paperback edition (1972), p. 78.

Page 142. C. S. Lewis, *That Hideous Strength*, p. 87.

Page 143. *The Life and Selected Writings of Thomas Jefferson*, edited and with an

Introduction by Adrienne Koch and William Peden (New York, 1944), pp. 729-730.

Page 143. *Ibid.*, p. 377.

Page 144. *Ibid.*, p. 377.

Page 144. *Ibid.*, p. 534.

Page 144. *Ibid.*, p. 727.

Page 144. Morrill Act, *United States Code Annotated* (St. Paul and Brooklyn, 1964), Title 7, Section 301.

Page 145. *Ibid.*, Section 304.

Page 145. Hatch Act, *United States Code*, Section 361b.

Page 145. *Ibid.*, Section 361b.

Page 145. *Ibid.*, Section 361b.

Page 145. Smith-Lever Act, *United States Code*, Section 341.

Page 145. William Belmont Parker, *The Life and Public Services of Justin Smith Morrill* (Boston and New York, 1924), p. 261.

Page 145. *Ibid.*, p. 262.

Page 146. *Ibid.*, p. 262.

Page 146. *Ibid.*, p. 263.

Page 146. Koch and Peden, *Writings of Thomas Jefferson*, pp. 632-633.

Page 150. "The Land Grant College Complex," *The People's Land: A Reader on Land Reform in the United States*, edited by Peter Barnes (Emmaus, Pennsylvania, 1975), p. 92.

Page 150. *Ibid.*, p. 90.

Page 151. Phil Norman, "UK Agriculture College touches many lives," *Louisville Courier-Journal*, October 10, 1976.

Page 151. Smith-Lever Act, *United States Code*, Title 7, Section 347a, paragraphs (a) and (c)

Page 151. House Committee on Agriculture, U.S. Congress, "Cooperative Agricultural Extension Work," *Report No. 110*, 63rd Congress, 2nd Session (1913), p. 5.

Page 151. Smith-Lever Act, *op. cit.*, paragraph (a).

Page 152. Sarah Shaver Hughes, "Agricultural Surpluses and American Foreign Policy 1952-1960," (Masters thesis, University of Wisconsin, 1964). Quoted in Darryl McLeod, "Urban-Rural Food Alliances: A Perspective on Recent Community Food Organizing," *Radical Agriculture*, edited by Richard Merrill (New York, 1976), p. 190.

Page 154. Andre Mayer and Jean Mayer, "Agriculture, the Island Empire," *Daedalus*, Summer, 1974, p. 87.

Page 154. *Ibid.*, p. 88.

Page 154. *Ibid.*, p. 91.

Page 154. *Ibid.*, pp. 86-87, 91.

Page 154. *Ibid.*, p. 94.

Page 158. W. Ross Winterowd, *The Contemporary Writer* (New York, 1975), p. 298.

Page 160. Earl O. Heady, "The Agriculture of the U.S.," *Scientific American*, September, 1976, pp. 107-127.

Page 161. F. H. King, *Farmers of Forty Centuries* (Emmaus, Pennsylvania, 1972).

Page 166. Sterling Wortman, "Food and Agriculture," *Scientific American*, September, 1976, p. 35.

CHAPTER IX

Page 170. Isaiah 5:8. Jerusalem Bible.

Page 170. Koch and Peden, *Writings of Thomas Jefferson*, p. 390.

Page 172. Philip M. Raup, "Needed Research Into the Effects of Large Scale Farm and Business Firms on Rural America" (testimony before the Subcommittee on Monopoly of the United States Senate Small Business Committee, March 1, 1972).

Page 175. Stephen B. Brush, "Andean Culture and Agriculture: Perspectives on Development" (paper presented at the International Hill Land Symposium, West Virginia University, Morgantown, West Virginia, October 5, 1976).

Page 179. Maurice Telleen, in correspondence.

Page 188. Thomas P. Cooper, University of Kentucky College of Agriculture Circular No. 306, November, 1937, pp. 3-4.

Page 192. *Farmers Home Journal*, January 2, 1892 (Louisville, Kentucky), p. 3.

Page 192. *Ibid.*, p. 8.

Page 192. *Ibid.*, p. 8.

Page 192. *Ibid.*, p. 2.

Page 193. St. John 12:24. King James Version.

Page 197. William Lockeretz, Robert Klepper, Barry Commoner, Michael Gertler, Sarah Fast, Daniel O'Leary, Roger Blobaum, "A Comparison of the Production, Economic Returns, and Energy Intensiveness of Corn Belt Farms That Do and Do Not Use Inorganic Fertilizers and Pesticides," Center for the Biology of Natural Systems at Washington University (1975).

Page 198. Barry Commoner, *The Poverty of Power* (New York, 1976), pp. 160-161.

Page 198. *Ibid.*, pp. 164-166.

Page 198. *Ibid.*, p. 172.

Page 199. *Ibid.*, pp. 174-175.

Page 199. *Ibid.*, p. 167-168.

Page 199. *Ibid.*, p. 167.

Page 200. *Farm Index* (United States Department of Agriculture, August, 1975), pp. 10-13.

Page 201. Earl L. Butz, speech to the American Chemical Society Centennial Meeting, New York, April 8, 1976.

Page 201. *Draft Horse Journal*, Winter, 1976, p. 47.

Page 202. *Ibid.*, p. 46.

Page 203. *Ibid.*, p. 47.

Page 203. *Ibid.*, p. 46.

Page 204. Earl L. Butz, *op. cit.*

Page 205. *Ibid.*

Page 205. *Ibid.*

Page 205. *Ibid.*

Page 205. *Ibid.*

Page 209. Maurice Telleen, in correspondence.

Page 211. "Agricultural Alternatives," *CBNS Notes*, March–April, 1972, p. 4.

Page 212. *Ibid.*, p. 3.

Page 212. *Ibid.*, p. 3.

Page 215. *Draft Horse Journal*, Autumn, 1976, p. 33.

Page 216. "Agricultural Alternatives," *op. cit.*, pp. 10-11.

Page 216. *Ibid.*, p. 11.

Page 216. *Ibid.*, p. 12.

Page 220. Koch and Peden, *Writings of Thomas Jefferson*, p. 390.

Page 222. "Michigan 'Episode,' " *The Shepherd*, July, 1976, p. 24.

Page 223. *Ibid.*, p. 24.